Nonverbal Communication and Marital Interaction

INTERNATIONAL SERIES IN EXPERIMENTAL SOCIAL PSYCHOLOGY

Series Editor: Michael Argyle, University of Oxford

A Related Pergamon Journal

LANGUAGE & COMMUNICATION*

An Interdisciplinary Journal
Editor: Roy Harris, University of Oxford

The primary aim of the journal is to fill the need for a publication forum devoted to the discussion of topics and issues in communication which are of interdisciplinary significance. It will publish contributions from researchers in all fields relevant to the study of verbal and non-verbal communication.

Emphasis will be placed on the implications of current research for establishing common theoretical frameworks within which findings from different areas of study may be accommodated and interrelated.

By focusing attention on the many ways in which language is integrated with other forms of communicational activity and interactional behaviour it is intended to explore ways of developing a science of communication which is not restricted by existing disciplinary boundaries.

*Free specimen copy available on request.

NOTICE TO READERS

Dear Reader

An invitation to Publish in and Recommend the Placing of a Standing Order to Volumes Published in this Valuable Series.

If your library is not already a standing/continuation order customer to this series, may we recommend that you place a standing/continuation order to receive immediately upon publication all new volumes. Should you find that these volumes no longer serve your needs, your order can be cancelled at any time without notice.

The Editors and the Publisher will be glad to receive suggestions or outlines of suitable titles, reviews or symposia for editorial consideration: if found acceptable, rapid publication is guaranteed.

ROBERT MAXWELL
Publisher at Pergamon Press

Nonverbal Communication and Marital Interaction

by

PATRICIA NOLLER
University of Queensland, Australia

PERGAMON PRESS
OXFORD · NEW YORK · TORONTO · SYDNEY · PARIS · FRANKFURT

U.K.	Pergamon Press Ltd., Headington Hill Hall, Oxford OX3 0BW, England
U.S.A	Pergamon Press Inc., Maxwell House, Fairview Park, Elmsford, New York 10523, U.S.A.
CANADA	Pergamon Press Canada Ltd., Suite 104, 150 Consumers Road, Willowdale, Ontario M2J 1P9, Canada
AUSTRALIA	Pergamon Press (Aust.) Pty. Ltd., P.O. Box 544, Potts Point, N.S.W. 2011, Australia
FRANCE	Pergamon Press SARL, 24 rue des Ecoles, 75240 Paris, Cedex 05, France
FEDERAL REPUBLIC OF GERMANY	Pergamon Press GmbH, Hammerweg 6, D-6242 Kronberg-Taunus, Federal Republic of Germany

First edition 1984

Library of Congress Cataloging in Publication Data
Noller, Patricia.
Nonverbal communication and marital interaction.
(International series in experimental social psychology; v. 9)
Includes bibliographical references and index.
1. Communication in marriage.   2. Nonverbal communication.   I. Title.   II. Series.
HQ734.N67   1984   306.8'7   83-24988

British Library Cataloguing in Publication Data
Noller, Patricia
Nonverbal communication and marital interaction.
(International series in experimental social psychology; v. 9)
1. Marriage   2. Interpersonal communication
3. Nonverbal communication
I. Title   II. Series
306.8'1   HQ728

ISBN 0–08–027927–9 (Hardcover)
ISBN 0–08–031313–2 (Flexicover)

The publisher gratefully acknowledges the assistance of Debbi and Mark Phillips, and Dr Joseph McDowall of the Psychology Department of the University of Queensland, in providing the photograph used on the cover of this book. .

Printed in Great Britain by A. Wheaton & Co. Ltd., Exeter

Acknowledgements

I wish to thank a number of people for their help in the undertaking of the research reported in this book as well as their help during the writing stages:

Professor Glen McBride and Dr Janet Khan who were the supervisors for my Ph.D. project and who provided encouragement and guidance;

The members of the Animal Behaviour Unit seminar group who endured many presentations of ideas and data and helped so much with comments and suggestions;

Members of the staff of the Psychology Department both technical and academic—particularly Mr Peter Pamment, Mr Fred Foenander and Dr Cindy Gallois, as well as those who worked so hard with typing the final manuscript;

Ms Vikki Uhlmann who did most of the coding of the videotapes—a demanding and tedious job;

Dr David Chant of the Department of Mathematics for help with the analyses;

My children who helped with various activities such as transcribing the videotapes—and for their tolerance and encouragement:

Dr Joseph McDowell who took the photograph on the cover and Debbi and Mark Phillips who posed for it;

My husband, Charles for his encouragement and for the help he has been as I've needed to "sound out" ideas—also for help with proof-reading;

The couples, themselves, without whom the project would not have been possible;

Dr Michael Argyle for his help and encouragement and his correcting of drafts.

Copyright Acknowledgements

The following authors and publishers are acknowledged for their co-operation in allowing the reprinting of material in this book.

Dr James Honeycutt and the National Council on Family Relations, 1219 University Avenue Southeast, Minneapolis, Minnesota, 55414, for Table 6.3 on p. 95 and Table 6.4 on p. 95 (copyrighted, 1982).

Professor John Gottman and Academic Press for Tables 3.4 and 3.5 on p. 35, Table 3.6 on p. 36, and quotations on p. 38 and p. 56 (copyrighted 1979).

Professor Harold Raush (and Jossey-Bass Inc.) for Table 3.2 on p. 33, Table 3.3 on p. 34, Table 4.6 on p. 61 and the quotations on p. 17 and p. 33 (copyrighted, 1974).

Professor Robert Rosenthal and the Johns Hopkins University Press for Tables 4.3 and 4.4 on p. 51, and Table 4.7 on p. 63 (copyrighted, 1979).

Dr Gary Birchler and the American Psychological Association for Tables 6.1 on p. 91 and 6.2 on p. 92 (copyrighted, 1975).

Ard, B. N. and Ard, C. C. and Science and Behavior Books Inc., Palo Alto, California, for the quotation on p. 189 (copyrighted, 1976).

The American Psychological Association for tables and figures adopted from papers by Noller for Figures 5.1, 5.2 on p. 80; Figure 6.1 on p. 99; Figure 8.3 on p. 123; Figure 9.1 on p. 134; Tables 5.2 and 5.3 on p. 73; Table 5.4 on p. 77; Table 5.6 on p. 79; Tables 5.7 and 5.8 on p. 81; Table 5.10 on p. 84; Table 5.11 on p. 85; Table 5.12 on p. 86; Table 6.6 on p. 98; Table 6.7 on p. 99; Tables 9.1 and 9.2 on p. 133 (copyrighted 1980, 1981, 1982).

Human Sciences Press Inc. for Table 10.2 on p. 161 and 10.3 on p. 162 (copyrighted 1980 in a paper by Noller).

Contents

1

The Scope and Functions of Nonverbal Communication in Marriage

The Impossibility of "Not Communicating"

In the marital situation, as in most others, it is impossible to, "not communicate"—communication can continue to occur, either nonverbally, or through the situation, long after the last word has been spoken. Many people do not understand this, because they limit their concept of communication to words. Even if they acknowledge the importance of nonverbal communication, they limit its scope to body language—facial expressions and gestures in particular—and thus fail to realize that communication is going on whenever we are in the presence of someone else, even if we are only communicating that we want to have nothing to do with them.

There are many common examples which illustrate the impossibility of not communicating. A person in a doctor's waiting-room, avoiding eye contact with everyone else in the room and concentrating on reading his magazine may think that he is not communicating. He is actually communicating a clear reticence to become involved with other people in that situation. A husband sitting behind his newspaper and responding to his wife with grunts may be communicating that he does not want to be disturbed and, at that point in time at least, is not interested in what she has to say.

If a wife walks out on a discussion with her husband and goes wandering in the garden, her absence may communicate to him a continuing unwillingness to deal with the issue. On the other hand, his failure to follow after her and keep the discussion going may communicate quite different things to her—perhaps a stubborn refusal to give any ground on the issue, or even a genuine respect for her that allows her time to go off and think more about a problem if she needs to. How they each interpret the other's behaviour will depend to some extent on the past history of the relationship and the present mood of each.

Effective marital communication, however, demands that the communicator gets across to the spouse the message that he or she intends. In our example, if the husband wants to communicate to his wife that he wants her to take time to think more about the issue, but she interprets his failure to follow her as meaning that he couldn't care less about her opinion, then a misunderstanding has occurred. Unless they talk to each other about their interpretations they will not increase their understanding of each other's communications, and they may be heading for an argument or increased feelings of resentment. When they do talk to each other *how* they say what they say will be even more important than *what* they say—the posture, the facial expression, the tone of voice, the volume, and any sighs, grunts, etc., which may accompany the words all may have a powerful effect on how those words are interpreted and the response which will follow them.

When a husband comes home from work and sits silently with hunched shoulders, a wife may interpret this behaviour as indicating that he is angry with her because she has somehow displeased him—how, she doesn't know. On the other hand, if he is upset about something that happened at work, how can she know that unless he tells her. While some would say that he has failed to communicate, a message has been communicated to his wife. But, the *intent* of the communication and the *impact* that it has on the spouse are quite different. Misunderstanding has occurred, and the potential for argument is great. Communication continues to occur in situations like this whether the interactants realize it or not. Stuart (1980) suggests that married couples can benefit enormously from discussing "the communicational dimensions of such daily routines as the way they enter their home after work and the way they get ready for bed, reviewing which aspects of these wordless experiences reflect mutual concern and which reflect mutual distance" (p. 213).

Defining Nonverbal Communication

We are continually communicating, then, with our spouses, whenever we are with them (and sometimes even when we are not), and there will be times when we use words and times when we do not. So, while nonverbal communication could perhaps be defined as the communicating we do when we are not using words, this is an inadequate definition of nonverbal communication, since much of the communicating that goes on when we are using words, the tone of voice, the volume at which we talk, the smile, the wink, the hand gesture, the nod, the grunt and so on, must also be included. Weitz (1976) emphasizes the importance of this type of nonverbal communication when she says,

> "The interactant is never confronted with a disembodied voice, but rather with a gesturing, expressive, positioned individual whose voice and language are only part of the message being conveyed."

Nonverbal communication, then, could be defined as that part of a message, which is not words, but which may accompany words or occur separately from words—and includes facial expressions, gestures, posture, spacing, tone of voice, pitch, volume, speed of talking, etc.

Functions of Nonverbal Communication

Argyle (1975) discusses six functions of nonverbal communication, and readers who feel they need to get a clearer idea of the scope of nonverbal behaviour may like to consult this book. Only three of these functions will be discussed here, because they are particularly relevant to the marital situation.

Conveying interpersonal attitudes

Conveying interpersonal attitudes, particularly towards other interactants, and the topic under discussion is an important function of nonverbal communication. Bateson (1962) described nonverbal communication as being particularly sensitive to "the nuances and intricacies of how two people are getting along". Since spouses vary with regard to how easily they convey their opinions and attitudes, needs and feelings to one another, one would expect that couples who have difficulty in communicating openly and honestly (probably most couples on some issues, while only some couples on most issues) may convey a great deal of information nonverbally. The problem is that this information is not always communicated accurately to the spouse, and the partners do not always realize when a misunderstanding has occurred, with further implications for the relationship. Information conveyed nonverbally in this way may include information about how each sees their relative status, how much they care about one another, how friendly they are, and how much they agree about the issue being dealt with.

It is important to realize that nonverbal communication is fairly ambiguous, and thus is capable of being misinterpreted. For example, a frown on the face of a spouse may mean that he is annoyed, or may indicate that he has a headache. To assume that he is annoyed, without checking out, may only lead to more misunderstanding and unnecessary argument. Also, there can be some discrepancy between one part of a communication and another, so the attitude that one wished to convey might not be conveyed at all. There is considerable evidence (Argyle *et al.*, 1970; Bugental, Kaswan & Love, 1970) that where the verbal and the nonverbal components of a message conflict, much more weight is given to the nonverbal part, despite its ambiguity.

Let us take an illustration related to status. Imagine a situation where a husband is trying to convey to his wife that he sees her as an equal in the relationship, and wants her to have an equal say in the decision-making, but she doesn't seem to believe him. This unbelief could be related to their past history, where he has been generally very dominating, and she may be hesitant to believe this present statement until he shows her by his actions that he means what he has said. However, the problem could well be in his nonverbal behaviour. If, on the one hand, he is saying that he does not want to dominate her, but is using rather dominant nonverbal behaviour (e.g.

TABLE 1.1. *When Verbal and Nonverbal Channels Conflict*
(An example related to dominance)

Possible explanation	Comment	Example	
		Verbal channel	Nonverbal channel
1. Intensity of feelings	E.g. coming on strong.	"I really want us to be equals in our relationship".	Pointing finger, intense loud voice, nodding head etc.
2. Lack of social skill	Either words or nonverbal behaviour doesn't obey normal rules for expressing that feeling or attitude.	You're going to be equal in our relationship—so there! (Verbal very dominant).	Nonverbal behaviour will probably also be very dominant (see above).
3. Ambivalence	Words express one feeling while nonverbal behaviour expresses other equally strong feeling.	Of course I think you and I should be equals in our relationship.	Some dominance, perhaps also sneer, negative voice tone.
4. Pretending	Words express socially desirable attitude while nonverbal indicates something of true feelings.	As above.	As above, but may be some clues to deception, e.g. avoidance of eye contact—speech errors etc.

pointing finger, leaning back, loud voice, etc.) then this dominance may be the overwhelming message which his wife receives, totally cancelling out his words. The crucial question is, why is he using such dominant nonverbal behaviour? A number of explanations are possible:

(a) He feels very strongly about the issue—in which case he probably means the words he is saying, but the intensity of his feelings on the issue is causing him to "come on strongly" and seem more dominant than he intends.

(b) He doesn't realize how dominant his nonverbal behaviour is, or the impact that it has on his wife—in which case he may mean the words, but lacks the social skill to convey the message appropriately.

(c) He feels ambivalent—at one level he would like his wife to be more equal in the relationship, but at another level he is uncertain of the consequences of such equality—in which case the apparently confused message is a true expression of his attitude at that point of time.

(d) He may be giving lip-service to the idea of equality, while his true attitude is one of continuing dominance—in that situation, his underlying attitude "leaks" out through his nonverbal behaviour. See Table 1.1 for a summary of the possible behaviours and explanations. Such an illustration conveys something of the complexity of marital communication, and particularly of the often delicate relationship between the verbal and nonverbal components of such communication.

Another illustration which comes to mind is related to the use of posture in conveying nonverbal information about attitudes. A couple were discussing an issue in their marriage. They were sitting side by side at a table. He had his arm on the table between them, and was turned slightly away from her, his shoulder creating a barrier between them. Almost everyone who has ever seen the tape of that interaction (and only the visual channel has ever been shown because the soundtrack is confidential) has commented on the way he is using his body as a barrier in that situation to cut himself off from her. Interestingly, this fits with the fact that in their discussion he is seeking to maintain the status quo, and refuses to take into account any of her suggestions or ideas. So, attitudes to one another can be conveyed in a number of ways—by the posture adopted, by spacing, amount of eye-contact, the kinds of looks exchanged, gestures, facial expressions, and amount of touching (if any).

Attitudes to the topic under discussion and the point of view being expressed are also likely to be conveyed nonverbally, by tone of voice, loudness or softness of the voice, facial expression and amount and intensity of gaze. One of the problems often encountered here is that the two sets of attitudes (that is, attitudes to the topic and attitudes to the interactant) often become intertwined, and it is difficult to express a negative attitude to a topic, without, at the same time, conveying a negative attitude to the person with whom one is discussing that topic, particularly if one is in disagreement with the other interactant. Mehrabian (1971) showed that when communications are inconsistent (that is, one channel is positive while the other is negative), the nonverbal channel tends to convey the attitude to the person, while the verbal channel conveys the attitude to the behaviour. Here, too, however, there are problems with trying to keep the two attitudes separate. After all, we respond to a total communication, not a single channel at a time.

The expression of emotion

The expression of emotion is also mentioned by Argyle (1975) as a function of nonverbal communication. How a person feels at a particular time is likely to be conveyed nonverbally—whether he/she is feeling happy or sad, depressed or confused, excited or disgusted. Such emotions may be expressed voluntarily and deliberately, as when a person feels sad and doesn't care who knows it, or may be "leaked" (Ekman & Friesen, 1969) as when a person is secretly pleased about a situation and would prefer that no-one realized that, but his pleasure still shows. A child who is pleased that his sister or brother is in trouble, or is happy that he's managed to get his parents angry would exemplify this type of emotion. The husband described earlier (see Table 1.1) who is saying that he would like his wife to have an equal say in their relationships but is only pretending, is "leaking" his true attitude through the nonverbal channel.

The accurate expression of emotion is important in marriage from two points of view—firstly in terms of communicating one's own feelings to the spouse—letting him or her know when one is pleased, excited, depressed, tense, or sad, so that the spouse can then respond appropriately. At the same time, expressing the emotion to the spouse enables the spouse to increase his/her understanding of the partner, and the emotions that the partner experiences in different situations. Imagine a wife who becomes very anxious about her husband's safety when he fails to let her know he will be late for dinner. It may be important for her to communicate these feelings to him so that he can take steps to avoid situations where she becomes so anxious in the future.

Secondly, the expression of emotion is important in terms of empathizing with the spouse in his/her emotional moments, and being able to communicate that empathy, so that the spouse experiences the shared feeling "laughing with those who laugh, and weeping with those who weep". It may be important that a husband can express shared grief that he and his wife may feel as a result of a miscarriage, or the wife share the disappointment that a husband may feel at missing a promotion, or it may be important that a wife share her husband's sadness at the death of a friend and that a husband share his wife's anxiety before a job interview.

Handling the ongoing interaction

The third function of nonverbal communication which is important in the marital situation is that of handling the ongoing interaction. This includes indicating interest in and attentiveness to the person with whom one is interacting. Posture and pattern of gaze (Argyle & Cook, 1976; Exline, 1972) are important behaviours, as well as nods and vocalizations like "uh-uh" which let the speaker know he/she is being heard, without interrupting the flow of conversation. Turn-taking and floor apportionment involve nonverbal behaviours such as pausing, dropping or raising the voice appropriately, looking at and looking away. Many married couples complain that their spouses are not interested in what they have to say, don't listen to them, or interrupt them frequently. One would expect that married couples who communicate well with one another would get to know each other's conversation patterns, and as well, understand the meaning of each other's nonverbal cues. It is also possible that they may learn the cues too well. I knew of a woman who could tell immediately if her husband's attention strayed to a letter on his desk while talking to her on the telephone.

Channels of Nonverbal Communication

Nonverbal communication, then, performs a number of functions and is sometimes related to speech and sometimes occurs instead of speech. Kahn

(1969) speaks of "the nonverbal components of communication which qualify and colour all messages transmitted through our basically standard vernacular" (p. 14). Many writers see communication as consisting of a verbal channel, and a nonverbal channel. In fact, "nonverbal channels" would be more accurate since, as we have already seen, the nonverbal component of the message may include visual aspects such as facial expression, gesture, posture and gaze, or vocal aspects such as voice quality, loudness, pitch, pausing, tempo (Knapp, 1972). Since, in this volume, we are mainly concerned with the nonverbal behaviour which accompanies speech, the terms "visual channel" and "vocal channel" will be used as defined above, while the term "nonverbal behaviour" will refer to all the nonverbal behaviours presented by a combination of these two channels.

Relationship between Verbal and Nonverbal Components of a Message

Content vs feeling

Watzlawick and his colleagues (1967) see the verbal component as carrying the basic content of a message, while the nonverbal channels carry the "relationship or command" part of the message—including indications of the attitudes of the participants to one another and of how the message is to be interpreted (e.g. as a joke, an order, or a request). Friedman (1979), on the other hand, while acknowledging that a complete understanding of a message must involve the integration of the verbal and nonverbal components, warns against assuming that the verbal part of a message expresses thoughts and ideas, while the nonverbal part expresses feelings and attitudes. Clearly, both feelings and attitudes can be expressed verbally as well as nonverbally. For example, a husband may see his wife doing something which angers him and he may say, "I get angry when you do that and I wish you would stop." Here the words clearly carry his attitude of displeasure, and would do so even if his facial expression and tone of voice were quite neutral. On the other hand, he could merely say, "What are you doing?" with very negative nonverbal behaviour (loud, harsh voice, frown, etc.), and he would achieve a similar effect, but in the second example, the attitude is not expressed through the words (which are neutral) but by the nonverbal behaviour accompanying those words, and there may be more ambiguity.

Reinforcement or contradiction

In any message the verbal and nonverbal channels may repeat or reinforce one another (Ekman, 1964), as when I say, "I like that", with a smile and pleasant voice tone. On the other hand, the channels may contradict one another, as when I say, "I like that", with negative voice tone and a frown. There may also be differences between the nonverbal channels, as when someone asks, "Do you know what that would cost?", with a negative voice tone, suggesting that the idea is outrageous, but with a grin implying some interest. Again, our earlier example summarized in Table 1.1 involves the verbal and nonverbal channels contradicting one another.

Relative importance of the channels

Psychologists have also been interested in the relative importance of verbal and nonverbal cues in the interpretation of a message. Argyle and his co-workers (1970) found that nonverbal cues combined with verbal cues of almost equal strength, had a much greater impact on the receiver of the message than did the verbal cues. However, this is a complex issue, since there is evidence that this effect depends on the type of message being conveyed by the different channels, and even the sex of the message-sender. (This issue will be taken up again in the chapter on channel inconsistency.) The important point to be made here is that any message consists of both verbal and nonverbal parts and the various parts may "modify or qualify one another" (Weakland, 1976, p. 117).

Communication as a Two-way Process

Communication is clearly a two-way process, and nowhere is this more obvious than in the marital situation. Messages generally have both a sender and a receiver and the impact that a particular message has on the relationship between the spouses will depend on both how the message is sent and how the message is received.

Skills of encoding and decoding

Researchers have shown (Rosenthal et al., 1979) that individuals differ in their ability to perform the roles of sending and receiving messages (encoding and decoding), and also that their ability may differ from one situation to another (Noller, 1981). Hall (1979, pp. 33, 34) describes these two sets of skills as "skills of action" and "skills of reception". Skills of action, involve the ability to send nonverbal cues effectively, to articulate one's thoughts, ideas and desires, to integrate in one's message the verbal and nonverbal components, and to act appropriately in communicative contexts. Skills of reception on the other hand, involve the ability to decode affect communicated nonverbally, to grasp the meaning of a communication, including the interpretation of verbal and nonverbal meanings and the ability to understand social contexts and roles.

Encoding and decoding errors

When a message between two people is misunderstood this may be because the message is not sent clearly, or because, even though the message is sent clearly, the other person has failed to receive it accurately. It is important to be aware that communicating, verbally or nonverbally, is a two-way process, with failures in communication being related to encoding, decoding or both. In a situation where a wife is telling her husband something, and he doubts her sincerity, the problem could be in the way the message is sent (an encoding problem) or the way the message is received (a decoding problem). Perhaps she is not being expressive enough in the way she is sending the message, or some underlying reticence or ambivalence is coming through to him. On the other hand, it may be that because of the way he is feeling at the moment, or because of something that has happened in the past, he doesn't believe her, even though her message is sent quite clearly. This issue will be taken up in more detail in the chapter on accuracy.

Summary

In this chapter the scope of nonverbal behaviour, as well as its many functions in the communication process, has been discussed. The complex interaction between the verbal and nonverbal components of any message, including the way the nonverbal part of a message may modify or qualify the meaning of the words has also been considered. Finally, the complexity of the communication process itself has been shown, with misunderstandings being discussed in terms of both encoding and decoding. All of these issues will be taken up in much greater detail in later chapters. This chapter is intended only to set the scene.

References

ARGYLE, M. (1975) *Bodily Communication*. London: Methuen.

ARGYLE, M. & COOK, M. (1976) *Gaze and Mutual Gaze*. Cambridge: Cambridge University Press.

ARGYLE, M., Salter, V., Nicholson, H., Williams, M. & BURGESS, P. (1970) The communication of inferior and superior attitudes by verbal and nonverbal signals. *British Journal of Social and Clinical Psychology*, **9**, 222–31.

BATESON, G. (1962) Exchange of information about patterns of human behavior. Paper read at symposium on information storage and neural control, Houston, Texas.

BUGENTAL, D. E., KASWAN, J. M. & LOVE, L. R. (1970) Perception of contradictory meanings conveyed by verbal and nonverbal channels. *Journal of Personality and Social Psychology*, **16**, 647–55.

EKMAN, P. (1964) Body position, facial expression and verbal behaviour during interviews. *Journal of Abnormal and Social Psychology*, **68**, 295–301.

EKMAN, P. & FRIESEN, W. V. (1969) Nonverbal leakage and cues to deception. *Psychiatry*, **32**, 88– 106. (a).

EXLINE, R.(1972) Visual interaction: the glances of power and preference. In COLE, J. K. (Ed.) *Nebraska Symposium on motivation*, Vol. 19. Lincoln: University of Nebraska Press.

FRIEDMAN, H. S. (1979) The concept of skill in nonverbal communication: Implications for understanding social interaction. In ROSENTHAL, R. (Ed.) *Skill in Nonverbal Communication*. Cambridge, Massachusetts: Oelgeschlager, Gunn & Hain.

HALL, J. A. (1979) Gender, gender roles and nonverbal communication skills. In ROSENTHAL, R. (Ed.) *Skill in Nonverbal Communication*. Cambridge, Massachusetts: Oelgeschlager, Gunn & Hain.

KAHN, M. (1969) Nonverbal communication as a factor in marital satisfaction. Doctoral dissertation, Southern Illinois University.

MEHRABIAN, A. (1971) *Silent Messages*. Belmont, California: Wadsworth Publishing Company.

NOLLER, P. (1981) Gender and marital adjustment level differences in decoding messages from spouses and strangers. *Journal of Personality and Social Psychology*, **41**, 272–8.

ROSENTHAL, R., HALL, J. A., DiMATTEO, M. R., ROGERS, P. L. & ARCHER, D. (1979) *Sensitivity to Nonverbal Communication: The Pons test*. Baltimore: The Johns Hopkins University Press.

STUART, R. B. (1980) *Helping Couples Change*. New York: The Guildford Press.

WATZLAWICK, P., BEAVIN, J. H. & JACKSON, D. (1967) *Pragmatics of human communication*. New York: Norton.

WEAKLAND, J. (1976) Communication theory and clinical change. In GEURIN, P. J. (Ed.) *Family therapy theory and practice*. New York: Gardner Press.

WEITZ, S. (1976) Sex differences in nonverbal communication. *Sex Roles*, **2**, 175–84.

2

Marital Communication and its Effect on the Marital Relationship

The Importance of Communication in Marriage

Bolte (1975) is one of many writers who emphasize the importance of communication between spouses to the satisfaction each gains from the marital relationship. For Bolte the communication system of the couple is a vital force, determining much of their happiness together. Navran (1967) carried out a study using the Primary Communication Inventory (Locke, Sabagh & Tomes, 1956) and concluded that any attempts at improving marital relationships must start with working on the communication between husband and wife.

Karlsson (1951, p. 153) raises a further important question when he comments that the strong association between communication and marital satisfaction undoubtedly exists, although the association could be due to the interaction between communication and satisfaction, or could be because communication is a result of satisfaction. If good communication is a result of satisfaction, then couples who have relatively few problems and feel good about each other should be able to communicate better with each other. There is probably some truth in such a contention, but Karlsson (1951, p. 153) goes on to maintain that in the light of clinical experience as well as theory, it seems likely that the process is two-way: that is, marital satisfaction affects communication, and communication affects marital satisfaction.

Eighty-five per cent of marital and family therapists questioned by Olson (1970), considered improved communication to be of primary importance to all of the families they were treating. Craddock (1980) surveyed marital therapists in three Australian state capitals and found that 92 per cent saw problems in communication and conflict management as being encountered very frequently in their practices.

Quality of Communication in Marriage

While many writers have focused on the importance of quality communication to marital satisfaction, "the notion of quality communication has

remained amorphous" (Montgomery, 1981). In this present chapter an attempt will be made to summarize both the theoretical issues, and the considerable empirical research which has been carried out. The literature on marital communication will be discussed under five main headings:
1. Amount of communication.
2. Types of communication.
3. Accuracy of communication.
4. Awareness of communication.
5. Effectiveness of communication.
An attempt will also be made to show how these different aspects of communication interrelate and affect marital satisfaction.

Amount of communication

Very little empirical work has been carried out with regard to the issue of how much communication is necessary for marital satisfaction. Unhappily married people frequently say, "We just don't communicate", implying that they don't communicate at all, and that their relationship would be more satisfactory if they communicated more. This type of thinking is, however, problematical on two grounds. Firstly there is the implication that it is possible to "not communicate". As we discussed in Chapter 1, there is almost always communication, even if all that is communicated is unwillingness to share feelings, to discuss issues, and to work out mutually satisfactory solutions to problems. Secondly, there is the implication that as long as communication (or more particularly talking) is taking place, the *type* of communication is unimportant. Clearly communication is a complex set of behaviours, and some communicative behaviours lead to high levels of marital satisfaction, while other behaviours lead to low levels of marital satisfaction. This issue will be taken up further in a later section when behaviours that help marital satisfaction, and those that hinder marital satisfaction will be discussed. Craddock (1980) found that the therapists he surveyed commented on the fact that couples experiencing marital difficulties either fail to attempt to communicate, or the attempts they do make prove unsatisfactory, often leading to arguments. Clients were seen as having difficulty in sharing their goals with one another and planning ways to achieve those goals.

Undoubtedly when communication proves unsatisfactory, the amount of time spent in communication is likely to decrease. The more often the process of communication proves to be unpleasant or ineffective, the less likely it becomes that the couple will attempt to communicate about, or talk through, similar situations in the future; that is, unsatisfactory communication has a punishing effect. Or perhaps it is more correct to say that the feelings that remain after unsatisfactory communication such as insults, put-downs and nagging, have a punishing effect. As well, there is often a

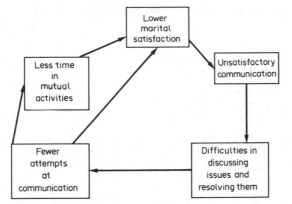

FIG 2.1. Diagrammatic representation of the relationship between amount of communication, difficulties in communication and marital satisfaction

circular effect, in that unsatisfactory communication leads to less communication and lower marital satisfaction, and the more that marital satisfaction drops, the less likely is the communication to be positive, rewarding and effective. A diagrammatic representation of the process can be seen in Fig. 2.1.

Navran (1967) used the Primary Communication Inventory (Locke, Sabagh & Tomes, 1956) and compared responses on that scale with responses on the Short Marital Adjustment Test (Locke & Wallace, 1959). He found that the happy couples in the sample talked more to each other, had a wider range of subjects on which they felt free to talk, and worked hard at keeping the channels of communication open. Matthews and Milhanovich (1963) found that the unhappy couples in their study were concerned about the amount of communication between their partners and themselves. They complained of sharing little companionship with their mates, and of being neglected, and receiving little affection, appreciation and understanding.

Some marital researchers (e.g. Mace & Mace, 1974) talk about the conflict-avoiding marriage where couples avoid discussing contentious issues in order to avoid putting strain on their relationship. The problem is that over time, a large number of issues may fall into this category, and the couple may end up with very few issues they feel safe discussing. Navran's (1967) finding that happy couples talked more to each other and had a wider range of subjects on which they felt free to talk, would lend support to the idea that unhappy couples spend less time in communication, and it is possible that this is because they avoid, rather than resolve, conflict. Of course, the avoidance may develop over time as a result of negative communication rather than be a cause of the problems.

Raush et al. (1974) found that a number of their couples used avoidance for coping with conflict, although in the experiment they couldn't actually avoid talking (because of the instructions and the demands of the situation).

TABLE 2.1. *Mean Scores for Wives on Areas of Change Questionnaire Items*

Item No.	Behaviour	Group 1	Group 2	Group 3
9	Start interesting conversations	0.50	1.06	1.63
11	Show appreciation for things I do well	0.31	0.88	1.69
24	Give me attention when I need it	0.31	0.56	1.31
31	Express his emotions clearly	0.38	0.81	2.38
34	Come to meals on time	0.06	0.18	0.81

They often used other methods of avoiding conflict, however, by denying that a problem existed, by refusing to share their feelings, or by blaming relationship problems on external circumstances. Such behaviours led to rather static interchanges, and to little resolution of the problems confronting them. Interestingly, these writers warn against assuming that avoidance as a way of handling conflict in marriage is always unsatisfactory. In fact they suggest that under certain conditions avoidance has a positive effect: when avoidance fits with the intrapsychic style of the individuals, when the partners' roles are clearly differentiated, and when their relationship includes real mutual affection. These researchers see such couples as being more likely to describe their marriages as happy and to have stable marriages than some couples who are more involved with one another.

Noller (1982) had couples fill in the Areas of Change Questionnaire (Weiss & Perry, Note 1) and the Short Marital Adjustment Test (Locke & Wallace, 1959) as part of an experimental procedure to be described in much greater detail in later chapters. Wives low in marital adjustment wanted their husbands to communicate with them more, and particularly to start more interesting conversations with them, to show more appreciation for the things they did well, to express their emotions more clearly, and to give them more attention. Table 2.1 shows the mean scores for each group (where 0 = no change required and 3 = I want my partner to perform the behaviour much more). On each of these variables there was a significant difference between subjects high in marital adjustment and those low in marital adjustment.

Types of communication

As has been suggested, the amount of communication is not necessarily the most important variable in discriminating between couples high and low in marital adjustment, although amount of communication will often decrease if the spouses engage in communication behaviours that are punishing, or that are ineffective. In the present section the types of communication behaviours that lead to high marital satisfaction, and those that lead to low marital satisfaction will both be discussed. Table 2.2 summarizes these.

Behaviours that lead to effective marital communication

Snyder (1979) showed that the best indicators of overall marital satisfaction were the couple's ability to express their feelings to one another, and their ability to discuss problems effectively (an issue to be taken up in the section on effectiveness of communication). Snyder suggested that communication skills are important not only because they provide the means for solving problems and differences, but make an increased level of intimacy possible. Lewis and Spanier (1979) in setting up their model of marital satisfaction and stability emphasize a group of variables which they label rewards from spousal interaction, and which include affective expression and problem-solving ability.

TABLE 2.2. *Behaviours Affecting Marital Satisfaction*

Behaviours that help	Behaviours that hinder
Self disclosure	Lack of communication
Boyd and Roach (1977)	Navran (1967)
Noller (1982)	Noller (1982)
Being sensitive to each other's feelings	Lack of responsiveness
Brody (1963)	Koren and Carlton (1980)
Navran (1967)	Rubin (1977)
Listening and responding	Lack of listening
Miller, Nunnally & Wackman (1975)	Raush *et al.* (1974)
	McNamara and Bahr (1980)
	Gottman *et al.* (1976)
Confirmation	Faulty behaviour change operations
Fisher and Spenkle (1978)	Billings (1970)
Montgomery (1981)	Jacobson and Moore (1981)
	Patterson and Hops (1972)
Expressing respect and esteem	Criticism, arguing and nagging
Vincent, Weiss & Birchler (1975)	Matthews and Milhanovich (1963)
Boyd and Roach (1977)	

(a) *Self-disclosure.* A number of studies have indicated the importance of spouses being able to express their feelings and needs to one another, what Miller, Nunnally and Wackman (1975) have called self-disclosure skills. Boyd and Roach (1977) found that subjects stressed the need for couples to send clear messages to one another, and Noller (1982) found that wives wanted their husbands to express their emotions clearly more often. Wives in this study complained that often they could tell that their husbands were upset, but it was very difficult to get husbands to talk about the reasons why they were upset and to express their real feelings on the issue. Montgomery (1981) in her discussion of quality communication in marriage emphasizes the need for openness which she sees as including "the act of revealing personal information to others" (Jourard, 1971, p. 2), but as also including the ability to receive similar personal information from others.

(b) *Being sensitive to each other's feelings.* The importance of being sensitive to the feelings of the spouse is stressed by a number of researchers. Brody (1963), for example, suggested that spouses in happy marriages have the capacity to put themselves in their partner's place and to empathize with them. Navran (1967) was also able to show that it was important for spouses to show sensitivity to one another's feelings. Showing sensitivity involves acceptance and understanding of the feelings of the partner when they are expressed (Miller, Nunnally & Wackman, 1975). It also includes awareness of those situations which are likely to cause the spouse distress and, where possible, seeking to avoid such situations. For example, a husband who knows that his wife becomes anxious if he doesn't let her know that he is going to be late, is not being sensitive to his wife's feelings if he repeatedly does not ring her and let her know that he has been held up. Likewise, a wife who knows that her husband is very concerned about staying within an agreed budget is not showing sensitivity to her husband's feelings if she repeatedly exceeds the agreed amount and spends the extra money on non-essentials.

(c) *Listening and responding.* Some writers have stressed the importance of listening in the communication process. Gottman and his co-workers (1977) emphasized the need for spouses to listen particularly to one another's complaints, so that partners know that their complaints have been heard and will be given consideration. In another study (Gottman, 1979) these researchers were able to show that happy husbands and wives were able to respond to negative comments or complaints from the spouse without themselves becoming unduly negative, and without escalating the conflict. Miller, Nunnally and Wackman (1975) also stress the importance of spouses' responding to one another's complaints in a cooperative and nondefensive way.

Boyd and Roach (1977), in their study of communication in married couples demonstrated the importance of active or empathic listening where spouses responded to one another's expressions of feeling by paraphrasing the content and reflecting the feeling so that the partner was given every possible indication that what they said had been clearly heard. This type of responding also gives partners the opportunity to indicate if they have been misunderstood. Imagine a situation where a husband says to his wife, "I'm feeling so frustrated at work. It doesn't seem to matter how careful I am or how much work I do I still seem to get criticized." An example of an active listening response would be, "Work's really getting you down because no matter how hard you try you don't seem to be able to please them".

(d) *Confirmation.* Fisher and Spenkle (1978), conducted a survey of 310 marriage and family counsellors who were asked to indicate which aspects of family functioning they felt were the most important. Confirmation responses (the ability to indicate acceptance of the other person as worth-while and important even when one disagrees with them), were considered to be crucial. Clarke (1973) showed that confirmation was related to marital satisfaction, while Cissna (1975) showed that skill at confirming one another was related to level of intimacy. Clearly a person is more likely to disclose his or her true feelings to someone who has shown that they can accept those feelings and understand them, even though that person may not feel the same themselves, or agree with the attitudes being expressed.

(e) *Expressing respect and esteem*. Boyd and Roach (1977) also found that another important communicative behaviour which discriminated between happy and unhappy couples was the ability to express respect and esteem for the spouse. This finding fits with that of Noller (1982) who showed that wives wanted their husbands to show more appreciation for the things they did well. Vincent, Weiss and Birchler (1975) also found that the level of marital satisfaction of a couple is directly related to how much they use positive reinforcement or rewards in attempting to change each other's behaviour.

Thus the communicative behaviours that seem to be positively related to marital adjustment include sharing feelings with one another as clearly as possible, expressing sensitivity to the partner's feelings, listening to the complaints of the spouse, being empathic, confirming the spouse, and expressing respect and esteem for the spouse.

Behaviours that lead to ineffective marital communication

(a) *Lack of listening*. Lack of listening is seen by many researchers as playing a crucial part in the breakdown of marital communication. Thomas (1977) described couples in unhappy marriages as being unwilling or unable to understand what is said. McNamara and Bahr (1980) found that unhappy spouses complained of a lack of listening on the part of their spouses. These researchers found that the most difficult role for spouses was what they called the "therapeutic" role, or listening to each other's problems, feelings and complaints—a role that is vitally related to the quality of communication within a couple. Raush *et al.* (1974) provide the transcript of an interaction in which a husband seems unable to listen to what his wife is saying, in the context of her wanting him to tell her why he seems upset (a problem discussed in the section on self disclosure).

"1 W Bob, would you like something to drink or some ice cream? (Pause) Bob? (Pause) Look, honey, I know you well enough to know that when something is wrong you often withdraw, you don't talk about it, I can't get anything out of you. I'm not the kind of person who can go on like that. I've got to explode and get it off my chest and talk about it. Now, something has been wrong for several days. Bob, is anything wrong at work? Have I done anything? We can't go on avoiding the situation. Please listen. Stop pouting, and tell me what's wrong.

2 H Did you feed the cat?

3 W Yes, but that has nothing to do with what we're talking about. Please talk to me. Tell me anything that's wrong. What is the matter with you?

4 H (Sighs) You know what's wrong.

Mrs Jones replies again at length, denying that she knows what's wrong, pointing out that they can't continue marriage ignoring one another, claiming that she loves him very much. To all this he replies 'Did you let the cat out?' The scene continues with her lengthy appeals to him countered either by his insistence that she knows what's wrong or his cool extraneous remarks ('Do you want a coke?', 'Did you cash the check?'). The scene ends with no resolution and the wife distraught." (Raush *et al.*, p. 72). In this example the husband is using tangential replies as a way of avoiding dealing with his wife's questions, since he either has difficulty with, or sees no point in, sharing his feelings with her. In any case, the message which comes through to the wife is that her issues are not being listened to or dealt with.

Gottman *et al* (1976) describe two other behaviours which they found to be common in unhappy couples: summarizing self and cross-complaining. Interestingly, each of these behaviours also involves a lack of listening. When spouses summarize self, they keep restating their own point of view, without taking into account the point of view of the other. The authors describe this as the blah-blah-yak-yak syndrome. One partner says, "What I'm trying to say is blah-blah", and the partner responds with, "But what I'm trying to say is yak-yak", and they continue in this vein, each ignoring the point of view of the other. When spouses cross-complain, one spouse states a complaint and the partner, instead of dealing with that complaint, merely states a counter-complaint. This behaviour could be epitomized as the "what about you" syndrome. Each of these behaviours involve the spouses failing to really listen to the partner, in the sense of taking into account what he/she has to say.

(b) *Lack of responsiveness*. Related to this lack of listening is the finding that spouses in unhappy marriages are generally less responsive to one another (Koren & Carlton, 1980). Rubin (1977) particularly comments on the husband's lack of responsiveness to the wife. This would fit with low marital satisfaction wives' complaints that husbands did not give them enough affection, and did not give them attention when they needed it (Noller, 1982).

(c) *Criticism, arguing and nagging*. Matthews and Milhanovich (1963) found a tendency for spouses to be critical and disapproving of one another.

They reported that the unhappy couples in their sample complained of being neglected, and receiving little affection, appreciation or understanding. These couples also complained that their spouses magnified their faults, belittled them, accused them unjustly and generally made them feel worthless and lacking in self-respect. Thomas (1977) listed the behaviours that unhappy couples complain about, including arguing, quarrelling, nagging, insults, put-downs, and talking past each other. Navran (1967) reported that the unhappy couples in his study seemed to use styles of communication which led to poor problem-solving and need frustration, and, as a consequence, a great deal of anger, anxiety and tension in the relationship. Miller, Nunnally and Wackman (1975) also emphasize the ineffective communication styles used by unhappy spouses, and poor communicators in general. This style (which they call Style II) involves such behaviours as nagging, directing, ordering, blaming, evaluating, demanding, defending, persuading and assuming.

(d) *Faulty behaviour change operations.* One common cause of arguments in married couples is the desire by one member of the couple for change in the spouse's behaviour. A number of writers have particularly commented on the faulty behaviour change operations used by unhappy married couples (Jacobson, 1981). Some researchers, in fact, see faulty behaviour change operations as the crucial factor in the breakdown of marital relationships (Birchler *et al.*, 1975; Patterson & Hops, 1972; Patterson, Hops & Weiss, 1975). Jacobson and Moore (1981) see unhappy couples as more often using punishment in order to change one another's behaviour, and using reinforcers less than other couples. Vincent, Weiss and Birchler (1975) claim that the level of marital satisfaction of a couple is directly related to whether the couple uses positive reinforcement or rewards in attempting to change one another's behaviour—or aversive control or coercion. While coercion can be effective in obtaining compliance (i.e. getting the other person to change in the desired direction), it can also produce counter-coercion and lack of cooperation (Barry, 1970; Weiss & Ford, 1977). This effect can be even more problematical in unhappy couples who have long-standing unsatisfactory marital relationships, since marital conflict is often about (at least implicitly) such issues as the nature of the relationship (Ard, 1967; Raush *et al.*, 1974) and who dominates whom (Barry, 1970; Weiss & Ford, 1970). Another problem with the use of coercion is that the very compliance which it demands serves to reinforce the use of coercion, and increase the probability of more coercion in future interactions (Patterson *et al.*, 1975). In other words, the spouse who gives in to coercive demands for behaviour change is more likely to face coercive tactics from the spouse the next time a change in behaviour is desired. This principle, to some extent, explains the escalation of conflict, and consequent deterioration of relationship so often encountered by both researchers and therapists. Jacobson (1981), for instance, comments on the extent to which unhappy couples coerce, threaten, intimidate and humiliate one another in order to achieve behaviour change, and Billings (1979) maintains that the proportion of hostile communication between unhappy spouses increases as the conflict continues.

Gottman (Gottman et al., 1977; Gottman, 1979) describes a process he calls "negative affect reciprocity". Using sequential analysis of problem-solving interactions between clinic and nonclinic couples, he was able to show that in the clinic couples, a negative statement by one member of the couple was more likely to be followed with negative from the other member than was true for couples who were not seeking marriage counselling at a clinic. These studies by Gottman and his co-workers will be described in greater detail in Chapter 3.

Other writers have also emphasized the progressive deterioration which seems to occur in marriages once they become involved in destructive communication patterns. Margolin, Christensen and Weiss (1975), for instance, see communication skills as critical if spouses are to have any possibility of circumventing or reversing downward trends in their relationship. Bardill (1966), for example, comments on the way that unhappy couples communicate progressively less well as time goes by and as the conflict becomes more intense, with ambiguous or contradictory communication being common, and arguments occurring over the simplest of tasks.

Accuracy of communication

While the kinds of communications that spouses are sending to each other are clearly important determinants of marital satisfaction, another important issue is the accuracy of the communication or the extent to which members of the couple send their messages to one another clearly, and understand one another (Boyd & Roach, 1977; Kahn, 1970).

One of the problems with regard to communication is that it cannot be assumed that communication has occurred just because a message has been sent. Some communication may occur, but a communicator cannot assume that the message that he intended is the one that is received. A number of communication theorists have discussed this problem, applying different conceptual frameworks and terminology. Watzlawick, Beavin and Jackson (1967) discuss two issues—the problem of the communicator getting his message across, and the problem of his being aware when the message fails to communicate, or is misinterpreted. In this section we will focus on the problem of accuracy in sending and receiving messages, and leave the question of awareness of how a message has been sent or received to a later section.

Importance of nonverbal communication to accuracy

Fletcher's (1973) contention that communicators must be aware of the importance of the nonverbal aspects of the message rather than just the words also relates to this same problem. Misunderstandings would seem to occur because of the failure by either the encoder or the decoder to take adequate account of nonverbal communication. For example, a decoder might not be looking at his/her spouse and may not notice the frown accompanying the agreement, and thus fail to clarify whatever hesitation the spouse still has about an idea he/she has proposed. Such a situation may lead to a spouse thinking the partner completely agrees when in fact, he/she does not, and further misunderstandings and disagreements may arise as a result. On the other hand, a preoccupied encoder may not realize that he/she is frowning when sending a message and is thus communicating more reticence to his/her spouse than is intended. In each of these situations, unless some clarification occurs, there is much potential for misunderstanding and argument.

Complexity of communication

Weakland (1976), in discussing the same problem, underlines the complexity of communication, noting that "people are always sending and receiving a multiplicity of messages by both verbal and nonverbal channels and these messages necessarily modify or qualify one another" (p. 117). Weakland focuses on the different channels of communication and the way these channels (for instance, verbal and one or more of the nonverbal channels) are related to one another. If the different channels are giving the same message, then they are supporting or confirming one another, and a clear unified message is the result. If, on the other hand, the different channels carry different messages, then they are modifying or qualifying one another. This situation generally leads to a message which is contradictory and difficult to interpret.

Completing communication cycles

Fletcher (1973) emphasized the importance of a communicator checking out the effects that his/her message has on the person receiving the communication, and thus ensuring that the message that has been received is the one that he/she intended. Mace and Mace (1974) in discussing communication in marriage call this checking out process "completing the communication cycles". The techniques described earlier of active or empathic listening can be very useful here.

TABLE 2.3. *The Talk Table Procedure*

Husband	Wife
1. Speaks	
2. Rates "intended impact"	
3. Yields floor	
	4. Rates "impact" of husband's message
	5. Speaks
	6. Rates "intended impact" of own message
	7. Yields floor
8. Rates impact of wife's message	
9. Speaks	
10. Rates "intended impact" of own message	
11. Yields the floor	
(And so on)	

Is inaccuracy due to encoding or decoding?

In a research project using a device which they called a "talk table", Gottman, Notarius and others (1976) compared intentions and effects of messages between spouses of different levels of marital adjustment. Spouses faced each other across a table and were asked to discuss a marital problem. After each utterance the encoder was asked to rate his/her intention on a 5-point scale from super-positive to super-negative, and the decoder was asked to rate the effect of the message on him/her on a similar 5-point scale. (See Table 2.3.) Comparisons of ratings of happy and unhappy couples showed that while the two groups did not differ with regard to the way they rated their intentions, unhappy couples rated the messages as having a significantly more negative effect on them than did the happy couples. While this result would seem to indicate that unhappy spouses decode more negatively than happy spouses, we cannot be sure that the problem was not in the way the messages from the unhappy spouses were actually encoded. It is possible that they sent these messages more negatively than they intended to.

Accuracy of encoding and decoding nonverbal communication

Gottman and his colleagues used videotapes of couples discussing an actual marital problem (Gottman, Notarius & Markman, 1977). They showed the importance of nonverbal communication in marriage when they found that distressed and nondistressed couples could be discriminated more clearly on the type of nonverbal communication accompanying their verbal statements, than on the verbal behaviour alone. These researchers found, for instance, that distressed couples were more likely than nondistressed couples to express their feelings about a problem with negative affect, and to express agreement with neutral or negative affect. (See Chapter 3.)

Some theorists and researchers have emphasized "person effects" on messages, noting that any message that is sent is not just made up of a number of parts or channels, but is affected in a more total way by the person sending it. Of course, the same kinds of effects occur with message-receiving, since the same message may be received quite differently by people with different backgrounds and histories—particularly if these people have different experiences with the message-sender. Newcomb, Turner and Converse (1965) comment that "messages are neither sent nor received by psychologically empty organisms" (p. 204).

Raush and his colleagues (1974) focus on the receiving process and the effects which the individual has on that when they comment "whatever is received is received according to the manner of the recipient". Kahn (1969, 1970) found that the level of marital satisfaction of a couple was related to the accuracy with which the members could understand each other's messages—particularly messages which relied heavily on the nonverbal channel for their meaning. Several studies have expanded on the work of Kahn (Gottman & Porterfield, 1981; Noller, 1980) and these studies will be described in greater detail in Chapter 5.

It is likely that Kahn's finding is related to the unsatisfactory perceptions which spouses with low satisfaction tend to have of one another (Murstein & Beck, 1972) with these perceptions leading to the distortion of the message by the decoder. It is also likely that a person's perception of the spouse's attitude to himself would be related to this type of decoding. For instance, a person who sees his spouse as always trying to dominate him could be more likely to interpret a message as controlling, while a person who saw his spouse as disliking him may be more likely to interpret remarks as criticisms. It is also possible that a spouse who has problems in the area of dominance may, in fact, send a more negative message to his/her partner, whether he/she intended to or not.

Relationship between communication accuracy and marital satisfaction

Figure 2.2 illustrates the relationship between accuracy at encoding and decoding communication, and marital satisfaction. This diagram particularly illustrates the circular nature of the relationship, with low marital satisfaction leading to problems in communication, and problems in communication leading to marital satisfaction.

Awareness of communication

While research has shown that communication accuracy is important to marital satisfaction, there is little data available on the relationship between communication awareness and marital satisfaction. Watzlawick, Beavin and

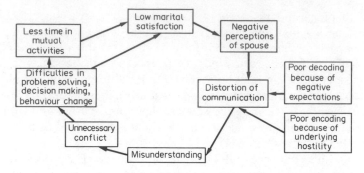

FIG 2.2. Diagrammatic representation of the relationship between low marital satisfaction and communication difficulties

Jackson (1967) claim that it is not only important for someone to be accurate in their communication, but it is also important for them to know when they have misunderstood, or been misunderstood. They describe the issue in terms of levels, with communication failing at one level when the encoder doesn't get across the message he/she intended, and at the second level when he/she doesn't realize that the message has not been understood, or has been misunderstood. As well, further problems may arise if the person receiving the message does not realize that he/she has not understood or has misunderstood. Table 2.4 illustrates the process.

Whether such a situation will be resolved or not depends on how ready the partners are to check out the communication to see whether there has been

TABLE 2.4

Encoder A	Decoder B
1. May not get message across.	1. May not decode message accurately.
2. May not realize message has not been understood.	2. May not realize has misunderstood.

Encoder A ————————————————→	Decoder B
1. Didn't we have chicken for dinner a few nights ago. (Meaning that he's pleased we are having chicken so often.)	1. Misunderstands and thinks that spouse is unhappy at having chicken so often.
2. Expects wife to be happy and can't understand why she is not.	2. Wife vows not to have chicken again for a month and feels angry because husband's comment seems unreasonable.

Each is puzzled by the reactions of the other and the partners end up out of sorts with one another.

any misunderstanding. The encoder is unlikely to check out, however, if he/she assumes that the message was sent clearly and therefore *must* be understood, and the decoder is confident that the message he/she heard was the one that was intended. As a counsellor, I have had the experience on a number of occasions of hearing a couple argue about the meaning of some past communication sent by one to the other. I have frequently been struck by how adamantly, decoders in particular, will hold to their interpretations, despite protestations from the encoder that something else was intended. The decoder's position could be characterized by the statement, "Don't tell me what you meant, I know what you meant. After all, I've been married to you for 10 years".

A study of communication awareness in married couples (Venardos, 1982) will be described in Chapter 7.

Effectiveness of communication

Peterson (1968) found effective communication to be related to the low incidence of many problems, and to the solving of others. That is, couples with an effective communication system may have the same kinds of issues coming up in their relationship, but they will have a greater chance than those with communication problems, of coming to a mutually acceptable solution. Peterson found, for example, that couples with effective communication had fewer problems in such areas as time spent together, conflict of religious views, family responsibilities, lack of closeness, sex relations, criticism, differences in expectations, and planning and decision-making in various areas. He also found that couples with good communication skills were more able to resolve problems in such areas as use of recreation and leisure-time, tenseness and low family morale, sex relations with mate, and criticism and fault-finding.

It is important to keep in mind, however, the distinction between communication skills (expressing one's feelings or point of view and taking account of those of the other person) and problem-solving skills which enable a couple to find mutually acceptable solutions to problems in their relationship (Epstein & Williams, 1981). While poor communication may lead to poor problem-solving, good communication will not necessarily lead to good problem-solving unless the couple have such skills as defining the components of a problem, collecting relevant information, generating alternative solutions, evaluating each of these solutions with regard to its advantages and disadvantages, choosing the appropriate solution, and defining the action that needs to be taken (Thomas, 1977). Negotiation and problem solving will be discussed further in Chapter 12.

Thomas (1977) comments that communication difficulties are the most common problem encountered in couples who seek assistance to improve their interpersonal relationship, and the effect of such difficulties on problem-solving is stressed by a number of writers. Matthews and Milhanovich (1963), for instance, found a general lack of ability to solve problems as crucial in the development of marital unhappiness. They found that, while for both happy and unhappy couples relatively few problems were actually solved but tended to remain as irritants, there were more detrimental effects for the unhappy couples. Royce and Weiss (1975) also describe unhappy married couples as having poor negotiation and problem-solving skills. So there would seem to be general agreement that married couples tend to have difficulties in working through issues to mutually acceptable solutions, and that unhappy couples have particular problems achieving such solutions because of the unhelpful behaviours they tend to engage in during the communication process.

In fact, there is considerable evidence, as Glick and Gross (1975) have maintained, that the process of interaction during conflict is a critical determinant of marital satisfaction. These researchers see interaction during conflict as linked to marital satisfaction through the making of decisions about the relationship and about joint activities (or failure to make such decisions), the intrinsic satisfaction (or lack of) obtained during the interaction itself, and the likelihood (or otherwise) of successful attempts to resolve issues in the future.

Some writers (Raush et al., 1974; Scanzoni, 1981) see a much greater potential for conflict in the contemporary couple because of the greater number of decision points to be faced due to the greater flexibility of roles in today's society, the fact that women are wanting more say in such decisions, and more consideration of their needs and wants than has been the case in the past. This position is supported by a recent study which showed greater levels of understanding between sex-typed spouses than was true for other couples. Of course, sex-typed couples have an accumulation of mutually accepted social rules to help them to understand one another, and they don't have to rely entirely on the communication process for gaining that understanding. Hallenbeck (1966) saw disagreement about ideal roles as a crucial factor in marital dissatisfaction, while Peterson (1968) emphasized that it was not just differences in norms and expectations that were important, but the failure to clarify what the differences were. Again the focus seems to be on the ability to express one's attitudes and feelings, and to resolve differences that exist.

Summary

A number of researchers have provided clues as to the reasons why communication is so often ineffective for unhappy couples, and why they fail to resolve issues:

(a) They do not share their true feelings with one another.

(b) If one spouse does share his/her true feelings, the other is likely to be unwilling to hear that message or to deal with it. Likely responses are a complaint of his/her own (What about you?), a statement of his/her own attitude that fails to acknowledge the expressed attitude of the spouse (What I'm trying to say is . . .), or a tangential response (Isn't it a lovely day?).

(c) The expression of a negative feeling by one member is likely to lead to a cycle of negative feeling statements which serve to escalate the conflict.

(d) Unhappy spouses are less likely to send clear messages to one another, and more likely to misunderstand one another, and are likely to have a more negative impact than they intend.

(e) Unhappy spouses are more likely to use negative behaviours such as threats, nagging, insults, put-downs, in order to change one another's behaviour, and are less likely to use reinforcement. However, many questions still remain unanswered, particularly with regard to non-verbal communication. Work by Kahn (1970), Gottman et al. (1976, 1977), Gottman (1979), and Noller (1980a, 1980b, 1982) will be described in greater detail in later chapters.

Reference Note

1. Weiss, R. L. & Perry, B. A. *Assessment and Treatment of Marital Dysfunction*, Oregon Marital Studies Program, University of Oregon, Eugene, Oregon.

References

ARD, B. J. (1976) Communication theory in marriage counseling: a critique. Paper presented at the National Council of Family Relations Annual Conference, 1967. In ARD, B. J. & ARD, C. C., *Handbook of Marriage Counseling* (2nd Ed.), Science and Behavior Books.

BARDILL, D. R. (1966) A relationship-focused approach to marital problems. *Social Work*, 2, 70–77.

BARRY, W. A. (1970) Marriage research and conflict: an integrative review. *Psychological Bulletin*, 73, 41–54.

BILLINGS, A. (1979) Conflict resolution in distressed and nondistressed married couples. *Journal of Consulting and Clinical Psychology*, 47, 368–76.

BIRCHLER, G. R., WEISS, R. L. & VINCENT, J. P. (1975) Multimethod analysis of social reinforcement exchange between maritally distressed and non-distressed spouse and stranger dyads. *Journal of Personality and Social Psychology*, 31, 349–62.

BOLTE, G. L. (1975) A communications approach to marital counseling. In GURMAN, A. S. & RICE, D. G. (Eds.) *Couples in Conflict*. New York: Jason Aronson.

BOYD, L. A. & ROACH, A. J. (1977) Interpersonal communication skills differentiating more satisfying and less satisfying marital relationships. *Journal of Counseling Psychology*, 24, 540–2.

BRODY, S. A. (1963) Husband-wife communication patterns related to marital adjustment. Unpublished Ph.D thesis, University of Southern California.

CISSNA, K. (1975) Facilitative communication and interpersonal relationships: an empirical test of a theory of interpersonal communication. Unpublished doctoral dissertation, University of Denver.

CLARKE, F. (1973) Interpersonal communication variables as predictors of marital satisfaction–attraction. Unpublished doctoral dissertation, University of Denver.

CRADDOCK, A. (1980) The impact of social change on Australian families. *Australian Journal of Sex, Marriage and the Family*, **1**, 4–14.

EPSTEIN, N & WILLIAMS, A. M. (1981) Behavioral approaches to the treatment of marital discord. In SHOLEVAR, G. P., *The Handbook of Marriage and Marital Therapy*. New York: Spectrum.

FISHER, B. & SPRENKLE, D. (1978) Therapists' perceptions of healthy family functioning. *International Journal of Family Counseling*, **6**, 9–17.

FLETCHER, C. M. (1973) *Communication in Medicine*. Rock Carling Monograph for Nuffield Provincial Hospitals Trust.

GLICK, B. R. & GROSS, S. J. (1975) Marital interaction and marital conflict: A critical evaluation of current research strategies. *Journal of Marriage and the Family*, **37**, 505–12.

GOTTMAN, J. M. (1979) *Marital Interaction: experimental investigations*. New York: Academic Press.

GOTTMAN, J., MARKMAN, H. & NOTARIUS, C. (1977) The topography of marital conflict: a sequential analysis of verbal and nonverbal behaviour. *Journal of Marriage and the Family*, **39**, 461–77.

GOTTMAN, J., NOTARIUS, C., MARKMAN, H., BANKS, S., YOPPI, B. & RUBIN, M. E. (1976) Behaviour exchange theory and marital decision making. *Journal of Personality and Social Psychology*, **34**, 14–23.

GOTTMAN, J. M. & PORTERFIELD, A. L. (1981) Communicative competence in the nonverbal behaviour of married couples. *Journal of Marriage and the Family*, **4**, 817–24.

HALLENBECK, P. (1966) An analysis of power dynamics in marriage. *Journal of Marriage and the Family*, **28**, 200–3.

JACOBSON, N. S. (1981) Behavioral Marital Therapy. In GURMAN, A. S. & KNISKERN, D. P. (Ed.) *Handbook of Family Therapy*. New York: Brunner/Mazel.

JOURARD, S. (1971) *The transparent self*. New York: Van Nostrand.

KAHN, M. (1969) Nonverbal communication as a factor in marital satisfaction. Doctoral dissertation, Southern Illinois University.

KAHN, M. (1970) Nonverbal communication and marital satisfaction. *Family Process*, **9**, 449–56.

KARLSSON, G. (1951) *Adaptability and communication in marriage*. Uppsala: Almquist and Wiksells Aktiebelag Bektrycheri.

KOREN, P. & CARLTON, K. (1980) Marital conflict: relations among behaviours, outcomes and distress, *Journal of Consulting and Clinical Psychology*, **48**, 460–8.

LEWIS, R. A. & SPANIER, G. B. (1979) Theorizing about the quality and stability of marriage. In BURR, W., HILL, R., NYE, F. I. & REISS, I. L. (Eds.) *Contemporary Theories about the Family* (Vol. 12). New York: The Free Press.

LOCKE, H. J., SABAGH, G. & THOMAS, M. (1956) Correlates of primary communication and empathy. *Research Studies of the State College of Washington*, **24**, 118.

LOCKE, H. J. & WALLACE, K. M. (1959) Short marital adjustment and prediction tests: their reliability and validity. *Marriage and Family Living*, **21**, 251–5.

MACE, D. & MACE, V. (1974) *We can have better marriages if we really want them*. London: Oliphants.

McMAMARA, M. L. L. & BAHR, H. M. (1980) The dimensionality of marital role satisfaction. *Journal of Marriage and the Family*, **42**, 45–55.

MARGOLIN, G., CHRISTENSEN, H. & WEISS, R. L. (1975) Contracts, cognition and change: a behavioral approach to marriage therapy. *The Counseling Psychologist*, **5**, 15–26.

MATTHEWS, V. C. & MILHANOVICH, C. S. (1963) New orientations on marital adjustment. *Marriage and Family Living*, **25**, 300–4.

MILLER, S., NUNNALLY, E. W. & WACKMAN, D. B. (1980) *Couple communication I. Talking Together*. North Strathfield: Family Life Movement of Australia.

MONTGOMERY, B. M. (1981) The form and function of quality communication in marriage. *Family Relations*, **30**, 21–30.

MURSTEIN, B. I. & BECK, G. D. (1972) Person perception, marriage adjustment and social desirability. *Journal of Consulting and Clinical Psychology*, **39**, 396–403.

NAVRAN, L. (1967) Communication and adjustment in marriage. *Family Process*, **6**, 173–84.

NEWCOMB, T. M., TURNER, L. H. & CONVERSE, P. E. (1965). *Social psychology: The study of human interaction*. New York: Holt, Rinehart & Winston.

NOLLER, P. (1980a) Misunderstandings in marital communication: a study of couples' nonverbal communication. *Journal of Personality and Social Psychology*, **39**, 1135–48.

NOLLER, P. (1980b) Gaze in married couples. *Journal of Nonverbal Behaviour*, **5**, 115–29.

NOLLER, P. (1981) Gender and marital adjustment level differences in decoding messages from spouses and strangers. *Journal of Personality and Social Psychology*, **41**, 272–8.

NOLLER, P. (1982) Couple communication and marital satisfaction. *Australian Journal of Sex Marriage & Family*, **3**:**2**, 69–75.

OLSON, D. H. (1970) Marital and family therapy: integrative review and critique. *Journal of Marriage and the Family*, **32**, 501–38.

PATTERSON, G. D. & HOPS, H. (1972) Coercion, a game for two: Intervention techniques for marital conflict. In ULRICH, R. E. & MOUNTJOY, P. (Eds.) *The experimental analysis of social behavior*. New York: Appleton-Century-Crofts.

PATTERSON, G. D., HOPS, H. & WEISS, R. L. (1975) Interpersonal skills training for couples in early stages of conflict. *Journal of Marriage and the Family* (1968), **37**, 295–302.

PETERSON, D. M. (1968) Husband-wife communication and family problems. *Sociology and Social Research*, **53**, 375–84.

RAUSH, H. L., BARRY, W. A., HERTEL, R. K. & SWAIN, M. E. (1974) *Communication, Conflict and Marriage*. San Francisco: Jossey-Bass.

ROYCE, W. S. & WEISS, R. L. (1975) Behavioural cues in the judgment of marital satisfaction: a linear regression analysis. *Journal of Consulting and Clinical Psychology*, **43**, 816–24.

RUBIN, M. E. Y. (1977) Differences between distressed and nondistressed couples in verbal and nonverbal communication codes. *Dissertation Abstracts International*, Oct, **38**, (4-B), 1902.

SCANZONI, J. (1975) Sex roles, economic factors, and marital solidarity in black and white marriages. *Journal of Marriage and the Family*, **37**, 130–44.

SNYDER, D. K. (1979) Multidimensional assessment of marital role satisfaction. *Journal of Marriage and the Family*, **41**, 813–23.

THOMAS, E. J. (1977) *Marital Communication and Decision Making*. New York: The Free Press.

VENARDOS, C. (1982) Communication awareness in married couples. Unpublished Honours Thesis, University of Queensland.

VINCENT, J. P., WEISS, R. L. & BIRCHLER, G. (1975) A behavioral analysis of problem-solving in distressed and nondistressed married and stranger dyads. *Behavior Therapy*, **6**, 475–86.

WATZLAWICK, P., BEAVIN, J. H. & JACKSON, D. (1967) *Pragmatics of human communication*. New York: Norton.

WEAKLAND, J. (1976) Communication theory and clinical change. In GUERIN, P. J. (Ed.) *Family therapy theory and practice*. New York: Gardner Press.

WEISS, R. L. & FORD, L. (1977) A social learning view of marriage. Draft distributed by the Oregon Marital Research Institute.

3

Nonverbal Communication and Marriage

So the impetus for the study of nonverbal communication comes mainly from two sources:

1. the evidence for the importance of communication to the marital relationship, and
2. the evidence for the importance of nonverbal communication to the whole interaction process.

If communication is important to marital satisfaction, and nonverbal communication is a crucial component of the communication process, then it makes sense that nonverbal communication is important to marital satisfaction, particularly since there is evidence that nonverbal communication tends to handle interpersonal attitudes and relationships (Argyle, 1975).

The problem is, in what way is nonverbal communication related to marital satisfaction? There are several questions that need to be answered.

1. Does the nonverbal communication system of a couple constitute a private message system which enables the couple to communicate in unique and idiosyncratic ways—and to get across messages to each other that are not necessarily understood by others. If this were the case, one would expect that such a private message system would work better for couples high in marital satisfaction, than for those low in marital satisfaction.

2. Is the communicative behaviour of happy couples different from that of unhappy couples:

(a) In the use of different verbal behaviours?
(b) In the use of different nonverbal behaviours?
(c) In the way the verbal and the nonverbal components are combined?

3. Do happy and unhappy couples perceive each others' communications differently?

4. If marital satisfaction is related to accuracy of communication for a couple, how important is nonverbal communication to this accuracy, and in what ways does nonverbal behaviour affect accuracy? Each of these questions will be dealt with in a separate section of this chapter.

TABLE 3.1. *Nonverbal Items on the Primary Communication Inventory*

Item 5	Does your spouse adjust what he (she) says and how he (she) says it, to the way you seem to feel at the moment.
Item 7	Do you know the feelings of your spouse from his (her) facial and bodily gestures?
Item 9	Does your spouse explain or express himself (herself) to you through a glance or gestures?
Item 11	Can your spouse tell what kind of day you have had without asking?
Item 15	How often does your spouse sulk or pout?
Item 18	You and your spouse are visiting friends. Something is said by the friends which causes you to glance at each other. Would you understand each other?
Item 19	How often can you tell as much from the tone of voice of your spouse as from what he (she) actually says?
Item 23	Do you understand the meaning of your spouse's facial expressions?

Private message system

Navran (1967) correlated scores on the Primary Communication Inventory (Locke, Sabagh & Tomes, 1956) with scores on the Short Marital Adjustment Test (M.A.T.) (Locke & Wallace, 1959). He found a high correlation between the two measures. It should be borne in mind, of course, that these are both self-report measures and would have similar susceptibility to social desirability effects. Navran also performed separate correlations between the verbal items (17 items) and the M.A.T., and the nonverbal items and the M.A.T. A higher correlation was found for the verbal items than for the nonverbal items. Table 3.1 shows the nonverbal items on the P.C.I. which emphasize understanding one another's nonverbal communication apart from words, as much as understanding the nonverbal communication that accompanies words.

As well, some of the verbal items on the P.C.I. also relate to the private message system of the couple. For example:

Item 6   When you start to ask a question, does your spouse know what it is before you ask it?

Item 14   Do you and your spouse use words which have a special meaning not understood by others?

Item 21   Do you feel that in most matters your spouse knows what you are trying to say?

Gottman (1979) reports a test of the private message system hypothesis. He compared the *impact* which a particular message had on the spouse with the way that message was coded by a third coder (using the Couples' Interaction Scoring System). (See Chapter 4.)

For wives in the clinic group there was a significant relationship between the two sets of ratings while there was no such relationship for the other wives or for the husbands in either group. These findings suggest some evidence for a private message system in the nonclinic couples.

Gottman (1979) presented, in detail, the data for the nonclinic wives as speakers, and showed that the observers tended to code less positively than the husbands. This finding could indicate that what private message system exists is related to recognizing positivity. Such a possibility fits with the original Talk Table data (Gottman *et al.*, 1976) since one could argue that the reason the impact for clinic couples is more negative than intended is that they do not have an established method of relaying positivity, so that it is easily recognized by each of the partners.

Gottman and Porterfield (1981) also tested the private message system hypothesis using a methodology to be described in detail in Chapter 5. Their results were consistent with the hypothesis that happy couples have a private message system, at least for the situation of wives as message senders, and husbands as receivers. This finding fits with that of the earlier study (Gottman, 1979).

Noller (1980) also tested the private message system hypothesis (or what she called idiosyncratic communication), but using a different criterion for what constitutes evidence for a private message system. While this study will be presented in greater detail in Chapter 5, it should be noted here that she also found evidence that the private message system particularly operates when wives are the message senders. In Gottman's (1979) study, however, the result applied generally, and was not related to marital adjustment level.

Different Communicative Behaviours

From the literature on marital communication reviewed in Chapter 2, there seems to be considerable evidence that husbands and wives in unhappy marriages communicate with each other differently from husbands and wives in happy marriages. The issue of interest to us here is the extent to which such differences are related to nonverbal behaviour.

Some self-report data. The Primary Communication Inventory (Locke, Sabagh & Thomas, 1956) contains questions about the use of facial expression, gestures, tone of voice, and nonverbal behaviours such as sulking and pouting, but little distinction is made between the positive and negative uses of such behaviours (see Table 3.1).

While Navran (1967) was able to show that the verbal items relate more to marital adjustment than the nonverbal items, there is no data as to whether some of the nonverbal items are more important in discriminating between happy and unhappy couples than are others. Venardos (1982) administered the P.C.I. as part of a study to be described in greater detail in a later section on awareness of communication. She found that for females the verbal part of the P.C.I. was related to marital adjustment, but this was not true for males. For the males she found that the correlation between scores on the

TABLE 3.2. *Six-Category Coding Scheme for Interpersonal Conflict*

Category	Description
1	Cognitive acts: neutral acts, suggestions, and rational argument.
2	Resolving acts: acts aimed at cooling the conflict or resolving the conflict issue.
3	Reconciling acts: acts aimed at reconciling the two partners emotionally.
4	Appealing acts: acts appealing to the other to grant one's wish.
5	Rejecting acts: acts showing a cold or nasty rejection of the other's argument or person.
6	Coercive acts or personal attacks: acts aimed at forcing compliance by power plays, guilt induction, or disparagement of the other.

From Raush *et al.*, 1974, p. 115.

nonverbal part of the P.C.I. and a measure of actual skill at decoding the spouse was greater for the happy husbands than for the others.

Of course, the data available here is self-report data and it is not at all clear that interactants are able to report accurately on what they do themselves, or what their spouses do. There is a dearth of behavioural data, however, related to this question.

Some behavioural data Raush *et al.* (1974) had couples participate in improvisations "designed to engage couples in quasi-experimental, quasi-naturalistic situations of interaction where because of the separate instructions given to each partner, a conflict of interest was created" (p. 56). The improvisations were audio-taped and transcripts were made from the tapes. Both the tapes and the transcripts were used in the coding, and formal analyses were based on a six-category coding system (see Table 3.2).

Using factor analysis these researchers isolated a group of couples (six) they labelled "discordant" who reported disagreement, unhappiness and doubts about the marriage, and a group they labelled as harmonious (seven). While the wives in the discordant group differed little from other wives overall, husbands in this group were different from other husbands in that they were more coercive and less cognitive, and used fewer reconciling acts. They were also more likely to respond to coercion from their wives with more coercion.

"Thus, in these couples the husbands are the ones who differ most from the rest of the sample, and they differ in the direction of greater punitiveness. These husbands seem to charge conflict with coerciveness, personal grievances and disparagement." (Raush *et al.*, 1974, p. 161).

Table 3.3 presents data on the use of the different categories of behaviour by the discordant couples as compared with the rest of the sample, and the harmonious couples as compared with the rest of the sample.

TABLE 3.3. *Comparison of Discordant and Other Couples in Four Scenes Combined*

Group	Consequent categories						
	Cognitive	Resolving	Reconciling	Appealing	Rejecting	Coercive	N
Discordant H	38.1	10.0	8.6	8.6	12.5	22.2	1417
Other H	46.0	9.8	11.5	10.5	10.9	11.4	6132
Discordant W	40.7	7.5	7.8	13.2	11.7	19.2	1420
Other W	44.4	8.0	8.0	12.0	12.4	15.3	6163

From Raush *et al.*, 1974, p. 158.

Issues vs Relationship

However, Raush and his colleagues used two different types of improvisations:

(a) Issue oriented (planning an anniversary celebration, and conflict over television).
(b) Relationship oriented (one where the husband was asked to be distant towards his wife, and one where the wife was asked to be distant towards her husband).

These researchers found that the discordant couples behaved very differently in the issue oriented scenes from the relationship oriented scenes.

In the issue oriented scenes the wives behaved more coercively than the husbands irrespective of the husband's antecedent behaviour, and they were more coercive than the rest of the wives. However, in the situations where spouses were being distant from one another (relationship oriented situations), the husbands became much more coercive and rejecting, and they tended to use fewer reconciling and resolving acts (see Table 3.3) than the rest of the husbands (in both the husband-distant and the wife-distant scenes). On the other hand, the wives in both scenes were less rejecting and coercive than the rest of the wives, and much less rejecting and coercive than their husbands. These findings suggest that wives are more negative and coercive in discussions about specific issues, while husbands become more coercive in discussions about the relationship.

One possible explanation is that these differences in behaviour were related to traditional sex roles, with males being able to handle the issue scenes fairly rationally while women became negative and emotional; on the other hand, in the relationship oriented scenes men whose marriages were not happy and secure may have become uncertain and afraid—emotions not normally acceptable for males, and a situation where males might be expected to react with aggression which is acceptable for males. Females on the other hand have been socialized with a concern for maintaining relationships.

TABLE 3.4. *Eight Summary Content Codes of the C.I.S.S.*

Code	Definition	Example
AG	Agreement	(a) Yeah.
		(b) You're right.
DG	Disagreement	(a) No.
		(b) Yes, but ...
		(c) No, because it's too late.
CT	Communication Talk	We're getting off the issue.
MR	Mindreading: Attributing thoughts, feelings, motives, attitudes, or behaviours to spouse	You always get mad in those situations.
PS	Proposing a solution to a problem or information exchange	Let's take out a loan.
SO	Summarizing other	(a) What you're saying is I drink too much.
		(b) We're both suggesting that we take a vacation.
SS	Summarizing self	(a) I told you that I'm not going because its too far to drive.
		(b) What I'm saying is that it's just too late.
PF	Problem information feelings about a problem	(a) The problem is that we don't have enough money.
		(b) That makes me sad.

From Gottman, 1979, p. 86.

Unfortunately Raush and his colleagues made no attempt to separate the effects of the verbal and nonverbal components (although both were clearly taken into account in the coding). Gottman (1979) who recoded the data using the Couples' Interaction Scoring System (see Chapter 4) showed that the couples in Raush's study behaved very similarly to the distressed and nondistressed couples in the study by Gottman *et al.* (1977) (at least, as far as could be determined from audiotapes).

In another study, Gottman and his colleagues (Gottman *et al.*, 1977; Gottman, 1979) made videotapes of couples who were asked "to come to a mutually satisfying resolution of the most troublesome of three problems". Videotapes were coded using both content and affect codes, with the content being coded from the transcript, and affect codes from the videotape and the soundtrack. Nonverbal behaviour was coded using facial expression, voice tone, body position and movement, in that order. The nonverbal behaviours of the listener were also coded. Table 3.4 presents the eight summary content codes used by Gottman (1979, p. 86) and Table 3.5 the cues used to code nonverbal behaviour. When the nonverbal behaviour could not be coded as positive or negative, it was coded as neutral. A number of reliability studies are reported (Gottman, 1979, Chapter 5).

Gottman analysed the nonverbal component of the interactions by summing positive, neutral and negative affect over all content codes. As can be

TABLE 3.5. *Cues Used to Code Nonverbal Behaviour in the C.I.S.S.*

Nonverbal channel	Cues			
	Positive		Negative	
Face	smile empathetic expression head nod		frown sneer fearful expression cry smirk angry expression disgust glare	
Voice	caring warm soft tender relieved empathetic concerned affectionate loving	satisfied buoyant bubbly cheerful chuckling happy joyful laughter	cold tense scared impatient hard clipped staccato whining	blaming sarcastic angry furious blaring hurt depressed accusing mocking laughter
Body	touching distance reduction open arms attention relaxation forward lean		arms akimbo neck or hand tension rude gestures hands thrown up in digust pointing, jabbing, slicing inattention	

TABLE 3.6. *Nonverbal Delivery of Messages Independent of Their Content—Univariate F-ratios for Distress Main Effect*

Variable	Univariate F-ratio	Distressed mean	Nondistressed mean
Neutral affect	11.67**	.65	.85
Positive affect	.09	.10	.12
Negative affect	35.36***	.25	.03

** $p < .01$.
*** $p < .001$.
From Gottman, 1979, p. 108.

seen from Table 3.6 distressed couples expressed significantly less neutral affect, and more negative affect than nondistressed, and there were no differences between the groups on positive affect.

As well, when Gottman compared the ratios of agreement/agreement + disagreement for the two groups he found significant differences between the groups (nondistressed higher than distressed) for both husbands and

TABLE 3.7. *Relationship between Type of Coding and Type of Data*

Type of Data	Type of coding discriminating between the marital adjustment groups
Verbal only	Positive (Highs more)
Nonverbal only	Neutral (Lows less) and negative (Lows more)
Verbal and nonverbal combined	Positive (Highs more) and negative (Lows more)

wives, implying that positive verbal (as against nonverbal) may be important in discriminating between the groups.

Birchler, Weiss and Vincent (1975) found that both positive and negative codes discriminated between distressed and nondistressed subjects, but they made no attempt to separate verbal and nonverbal codings. Table 3.7 summarizes the data and shows that there is some evidence that there is a relationship between the kind of data examined, and the types of behaviours found to discriminate between happy and unhappy couples.

Noller (1982) obtained videotapes of couples interacting and coded them four separate times:

(a) Verbal channel (words from transcript).
(b) Vocal channel (words plus tone of voice from audiotape).
(c) Visual (picture only from videotape with sound removed).
(d) Total channel (videotape with sound and transcript).

This experiment will be described in greater detail in Chapter 8, and at that point the results will be compared with results discussed here.

Relationship between Verbal and Nonverbal

Gottman's data (Gottman *et al.*, 1977; Gottman, 1979) were also analysed to look for relationships between content codes and affect codes; each set of content codes was analysed separately for each affect type using multivariate analysis of variance. Distressed subjects were significantly different from the nondistressed subjects for both neutral and negative affect, and there were no gender effects. Univariate F-tests showed that nondistressed spouses were more likely to express agreement with neutral affect than were distressed spouses, and were less likely to state their feelings about a problem ($p < .001$), mindread ($p < .001$), or express agreement ($p < .05$) or disagreement ($p < .01$) with negative affect than were distressed spouses.

These are very important results since they indicate that including the affect codes, rather than relying on content analysis by itself, greatly increases the discriminating power of the variables. For example, distressed and nondistressed couples did not differ on the extent to which they expressed feelings about a problem, or used mindreading statements, but they differed significantly on the extent to which they performed these behaviours with negative affect.

Frequency of Different Nonverbal Behaviours

To summarize then, Raush *et al.* (1974) found differences between their discordant and harmonious couples in the extent to which they used coercive and rejecting, or reconciling and resolving behaviours, and Gottman *et al.*, 1977) has shown the extent to which codings of the affect which accompanies statements coded for content, increases the power of the content codings to discriminate between distressed and nondistressed married couples. What we do not know, however, is whether there are differences between happy and unhappy couples in the frequency with which they use certain nonverbal behaviours. This is not quite the same question as whether there is a difference in the way the nonverbal behaviour is coded on a particular dimension. At present a study is being carried out at the University of Queensland (in collaboration with Dr Cynthia Gallois), to investigate this question. The frequency of behaviours such as smiles, frowns, eyebrow raises and lowers, head nods etc. is being recorded and this data will be analysed using such independent variables as gender, marital adjustment level, and type of message.

Perceptions of Communication by Spouses

An important study in the area of spouses' perceptions of each other's communications is the Talk Table study by Gottman *et al.* (1976) which was described in some detail in Chapter 2, and discussed in detail in the section of this chapter headed "private message system". These researchers had couples rate both the *intent* of the messages as they sent them, and the *impact* of messages from the partner. Gottman (1979) discusses the possibilities in terms of three models: the impact model, the intent model, and the communication model.

> "It may be that, regardless of the speaker's intended impact, the messages of nondistressed couples will have a more positive *impact* than the messages of their distressed counterparts. This is the *impact* model. On the other hand, it could be that the *intent* of messages, not impact, discriminates the two groups. This is the *intent* model. Alternatively, it could be that the relationship between intent and impact might discriminate the two groups. For example, it could be the case that there is less discrepancy between the intended impact and the actual impact of messages exchanged in nondistressed marriages. This is a *communication* model, in which "good communication" would be defined as low

discrepancy between intent and impact and hypothesized as more characteristic of high satisfaction marriages. The communication model is independent of the previous two models, since, if distressed couples intend their messages to be more negatively received than do the nondistressed couples, the intent–impact discrepancy of the two groups would not differ even if the impacts of their messages were more negative." (Gottman, 1979, p. 219).

To recapitulate, what Gottman and his colleagues found was that distressed and nondistressed spouses did not differ with regard to the *intent* of their messages (as they rated them) but that messages between distressed spouses had a more negative *impact* than messages between nondistressed spouses. The results, then, support the *impact model*, that distressed spouses have a more negative impact on their partners than nondistressed spouses, even though intent does not differ. Results also support the *communication model*, that there is a greater discrepancy between intent and impact for distressed spouses than for nondistressed spouses.

The discrepancy between intent and impact could be explained in several ways.

1. It is possible that the distressed spouses decoded communications from their partners negatively, perhaps because of negative expectations, past history etc.
2. It is possible that the distressed spouses sent more negative messages than they intended because underlying feelings of hostility etc. toward the spouse "leaked" through and affected the sending of the message (Ekman & Friesen, 1969).
3. It is also possible that the ratings of intent were affected by social desirability, while those of impact were not (since these were not ratings of oneself).

One of the problems with this Talk Table task is that there is no way of separating encoding and decoding effects, and thus it is difficult to decide whether the decoding explanation is more likely, or the encoding explanation, or some combination of the two.

Gottman (1979) reports a doctoral dissertation (Markman, 1977) which aimed to assess the usefulness of Talk Table measures to predict marital satisfaction for couples planning to marry. *Impact* differences at the first testing (pre-marriage) were able to predict differences in relationship satisfaction two and a half years later. On the other hand, the correlation between relationship satisfaction at the initial testing and impact ratings two and a half years later were nonsignificant or negative. Of course, this latter finding could be because there was little variance in scores on the relationship satisfaction measure at the initial testing (as one would expect from couples about to marry) and much more variance in impact ratings later, leading to little correlation.

Markman also tested the power of the communication model at predicting relationship satisfaction and found that "initial intent–impact discrepancy was a poor predictor of later relationship or marital satisfaction but that impact ratings were excellent predictors" (Gottman, 1979, p. 231). Since impact measures are about positivity/negativity, what these results mean is that marriages where spouses have a negative impact on one another are likely to be low in marital satisfaction, while those where spouses have a positive impact on one another are likely to have high marital satisfaction. However, whether the impact is likely to be because of the way messages are sent, or the way they are decoded is still not clear.

In any case, whatever the explanation, it seems clear that unhappy spouses do not understand one another as well as happy spouses do, and the misunderstandings are likely to be in a negative direction. This leads to the question of accuracy.

Accuracy of Communication

Kahn (1970) tested the hypothesis that marital satisfaction is related to the spouses' ability to understand one another's nonverbal communication, and he was able to show that couples low in marital satisfaction made more errors in receiving messages from each other than did couples high in marital satisfaction, in a situation where the nonverbal part of the message was crucial to its interpretation.

As mentioned earlier, Gottman and Porterfield (1981) have expanded on the work of Kahn with a study designed, not only to replicate Kahn's findings, but to test whether the difference in accuracy occurs because happy couples have a private message system which enhances their communication, or because a skills deficit exists in unhappy couples. Noller (1980) also conducted a study which aimed to extend the findings of Kahn, and to explore the question of whether misunderstandings occurred because of poor encoding, or poor decoding, whether males and females were equally skilled or there were sex differences, and whether misunderstandings occurred more on some types of messages than others. These studies of accuracy will be described in detail in Chapter 5, after we have addressed some of the methodological issues involved in designing research into nonverbal communication in married couples.

References

ARGYLE, M. (1975) *Bodily Communication*. New York: International Universities Press.

BIRCHLER, G. R., WEISS, R. L. & VINCENT, J. P. (1975) Multimethod analysis of social reinforcement exchange between maritally distressed and non-distressed spouse and stranger dyads. *Journal of Personality and Social Psychology*, 31, 349–62.

GOTTMAN, J. M. (1979) *Marital Interaction: experimental investigations*. New York: Academic Press.

GOTTMAN, J., MARKMAN, H. & NOTARIUS, C. (1977) The topography of marital conflict: a sequential analysis of verbal and nonverbal behaviour. *Journal of Marriage and the Family*, **39**, 461–77.

GOTTMAN, J., NOTARIUS, C., MARKMAN, H., BANKS, S., YOPPI, B. & RUBIN, M. E. (1976) Behaviour exchange theory and marital decision making. *Journal of Personality and Social Psychology*, **34**, 14–23.

GOTTMAN, J. M. & PORTERFIELD, A. L. (1981) Communicative competence in the nonverbal behaviour of married couples. *Journal of Marriage and the Family*, **4**, 817–24.

KAHN, M. (1970) Nonverbal communication and marital satisfaction. *Family Process*, **9**, 449–56.

LOCKE, H. J., SABAGH, G. & TOMES, M. (1956) Correlates of primary communication and empathy. *Research Studies of the State College of Washington*, **24**, 118.

LOCKE, H. J. & WALLACE, K. M. (1959) Short marital adjustment and prediction tests: their reliability and validity. *Marriage and Family Living*, **21**, 251–5.

MARKMAN, H. (1977) A behavior exchange model applied to the longitudinal study of couples planning to marry. Unpublished doctoral dissertation, Indiana University at Bloomington.

NAVRAN, L. (1967) Communication and adjustment in marriage. *Family Process*, **6**, 173–84.

NOLLER, P. (1980) Misunderstandings in marital communication: A study of couples' nonverbal communication. *Journal of Personality and Social Psychology*, **39**, 1135–48.

NOLLER, P. (1982) Channel consistency and inconsistency in the communications of married couples. *Journal of Personality and Social Psychology*, **43**, 4, 732–41.

RAUSH, H. L., BARRY, W. A., HERTEL, R. K. & SWAIN, M. E. (1974) *Communication, Conflict and Marriage*. San Francisco: Jossey-Bass.

VENARDOS, C. (1982) Communication awareness in married couples. Unpublished Honours Thesis, University of Queensland.

4

Assumptions, Paradigms and Tasks in Research on Nonverbal Communication

Research in nonverbal communication has aimed to answer at least two very different types of questions about this complex and wide-ranging set of behaviours.

(1) What is the typical nonverbal behaviour in a particular situation (for example, when taking turns in a conversation or when greeting someone at a party (Kendon & Ferber, 1973))? Such research tends to use a small number of subjects and a small sample of behaviour, but this behaviour is usually analysed in great detail (Ekman & Friesen, 1978).

(2) What are the important variables which are related to particular types of nonverbal behaviour or to various levels of nonverbal skill? Such variables as sex (Hall, 1979; Henley, 1973), age (Dimitrovsky, 1964; Zuckerman & Przewuzman, 1979), race (Gitter, Black & Mostofsky, 1972; Gitter, Kozel & Mostofsky, 1972), academic ability (Weisgerber, 1956) and personality (Buck, 1977; Buck, Miller & Caul, 1974; Cunningham, 1977) have all been used as independent variables in such research. Rosenthal and his colleagues have also tested a number of variables in relation to decoding ability in their work on the PONS (Profile of Nonverbal Sensitivity) Test, a test of ability to decode nonverbal communication over a number of different channels (Rosenthal *et al.*, 1979) and this will be described in greater detail later.

Types of Data

An important question for researchers in this area is the type of data that should be collected, and in this section some of the alternatives available to the researcher will be discussed. An important distinction needs to be made between questionnaire data, and observational data, where samples of actual behaviour are obtained, and scored or coded in some way. Observational and behavioural data may also be obtained in different ways, but the main choices open to the researcher are between using an experimental task or obtaining a sample of more natural interaction.

Questionnaires

Both Scheflen (1968) and Ahammer (1973) emphasize the importance of first-hand observations of behaviour in research on nonverbal communication, rather than using questionnaires. Asking people what they do, or what others do may only lead to the reporting of "feelings about behaviour, or cultural or idiosyncratic myths about behaviour" (Scheflen, 1968, p. 87). Certainly there is evidence that people generally have little awareness of whether they are communicating effectively or understanding the communications of others (DePaulo & Rosenthal, 1979; Friedman, 1979; Rosenthal *et al.*, 1979; Zuckerman & Larrance, 1979).

Zuckerman and Larrance developed questionnaire measures of Perceived Encoding Ability (PEA) and Perceived Decoding Ability (PDA) and measured the validity of the instruments by comparing subjects' scores on the tests, with scores on various encoding and decoding tasks. They obtained positive, but generally low correlations between the questionnaire measures and measures of actual skill. Such a finding would seem to support the contentions of Scheflen (1968) and others, that observations of actual behaviour should be used in nonverbal research. As Zuckerman and Larrance note:

"It is too early to suggest that paper and pencil scales can replace actual encoding and decoding measures" (p. 191).

Locke, Sabagh and Tomes (1956) developed the Primary Communication Inventory specifically for the marital situation. This questionnaire includes items designed to measure both verbal and nonverbal communication in marriage. The verbal items measure perceived frequency of communication in various areas, together with disagreements, avoidances of topics etc. while the nonverbal items tend to measure perceived skill at communicating with one another without the use of words—such as through the use of gestures, meaningful glances etc.

It should be kept in mind that questionnaire data may not be as useful in many ways as data obtained from observations of behaviour but such material can be very useful in giving information about how subjects perceive the communication process, and their own communication ability—and in the marital situation, their perception of the communication ability of the spouse. Questionnaires can also be used in conjunction with behavioural or observational data, and can provide the researcher with important information that can then be related to actual behaviour or skill.

White (1982) had subjects participate in an interaction and then had them fill in a questionnaire about the interaction. Subjects were asked such questions as how well they thought they understood the other interactant and how well they thought the other interactant understood them. She was then able to get a measure of accuracy by comparing the two sets of perceptions.

Observations of behaviour

However, while there is general agreement that the study of actual communicative behaviour is desirable, there remains the question of how to obtain such data. In other words, what type of task should be used for obtaining measures of actual encoding and decoding ability. Studies of nonverbal communication generally follow one of three paradigms:

1. An experiment in encoding or decoding nonverbal communication (Argyle *et al.*, 1970).
2. The study of interaction in a laboratory setting (Birchler, Weiss & Vincent, 1975; Gottman *et al.*, 1976, 1977).
3. Studies of naturally occurring interaction (e.g. Bugental, Love & Gianetto, 1971).

The first part of this chapter will discuss issues related to selecting experimental tasks, while the second part of the chapter will discuss problems related to studying interaction. Table 4.1 sets out examples of the different types of paradigms used.

Experimental tasks

Encoding tasks. A number of different encoding tasks have been used in nonverbal research. In laboratory experiments the type of task has depended on which channel or channels were being studied, and, related to that question, whether verbal material is included. Where only the visual channel is the focus of study, the researcher does not have the problem of sorting out the separate effects of verbal and nonverbal channel in the way that he/she does if the task used involves speech.

Tasks not involving words. Asking subjects to pose is common, but as Harper, Wiens and Matarazzo (1978) have pointed out, there are both advantages and disadvantages in using posed nonverbal behaviour. They claim that an advantage of using a posing task is that giving a subject instructions to pose also gives that person permission to ignore display rules that may inhibit them in spontaneous situations. In other words, a person asked to pose may behave more "naturally" than someone in a spontaneous situation who believes those around him are monitoring and evaluating his behaviour. Rosenthal and his colleagues (1979), on the other hand, claim

TABLE 4.1. *Summary of Paradigms and Tasks used in Nonverbal Research*

Type of paradigm	Examples	Task	Type of data	Advantages	Disadvantages
1. Laboratory Experiment	Kahn (1970)	Encoding and decoding of standard content messages.	Scores as to accuracy of couple at decoding one another.	Verbal channel controlled and only nonverbal varied.	Stylized interaction—may not be meaningful. No way to separate effects of sex, or encoding/decoding.
	Noller (1980)	As above but items videotaped for showing to judges	Scores for encoding and decoding.	Effects of sex and nonverbal can be separated.	Stylized interaction—may not be meaningful.
	Gottman et al. (1976)	Spouses talk together but rating intent of own messages and impact of spouses' after each statement.	Ratings of intent and impact.	Closer to natural interaction.	Flow of conversation interrupted by rating procedure. Verbal channel not controlled. Social desirability problems with self-ratings.
2. Laboratory Interaction a. Free discussion of a topic or issue.	Gottman et al. (1977) Birchler, Weiss & Vincent (1975)	Discussion of conflict issue.	Coding using Couples' Interaction Scoring System (content and nonverbal behaviour.	Even closer to natural interaction—discuss personal issue—but may be affected by recording procedure. Conflict ensured.	Verbal channel not controlled—conflict artificially contrived.
b. Improvisations	Raush et al. (1974)	Act as though involved in a particular situation. Set by experimenter (e.g. conflict over T.V.).	Coding using scoring system.	Subjects encouraged to act as though resolving conflict—feelings etc. likely to be generated.	Issue not necessarily relevant. Subjects may "act rather than interact". Problems with generalizability.
	Rubin (1977)		Coding using Couples' Interaction Scoring System.		
3. Naturally occurring Interaction	Bugental, Love & Gianetto (1971) Noller (1978)	Interaction of a family in a waiting room. Videotapes of parents leaving children at pre-school.	Ratings of facial Expressions and words. Frequency and duration measures of behaviours.	Generalizability ensured. Natural behaviour likely.	Limited situations possible—ethical issues.

that posed behaviour may be stereotyped and unnatural, or may be idio-matic, if trained actors are used as the encoders. The problems of posing nonverbal behaviour would seem to be minimized if the subjects are, as Ekman (1966) suggests, able to concentrate on sending a verbal message, and just let the nonverbal behaviour happen.

While, in some early research, subjects were merely asked to encode a certain emotion nonverbally (Osgood, 1966) other studies have used more complex tasks in which to study nonverbal behaviour. Mehrabian (1972), for instance, asked subjects to imagine that a hatrack was a person of a certain sex, status etc., and then to talk to the hatrack as though talking to a person. Appropriate ratings of distance, posture and gaze could then be made.

Other researchers have relied on stimuli in the environment to cause the subject to encode a certain emotion. The use of pleasant and unpleasant slides in the research by Buck (Buck, 1979; Buck, Miller & Caul, 1974; Buck et al., 1972) would be an example of this kind of research. Subjects' nonverbal behaviours were recorded while they were watching the slides and their reactions measured. A problem with this paradigm is the assumption that subjects are affected in similar ways by similar experiences, an assump-tion that is not necessarily valid.

Ekman (1966), as mentioned earlier, has suggested that more natural nonverbal behaviour may be obtained by having subjects send a verbal message as part of the task. However, having the verbal component of the interaction included in the experimental task creates new problems for the researcher, as the effects of this verbal part of the message have to be separated from the effects of the nonverbal components. To overcome this difficulty researchers have typically used methods such as meaningless content or standard content in designing their experimental tasks.

Meaningless or standard content tasks. Davitz and Davitz (1959) used a meaningless content methodology when they asked subjects to recite the alphabet once through to express each of fifty different feelings, a task that would seem to be quite artificial and difficult, and to emphasize an individual rather than a relationship model of communication. Argyle and his co-workers (1970) also used the meaningless content method when they had subjects count in ways that expressed superior, neutral or inferior status in interaction with another person. While this task is also artificial, it seems simpler than that required by Davitz and Davitz, and by asking that the attitude be expressed to another person, the researchers were assuming a more relationship-oriented model of communication.

Different from the meaningless content task in some ways is the standard content task. In the standard content task subjects use the same words a number of times, but change the meaning of those words by varying the nonverbal behaviour which accompanies those words. Mehrabian and

TABLE 4.2. *Example of Marital Communication Scale Item*

Wife Message

Situation	Your husband just presented you with your birthday present. You had been expecting a completely different gift.
Possible Alternative Intentions	(a) You are quite satisfied with the gift although you really would have preferred what you were expecting.
	(b) You are very disappointed and annoyed that he didn't get you what you had expected.
	(c) You are pleasantly surprised by the unexpected gift.
Statement	You really surprised me this time.

Husband Message

Situation	Your wife is modelling a new outfit for you that she just bought. She asks you how you like it.
Possible Alternative Intentions	(a) You are curious to know how she managed to save the money to buy such an outfit.
	(b) You think the outfit looks good, are pleased with the purchase, and are pleasantly surprised that she could afford such an expensive looking outfit.
	(c) You think the outfit is totally unbecoming on her and therefore do not think it is worthwhile.
Statement	Oh, that's really something. Where did you get the money for an outfit like that.

Ferris (1967), for instance, had subjects use the word "maybe" in this way, to communicate attitudes of like, neutrality, and dislike toward another person. Duckworth (1975) had his subjects ask the question, "What are you doing" in ways that expressed different feelings such as anger, interest or surprise. Kahn (1969; 1970) had married couples send each other ambiguous messages which could have three different meanings, depending on the nonverbal behaviour accompanying the message. An example of this type of message can be seen in Table 4.2. The person who is sending the message is given the context, the words to be used and the intention to be communicated. The receiver is given the context and three possible intentions from which he/she has to choose the one the spouse is trying to convey. Several studies using this type of experimental task with married couples, and carried out by the present author will be described in later chapters.

Problems related to standard content tasks

While the standard content type of task would seem easier for the encoder in an experiment than the more stylized tasks mentioned earlier, there are also problems associated with using this methodology. Harper, Wiens and

Matarazzo (1978) outline four problems they see with using standard or constant content methods in designing tasks for nonverbal communication research.

The first of these problems is related to the *meanings which the words, set by the experimenter, may have for the encoder, or in marital communication research, for the couple in the context of their married lives.* In one of the studies which I conducted, for instance, a wife had to decide when her husband sent her the message, "Do you know what a trip like that costs?", which of three possible meanings he intended. The three possibilities were:

1. He felt that a trip to that place was unappealing and would hardly be worthwhile.
2. He was pleased that she would want to go with him on such a trip and would like to make serious enquiries about it.
3. He was interested in finding out whether she knew the approximate cost of such a trip before committing himself one way or the other.

Although the husband actually attempted to send all three of the messages at different times, the wife, who saw her husband as generally unwilling to spend money on holidays, interpreted each message as negative.

Kahn (1969; 1970) overcame this problem to some extent by giving subjects some choice about the messages they sent. Rosenthal and his colleagues (1979) faced a similar problem when making the videotapes for the PONS Test, and they decided to exclude from the scenes the encoder was asked to portray those which were "so alien to the portrayer's own experience that she felt unable to enact them" (p. 28).

Excluding items because they are alien to the subject's experience may be a sensible approach, but excluding items, especially in research on marital communication, because the item is an issue for that couple, could lead to excluding the really important data. If couples do, in fact, distort the meanings of messages where those messages relate to areas that are problematic in their lives, this process is of great interest to the researcher.

Problems may also arise because the actual words used in the message designed by the experimenter are different from those which could be normally used by the encoder. This problem can be lessened to some extent by the researcher being careful to use standard, conventional, conversational English in designing messages, and ensuring that the English is appropriate for the target group.

Another way that the effects of this problem can be minimized is by having a variety of items to be encoded so that each subject should have a number of messages to send that he/she is comfortable with, even though there may be some that he/she is not comfortable sending. Problems with encoding may be due to the wording, or to the fact that the item is alien to the encoder's experience or because the item relates to some area that is a problem. A number of researchers (Ekman & Friesen, 1967; Harper, Wiens & Matarazzo, 1978; Rosenthal, Hall & Zuckerman, 1978; Rosenthal *et al.*, 1979) have emphasized the need to use a variety of different emotions or messages in the encoding task, particularly in studies where accuracy is being measured.

A second problem that Harper, Wiens and Matarazzo (1978) have seen with standard content methods is *"microphone fright"*, and of course, a related problem is "camera shyness". Both of these problems are caused by the fact that people become very self-conscious when they know that their behaviour is being monitored or recorded. To some extent such problems can be overcome by giving subjects time to adapt to the presence of a recording device (and the evidence is that they do), by giving them practice items, and by ensuring that the standard content task occurs at a point in the session where subjects have had time to relax and to adapt to the situation.

The third problem raised by Harper, Wiens and Matarazzo (1978) is that *individual differences in speech-related paralinguistic phenomena (tone of voice, accent etc.) may be confounded with voice quality*. This should not be a problem where subjects know one another well (for example, married couples decoding one another) but may be relevant where subjects are sending messages to strangers, or decoding strangers.

The fourth problem referred to by Harper and his colleagues is that *characteristics such as dominance are characteristics of relationships and may not be present in standardized individual situations, but only in interaction situations*. To deal with this problem, Rosenthal and his colleagues (1979) report that they used an off-camera interactant when they were making the videotape for the PONS Test. This procedure gave the encoder a focus for her attention, and made her feel more as though she were involved in an interaction rather than in a monologue. In the situation of married couples, one would assume that problems which are part of their normal interaction (such as dominance) would carry over to the standard content situation as well. For example, a wife who saw her husband as constantly checking up on her would be likely to interpret questions such as "What are you doing?" or "Did you do that?" within this framework, and be annoyed by such messages irrespective of the accompanying nonverbal. As well, the husband who feels he has the right to check up on his wife would be likely to be affected by this belief when he is asking the question.

When standard content methods are not used, but research is based on interactions in which subjects use their own words, researchers are faced with the problem of trying to separate the effects of the verbal message from the nonverbal (paralinguistic) aspects. This issue will be taken up in a later section. Meanwhile, it is important to look at the kinds of judgements that decoders in nonverbal research are generally asked to make.

Types of decoding tasks

Decoders in nonverbal research may also be called on to make a variety of different decisions. One common task especially in earlier research was for subjects to be asked to name the particular feeling being expressed by an encoder. This type of task would generally be used in experiments where subjects were asked to pose a number of emotions such as surprise, fear, anger etc., or in studies using meaningless content, such as that by Davitz and Davitz (1959).

Another common task given to subjects in research on nonverbal behaviour is to make ratings on semantic differential type scales (e.g. angry–pleased), where the subject has to rate the impression created by the target person's nonverbal behaviour. Studies by Ekman (1966), Argyle and his co-workers (1970) and Summerfield (1975) fall into this category. A number of studies of this type have been carried out recently at the University of Queensland (Australia) using newsreaders (Owens, 1982) and immigrants (Gallois & Callan, 1981) as target groups. A similar but different task involves asking subjects to choose from a list of possible behaviours and qualifiers, which ones they think apply to the target person at a particular point in time. Such a study has been carried out using a baby as the target and groups of students as the raters (Hayes & Noller, 1982).

Studies of accuracy in nonverbal communication have also asked subjects to choose from among three possible meanings for a message (Kahn, 1969; 1970). Kahn used married couples as his subjects and their task was to decode each other's messages, with the messages used being of the type described earlier (see Table 4.2) where the wife had to decide her husband's attitude to going on a trip from the way he asked, "Do you know what a trip like that costs?"

In the PONS Test, subjects have to choose from two alternatives, the situation in which they thought the person they were watching or listening to, had been involved. Situations were chosen so that they varied on two dimensions—in terms of degree of pleasantness, and degree of dominance. Examples of situations used and how they related to each of the dimensions can be seen in Table 4.3. Table 4.4 gives examples of verbal behaviour used by the interactant in each of the four affect quadrants.

Particular problems of accuracy studies

Encoding or decoding studies involving accuracy of interpretation of nonverbal communication, or choosing the correct alternative, have the problem that it is often difficult to tell whether errors (or lack of agreement between the sender and the receiver as to the meaning of the message) are due to the encoding or the decoding process. Kahn (1970) had spouses send

TABLE 4.3. *Scores used in PONS Test in Four Affect Quadrants*

| Positivity | Dominance | |
	Submissive	Dominant
Positive	Helping a customer Ordering food in a restaurant. Expressing gratitude. Expressing deep affection. Trying to seduce someone.	Talking about one's wedding. Leaving on a trip. Expressing motherly love. Admiring nature. Talking to a lost child.
Negative	Talking about the death of a friend. Talking about one's divorce. Returning a faulty item to a store. Asking forgiveness. Saying a prayer.	Criticizing someone for being late. Nagging a child. Expressing strong dislike. Threatening someone. Expressing jealous rage.

(From Rosenthal *et al.*, 1959, p. 30.)

TABLE 4.4. *Examples of PONS Test Items (Verbal Channel)*

| Positivity | Dominance | |
	Submissive	Dominant
Positive	"Oh, thank you! I thought I'd lost that. I just can't thank you enough!" (Expressing gratitude.)	"Are you sure you're warm enough, dear? Why don't you put on a sweater? That's good. Have a good time." (Expressing motherly love.)
Negative	"I'm terribly sorry but this clock I bought just doesn't work, at least it doesn't seem to. Could I exchange it?" (Returning faulty item to a store.)	"How many times have I told you not to leave things all over the house? It just makes it a mess." (Nagging a child.)

(From Rosenthal *et al.*, 1979, p. 47, 48.)

each other ambiguous messages, and the decoder was scored as correct when the intention he/she chose (from the three possible alternatives) was the same as the encoder had meant to send. If, however, the decoder did not choose the alternative that the encoder had intended to send, and was marked as wrong, there was no way to tell whether this was because the message was not sent clearly, or whether, even though the message was sent clearly, the decoder was inaccurate in his interpretation. To return to our example of the husband and wife and the trip, while it is likely that the wife's expectation that her husband would not want to spend money on a trip affected her decoding, it is also possible that her husband's actual attitude affected the way he sent the message. In this situation, then, we are uncertain whether the wife has made a decoding error, because of her perception of her husband's attitude, or the husband has made an encoding error perhaps leaking his lack of interest. Yet this may be very important information, particularly for the many items where we have no knowledge of the interactants' attitudes. A further possibility, of course, is that both processes have been going on together, and the error is a combination of his encoding and her decoding. However, it is unlikely that the two processes are equally responsible on any particular occasion, and researchers may need to determine which process is more important for a particular communication error.

What Kahn (1970) did in his experiment was to give each subject a score equal to the number of items on which his/her decoding was the same as the encoder's intention. He then added together the score for the wife and the score for the husband, on the assumption that each member of the dyad contributed equally to each item. However, this assumption of equal contribution to the score on the part of each member of the dyad is not necessarily valid. For instance, if a subject continually encoded poorly, then even if the spouse were a good decoder, he/she would not get the chance to make his/her contribution and show his/her decoding skill. The score in this instance would really reflect the poor encoding of the one spouse, but would not really reflect the decoding ability of the other. On the other hand, if one spouse were a good encoder and the other spouse a poor decoder, the score would reflect the poor decoding but not the good encoding. In each of these cases, the score in Kahn's experiment could be exactly the same, but for very different reasons.

Gottman and his colleagues (Gottman *et al.*, 1976) encountered similar problems. They had each message sent during an interaction rated by both the spouse who was sending it and the spouse who was receiving it on a 5-point scale of positivity (i.e. from super-positive to super-negative). These researchers were able to compare happy and unhappy couples with regard to the relationship between the intent of their messages (as they rated them) and the impact that these messages had on their spouses. What they found was that messages sent to unhappy spouses had a more negative effect than messages sent to happy spouses. However, the methodology they used did not enable them to decide whether the discrepancies they obtained were due to the way the messages were sent or the way they were received.

Criterion of accuracy

In the series of studies which are the basis for this book, the aim was to use the standard content methodology designed by Kahn (1969; 1970) for studying the accuracy of nonverbal communication in married couples, but to be able to answer questions that could not be answered by Kahn with regard to sex differences, type of message differences, and differences in rates of errors related to encoding or decoding. In order to be able to decide whether a message was incorrectly decoded because of the sender or the receiver, each message was videotaped and shown to panels of judges, as suggested by Ekman (1966) so that the responses of this group of receivers could be used to distinguish between messages sent clearly, and those not sent clearly.

Rosenthal and his colleagues (1979) discuss the problem of choosing a criterion of accuracy, since using the intention of the sender can be subjective, or even misleading, while the judgement of a group of decoders may not necessarily be related to the intention of the sender (particularly if the judges are different in any way from the sender). This could be a particular problem when studying married couples, who presumably know one another well, and could be expected, therefore, to decode one another more accurately than any group of judges could. For the purpose of this group of studies, it was assumed that considerable agreement among a group of judges that the message was as the sender intended, implied a clearly sent message, while disagreement among the judges, or agreement that the message was other than the sender intended, indicated a poorly encoded message. Thus the criterion of accuracy used was agreement between the intention of the sender and ratings of the judges.

Dealing with social desirability

Using standard content methodology, in this situation has the advantage that the encoder's intention is set by the experimenter, and so there is less likely to be a problem related to social desirability. When standard content methodology is used subjects are virtually given permission by the experimenter to encode socially undesirable responses. It is possible, for example that the differences found by Gottman and his colleagues (1976) between the intention of the message, and the impact of the message on the spouse were affected by the unwillingness of spouses to admit to their negative intentions. In a situation where standard content methodology was used this problem may not have arisen because the subject would have had the negative intention set by the experimenter. Of course, it must also be remembered that if such behaviour is not a normal part of the subject's repertoire then there remains the question of the generalizability of the data.

Effects of message type

Because of evidence from previous research that some feelings are transmitted more accurately than others (Osgood, 1966) and that judges do better when asked to make a number of judgements, it seems important that subjects be asked to send each other and decode from each other a fairly large sample of messages, and that these messages range from positive, through neutral to negative types of communications. Also, type of message needs to be taken into account as an independent variable whenever possible. Some researchers have varied messages on dimensions other than the pleasantness or positivity dimension. For examples, as has already been noted, Rosenthal and his colleagues (1979) included both positivity and dominance in their design of the PONS Test. Kahn (1969; 1970) varies his items only on the positivity dimension. Clearly though, some of the items used for the couples to send to one another involved the dominance dimension as well, and messages could be rated as negative because they gave the impression of being attempts to dominate. Items such as "Did you do that?" would be particularly susceptible to this type of interpretation.

Advantages of standard content methodology

The standard content methodology based on the Marital Communication Scale (Kahn, 1969; 1970) allows for diverse but representative examples of behaviour, while allowing the encoder to send the message in his own way, nonverbally at least, and encoders are able to concentrate on sending the words and just let the nonverbal happen. The tasks of both sender and receiver are based on real life tasks, and take full account of the roles of both encoder and decoder. Effective communication is said to have occurred when the encoder is able to get his intention across to the receiver (at least intention as set by the experimenter), but failure to communicate to the spouse is not necessarily taken to indicate that the sender provided wrong or misleading information, or conversely, that the receiver was inattentive or incompetent, since inaccuracy can be due to either the sender or the receiver.

This section has concentrated on methodological issues related to conducting experiments to assess nonverbal communication, particularly in the marital situation. In the next section, issues related to assessing nonverbal communication in interaction settings will be discussed.

Using Interaction Tasks

While a great deal of the research in nonverbal communication has involved testing people in the kinds of situations described in the last section there has been a great deal of debate about the relationship between behaviour or accuracy in the stylized situation used in experiments, and the naturally-occurring behaviour of an individual, or his accuracy in everyday situations. For this reason researchers have attempted to design experiments in such a way that the relationship between the experimental task and more naturally-occurring behaviour is more obvious and less questionable. In marital research, samples of interactive behaviour have been obtained, and there has usually been some attempt to structure the interaction between the couple in some way, particularly in order to obtain some level of conflict, since this has been considered important in differentiating between couples high and low in marital adjustment (Gottman *et al.*, 1977). An important consideration in this type of research is the nature of the task which subjects are asked to engage in, and when the subjects are married couples, the choice of task becomes even more important.

Tasks used in interaction studies

Gottman and his colleagues (1977) comment that there seems to be a hidden assumption among researchers that the nature of the task is unimportant, yet in earlier work these researchers (Gottman *et al.*, 1976) found that differences in interaction patterns between happy and unhappy couples were dependent on whether the task involved the couples in high or low levels of conflict, with differences between the two groups being greater when the task was a high conflict one.

Revealed differences technique

Many of the tasks that have been used for assessing couple interaction are based on games, or the "revealed differences technique" (Strodtbeck, 1951) where couples answer questions separately, and then are asked to come to mutually agreed answers to the same questions. For example, Strodtbeck (1951) had the couples choose three families both of them knew well, and then answer separately 26 questions about these families, such as which was the happiest, the most religious, etc. The husband and wife then compared their answers to the questions and were asked to resolve any discrepancies. Ferreira and his colleagues (Ferreira & Winter, 1973; Winter, Ferreira & Bowers, 1973) used a similar technique, but their questions involved personal and family choices, such as a country to visit for a year, a meal to choose in a restaurant, and the choice of colour for the next car.

Structured differences

Some researchers, rather than relying on differences being revealed during the task, have structured differences between the couple into the situation. The two most frequently used tasks of this type are the Color Matching Test (Ryder, 1968) and the Inventory of Marital Conflicts (Olson & Ryder, 1970). In the Color Matching Test, patches of colour are named differently for each spouse, and the members of the couple find themselves involved in insoluble arguments over the trivial question of which patch of colour is most like some other patch. Using the Inventory of Marital

Conflicts involves giving each member of the couple a description of a number of disagreements between hypothetical couples. While each spouse is given descriptions of the same conflicts, they are given discrepant views of the conflict. For instance, the wife would have the conflict described in such a way that the husband seemed the most at fault and then the husband would have the conflict described in such a way that the wife seemed to be most at fault. The couple's task would be to discuss the case and agree as to who seemed the most blameworthy in the situation. While this is again a relatively insoluble task because of the structured disagreement, couples were found to become very involved in resolving such conflicts, and particularly when the conflict was relevant to their own situation. Also, it should be kept in mind that actual marital conflicts frequently involve different views of who is to blame for a particular occurrence, who should give in on an issue, and so on. So while the couples tended to discuss the cases as those of other people they were also able to inject something of their own feelings into the situation, as well as attitudes and conflicts that were part of their relationship in everyday interactions.

Improvisations or role-playing

Raush *et al.* (1974) had the couples in their study actually act out hypothetical marital situations (what they called improvisations) according to directions given to them by the experimenter. For instance, in one situation, each of the partners had arranged a secret anniversary celebration, the wife a special dinner at home, and the husband a visit to a restaurant and the theatre. Each couple then had to act out how they would deal with resolving the situation. In another situation, the problem was a clash of interests about what to watch on television. These researchers found a high level of involvement by couples in the improvisations, but they also found that couples became particularly involved in situations that were issues for them.

Rubin (1977) also used improvisations related to areas such as sharing events of the day, money, sex, in-laws and the decision to have children. This study is described in detail by Gottman (1979). Table 4.5 details the nature of some of the improvisations, and the positions taken by husband and wife. Coaches were used to administer the improvisations to the couples.

> "Each improvisation contained designated points at which the coach was to elicit information from the spouse that would individualize and personalize the situation for the particular couple. The intent of using the improvisations was to have a set of standardized tasks but at the same time to increase the couples' potential for involvement and identification with the tasks by engaging them in providing details from their own lives in developing each situation." (Gottman, 1979, p. 138).

TABLE 4.5. *Some Improvisations used by Rubin (1977) in studying Married Couples*

Topic	Husband's Instructions	Wife's Instructions
Sharing events of the day	Husband excited about sharing something.	Feeling harassed and needing privacy.
Money	Has agreed to a tight budget but feeling short of pocket money and wants to let wife know he needs more money.	Has agreed to tight budget but managed to save food money to buy something special which wants to share with husband.
Sex	Wants to complete an activity of his choosing without being disrupted.	Wants to be close and make love.
In-Laws	Wants to visit his family for 4 days during Christmas holidays.	Reluctant to go because of problems in relationships with in-laws.

Discussing personally relevant issues

Royce and Weiss (1975) emphasize the need for experimenters to structure experimental situations, in order to make them as much like the real
situation as possible. Glick and Gross (1975) claim that experimenters will
be most likely to achieve this situation by permitting couples to discuss
personally relevant conflict issues, and by structuring the task so that
subjects have minimal guidance about the way the conflict should be
handled. Gottman and his co-workers (1977) had couples focus on trying to
resolve an "existing salient marital issue", while Hawkins, Weisberg and
Ray (1977) used various methods, such as a sentence completion exercise,
discussion of a marital problem, and the sharing of what they liked about
each other. These researchers aimed to see "how couples verbally manage
the exploration of affectively loaded intrapersonal and interpersonal content" (Hawkins, Weisberg & Ray, 1977, p. 479). It is interesting to notice
here that these researchers involved the couples in expressing positive affect
as well as the negative affect related to conflict. After all, it is possible that
happy and unhappy couples also differ with regard to how they manage the
expression of positive feelings and not just negative feelings. Rubin (1977 in
Gottman (1979)) used a deck of cards which he called the "fun deck". Each
card had written on it things that some couples enjoy doing together.
Subjects were asked to respond to these ideas either by reminiscing,
planning or talking, and to generally have an enjoyable conversation. Here
again the focus was on positive communication (Gottman, 1979, p. 139).

Another possibility is to have the members of a couple fill in questionnaires
about their marriage individually, without any consultation with the spouse,
and then to have the couples talk about this experience together. This task
also gives the couple the opportunity to deal with affectively laden material,
both positive and negative, discuss problem situations and cope with conflict,

all in their own way. A study using this type of method and carried out by the present author will be described in a later chapter of this book. A problem with this method is that couples with more problems (and lower marital adjustment) are likely to be involved in more negative and fewer positive behaviours. Nevertheless, interesting information about the communication process can be obtained.

Use of direct observations or recordings

Another important question related to assessing interaction patterns is whether observations should be made directly, or the interaction recorded and observations made later. Researchers generally agree that having an observer or observers present during an interaction segment creates a number of serious problems. An important problem is the possibility of confounding due to observer reactivity (Patterson & Reid, 1970; Weiss & Margolin, 1975). Patterson and Reid (1970) for instance, found that when observers were present, family members increased the frequency of positive social reinforcers and decreased the frequency of punishers. An important question for marital research is whether all types of couples (happy to unhappy) change their behaviour in the same way when observers are present, or whether happy and unhappy couples alter their behaviour in different ways.

Types of recording methods

The presence of observers can be avoided by the use of recording methods such as audiorecording (Ferreira & Winter, 1973; Raush et al., 1974) or videotaping (Engel & Weiss, 1976; Gottman et al., 1976; 1977; Vincent, Weiss & Birchler, 1975). It is important that the equipment be set up in such a way that it does not need to be monitored, at least not by someone in the same room. And, of course, it is important to realize that even the presence of equipment may modify the behaviour of interactants to some extent, and this may be particularly true for married couples, because of the sensitivity which couples in our society tend to have about revealing information about their marriages (what Mace and Mace (1974, p. 115) have called, the inter-marital taboo).

However, it is likely that the degree to which the behaviour on the videotape resembles normal behaviour will depend not only on whether the interactants know they are being recorded, but also on the task the couple is given to do. If the couple become very involved in the task, then awareness of the presence of recording equipment is likely to be minimized.

Problems of recording methods

On the other hand, while recording may minimize the effects of observers to some extent, a new set of problems is created, because recording devices, and particularly cameras, are limited in the amount of behaviour they can record. Only behaviour occurring within the range of the camera lens can be recorded, and much of the flexibility of having an *in vivo* observer is lost. As well, much of the contextual information about the behaviour which is recorded may be missing, making the task of the coder that much more difficult. *In vivo* observers can often be aware of, and record, a lot of contextual information, but they are also limited by time. After all, their observations have to be made in real time, and the behaviour cannot be slowed down, repeated, or reviewed. One solution to this problem is to limit the movement of interactants to the range of the camera, and to have them engaged in a task that will keep them within that space. Such a situation is simple to achieve when adults such as married couples are the subjects of study, but much more difficult when children are involved, such as in family research.

Advantages of recordings

Eisler, Hersen and Agras (1973) explored the question of the relative reliability of coding, from live interactions or from videotaped recordings and found that the reliability was equally high, if not higher when videotapes were used. They also found that coding from the videotape had distinct advantages, especially related to precision in defining and measuring behaviours, since videotapes can be replayed numerous times for checking, clarifying and describing. Another advantage is that the various channels (visual and vocal) can be examined separately, as was done by Bugental and her colleagues (Bugental, Love & Gianetto, 1971) in their study of parents and children. Other advantages of using videotapes include the ability to go back to the tapes and collect other data not considered important when the study was designed, to modify the dependent variable, if necessary, and to collect several sets of dependent measures from the same interactants.

Coding of Interaction

Focus on outcomes

Marital and family interaction has been coded by researchers in a number of different ways, depending on whether the focus of the research has been on the outcome of the interaction (for example, who wins or loses in a conflict situation), or on the process of interaction, or both. Bauman and

Roman (1966), who were primarily interested in the outcome of interaction between married couples divided the responses of the couple in their study into four types: dominance (where one member of the couple influenced the final outcome and the other did not), combination (where the outcome was a compromise between the two individual responses), reinforcement (where their initial responses agreed) and emergence (where the final outcome was a new response, different from the initial responses of either). Strodtbeck (1951) focused on the number of decisions which a person won, but also on the amount of talking he/she did compared with the partner.

Focus on process of interaction

Researchers focusing on the process of interaction have also measured a variety of dependent variables. Chapple and Lindemann (1942) used a set of measures of time characteristics of dyadic interaction, including tempo, activity, initiation, dominance, and synchronization. Winter, Ferreira and Bowers (1973) used measures of decision time, time spent in silence, interruptions, explicit information, and degree of politeness. Farina and Holzberg (1968) in their work with families of schizophrenic boys used measures of frequency of simultaneous talk, failure to reach agreement, interruptions, disagreements and aggressions.

Coding systems

Some quite elaborate coding systems have been developed for dealing with interaction between married couples. Raush and his colleagues (Raush *et al.*, 1974) used audiorecording for their analyses, and their categories are based primarily on verbal behaviour which they divide into three categories—affiliative (or positive), cognitive (or neutral) and coercive (or negative), with subcategories within each group. These researchers found, however, that in order to be able to code reliably, they had to combine categories that were fairly disparate, and, in the process, lose much valuable descriptive material from their data. (See Table 4.6 for examples.) An examination of the sample items indicates that many of the messages could have different meanings than those assigned depending on the nonverbal behaviour accompanying them. Coding would need to take into account both verbal and nonverbal behaviour.

Marital Interaction Coding System (M.I.C.S.). At the Oregon Marital Research Institute researchers have devised the Marital Interaction Coding System which has been used by a number of researchers (Birchler *et al.*,

TABLE 4.6. *Coding Categories Used by Raush* et al.

Type	Characteristics	Example
Affiliative	Showing concern for other's feelings. Seeking reassurance. Accepting the other's plans etc.	What's bothering you, honey. You do love me, don't you. OK. That's fine with me.
Cognitive	Seeking information. Conventional remark. Suggesting a course of action.	What are you making? Nice day isn't it? How about going out to dinner?
Coercive	Rejecting the other. Disparaging the other. Threatening the other.	I don't want to talk to you. That's a stupid thing to say. You do that, and that's the end.

(Raush *et al.*, 1974.)

1975; Hops *et al.*, 1971; Vincent *et al.*, 1975). The codes used have been validated through research such as that of Royce and Weiss (1975) who found that a number of cues their untrained judges reported using to discriminate satisfied and dissatisfied married couples, were the same as cues included in the M.I.C.S. The M.I.C.S. involved 28 individual code categories, including both positive and negative, and verbal and nonverbal behaviours. (See Table 6.1 in Chapter 6.) Again, however, researchers have found the need to lump categories together. Birchler, Weiss and Vincent (1975), for instance, use only two categories in their analysis, positive and negative. (See Chapter 6 for more detail on this study.)

Couples' Interaction Scoring System. Gottman and his co-workers (Gottman, Notarius & Markman, 1976) have devised the Couples' Interaction Scoring System, which codes content (or verbal), affect (or nonverbal), and context (or listener nonverbal) separately. Affect is coded as positive, negative or neutral, depending on whether the unit being coded contributes to a more pleasant climate of interaction (+), a more unpleasant climate (−), or does not change the climate. It is suggested that face, voice and body are each coded, with coders being assured that there is no need for codes assigned to each channel to agree. While Gottman and his research team suggest that it is best for content and affect to be coded separately, they allow the different nonverbal channels to be coded together. Tables 3.5 and 3.6 (in Chapter 3) summarize the content and nonverbal codes used in the Couples' Interaction Scoring System (Gottman, 1979, pp. 86, 87).

The Couples' Interaction Scoring System (Gottman *et al.*, 1976) is seen as having two main advantages over other systems of coding marital interaction. The first advantage is that coding and analysis have been successfully carried out without the need to combine categories (Gottman *et al.*, 1977).

While this feature is not fully exploited in the research to be described later, because the emphasis is on nonverbal communication rather than on content coding, nevertheless the various categories used for coding content have been found helpful in making decisions about how a particular statement should be coded.

The second advantage is that this system recognizes that a statement may be a different message depending on how it is delivered nonverbally. For example, while most systems assume that a statement of agreement is a positive statement, C.I.S.S. recognizes that this is not always so, and enables agreement with positive affect to be coded quite differently from grudging agreement with negative affect. Gottman and his co-workers (1977) found that such measures powerfully discriminated between satisfied and dissatisfied married couples.

Separating Verbal and Vocal Components

Another problem that arises in interaction research is that of separating content or verbal parts of the message, from the vocal components, in order to assess the separate impact of each. Three different methods can be used for dealing with this problem: statistical analysis, content filtering, and random splicing.

Statistical analysis

The method of statistical analysis involves designing the research in such a way that the vocal and verbal channels can be compared. While the verbal channel (the words said) can be coded separately from the tone of voice (for example, by using a typescript from which to code), the vocal channel is much more difficult to separate from the words. Coding from an audiotape involves listening to both words and tone of voice together, and any coding of this kind will involve both sets of cues in an inseparable way. However, if coding of the words separately, is compared with the coding of the words combined with the vocal channel, any difference between the two sets of codings can be assumed to be a result of the tone of voice.

Content-filtering

The second method for dealing with this problem of separating the verbal and vocal channels is content-filtering (Rogers, Scherer & Rosenthal, 1971) which uses the technique of masking the higher frequency sounds in speech, and thus making the speech unintelligible. Harper, Wiens and Matarazzo (1978) outline several problems associated with the method, including uncertainty about whether high frequencies are important to understanding

TABLE 4.7. *Eleven Types of Stimuli Used in PONS Test*

| | Vocal Channel | | |
Visual Channel	CF (Content filtered)	RS (Random-splice)	No Sound track
Face (face only)	*	*	*
Body (shoulder to mid thigh)	*	*	*
Figure (face and trunk)	*	*	*
No visual channel	*	*	

(From Rosenthal *et al.*, 1979)

emotional content, repeated exposure to filtered speech leading to understanding (Kramer, 1964), the finding that filtering leads to changes in ratings made on the basis of voice (Kramer, 1963) and the fact that, while frequency and amplitude are changed by the filtering process, other variables remain unchanged. Another problem with the method is that subjects find the task of making ratings using filtered speech very difficult (Owens, 1982).

Randomized splicing or copying

The third technique which is often used for separating the effects of the vocal channel from those of the words is randomized splicing or copying. This method was introduced by Scherer (1971) in an attempt to overcome the problem of sequence remaining unchanged when content filtering is used, and involves scrambling the order of the speech so that the speech is again unintelligible, but frequency and amplitude remain unchanged. A problem with this technique is that the sequence of nonverbal phenomena may be important to the understanding of the emotional content, and hence to the coding or the rating of the nonverbal channel (e.g. as in the rising crescendo of anger). Some researchers (Rosenthal *et al.*, 1979) have claimed that the problems associated with each of these last two methods are overcome if both methods are used in a study. The PONS Test uses stimuli in 11 different forms—with different combinations of visual and vocal channels (see Table 4.7).

Designing research for nonverbal communication

Dittman (1972) has emphasized four aspects of communication which need to be taken into account in designing research in nonverbal communication—the information contained in the message, the coding process (both encoding, or message-sending, and decoding, or message-receiving), the capacities and limitations of the channels employed, and the effects of "noise" (or factors detracting from the clarity of the message) on how accurately the message comes across. As Harper, Wiens and Matarazzo (1978, p. 12) comment, "the research, in most instances, does not reflect the sophistication of the theory".

In the experiments to be described in this book, an attempt has been made to deal adequately with each of these points. The information contained in a message is controlled in the experiment using the Marital Communication Scale by using this set of standard ambiguous messages, and thus ensuring that information about the positivity or otherwise of the message is imparted nonverbally. With regard to the interaction segment, the information from each of the channels important in the type of communication being studied (verbal, visual, vocal) will be examined separately. Both encoding and decoding processes will be taken account of in the research, and the contributions of both encoder and decoder will be assessed separately. Using judges to rate the communications sent between spouses takes into account the concept of "noise", since communications with excess "noise" will be unlikely to qualify as effectively encoded.

Assessment of Marital Adjustment

A number of terms are used in the literature to describe a couple's positive or negative evaluation of their marital state. As McNamara and Bahr (1980) point out, "happiness", "adjustment", "success", "satisfaction" are all used on the positive side, while on the negative side "distress", "unhappiness", "dissatisfaction", "discord" and "maladjustment" are used. Brody (1963, p. 84) defines marital adjustment as "the extent to which a husband, wife or couple have adapted to the marital situation to the extent that there is companionship, agreement on basic values, affectional intimacy, accommodation and a sense of euphoria or well-being". Such a definition would seem to combine the ideas of adjustment, happiness, satisfaction and success, and will be what is meant when any of these words is used throughout this volume. The concept of marital adjustment will be seen as a continuous variable ranging from extreme satisfaction on the one hand to extreme dissatisfaction on the other, and as a basically "global" concept (McNamara & Bahr, 1980) "representing the balance between positive and negative aspects of the marriage" (p. 46).

The Marital Adjustment Test

One of the most frequently used measures of marital adjustment is the Short Marital Adjustment Test (Locke & Wallace, 1959). This is a paper and pencil self-report instrument which can be filled in individually (the usual method) or jointly (Brody, 1963). If the test is filled in individually, the experimenter obtains the view of the marriage held by each member of the couple, although these will often be quite divergent and make the assessing of the couple as a whole more difficult. Joint filling in, on the other hand, gives a single score, but one cannot be sure whose view of the marriage is obtained, almost certainly that of the dominant partner. Spanier (1972, 1973) criticizes the Marital Adjustment Test because correlations between husband and wife scores tend to be low. However, it is quite conceivable that one member of a couple can feel quite satisfied because his/her expectations are low and basic individual needs are being met, while the other member can feel neglected and unloved. It would seem particularly easy for the husband, for whom the marriage is only a minor part of his life to be quite satisfied, while unaware of his wife's dissatisfaction.

Validity and reliability

Test items were selected for the Short Marital Adjustment Test because they covered the areas of marital adjustment viewed as important by the authors, because they showed the highest level of discrimination between satisfied and dissatisfied couples in earlier studies, and because they did not duplicate other included items. The items were also chosen to reflect what Locke (1951) considered as important indications of intimate communication in marriage. The test items largely concentrate on measuring the attractions within marriage.

Locke and Wallace (1959) report that the reliability coefficient of the adjustment test, computed by the split-half technique (with Spearman–Brown correction) was .90, with 236 subjects. They also compared 48 couples known to be poorly adjusted in marriage with 48 matched couples in the sample whose friends considered them to be exceptionally well-adjusted. The mean adjustment score for the well-adjusted group was 135.9 (highest possible 152) while for the poorly adjusted the mean was 71.7, with 96 per cent of the well-adjusted group obtaining adjustment scores above or equal to 100 and only 17 per cent of the maladjusted group obtaining scores of 100 or more. Locke and Wallace (1959, p. 255) conclude, "The above figures indicate that this Short Marital Adjustment Test clearly differentiates between persons who are well-adjusted and those who are maladjusted in marriage".

Problems with the Short Marital Adjustment Test

There is some evidence that the Short Marital Adjustment Test suffers from susceptibility to social desirability distortion. However, while some researchers conclude that the effects are minimal (Hawkins, 1966; Murstein & Beck, 1972) others have concluded that scores on the test are significantly affected by such distortions (Cone, 1967, 1971; Edmonds, Withers & Batista, 1972). Murstein and Beck (1972) conclude that the main problem is that happily married people exaggerate their spouses' good qualities—a factor which may lead to a greater spread of scores, but not affect too much the placing of subjects into groups according to their level of marital adjustment.

Margolin and her co-workers (1975, p. 6) maintain that the Marital Adjustment Test "remains one of the most internally consistent self-report measures" while Weiss and Margolin (1975) comment on its high test–retest reliability. Margolin and her co-workers (1975) see the Marital Adjustment Test as suffering from another defect—its association with the acceptance of traditional marital values. While this is undoubted (for instance, points are given if the wife is the one who frequently gives in on disagreements, but no points are given if the husband is the one who gives in), it would not seem to be a crucial problem at this stage. However, the problem may increase as time passes and less traditional values are more widely accepted. The value of the test would then be diminished. Snyder (1979) also sees global measures of marital satisfaction such as that of Locke and Wallace (1959) as failing to provide "a comparative assessment of the different dimensions of marital interaction" (p. 813). Nevertheless, it has to be agreed that couples who score high on the Short Marital Adjustment Test see themselves as happy, agree in most of the basic areas relevant to married life, settle their arguments by mutual give and take, never or rarely wish they had not married, declare that they would marry the same person again, and engage in activities together.

Choosing cut-off points

Birchler, Weiss and Vincent (1975) used a three-phase selection procedure for grouping their subjects as to their marital adjustment level. They first had couples fill in the Short Marital Adjustment Test (Locke & Wallace, 1959). Couples where both members scored above 120 were included in the satisfied group, while those where at least one member scored 95 or less were included in the dissatisfied group. These researchers also had couples tick a list of marital conflict items, with couples having to indicate conflict on at least 15 items, as well as extreme desire for behaviour change by at least one of them to be included in the dissatisfied group. The third phase of the selection procedure was a rating of the couple from their interview behaviour. This selection procedure was validated by the fact that all couples in the distressed group sought marital counselling within 12 months of the completion of the study, while none of those in the satisfied group had done so up to the time of publication of the study.

In the studies described in this book couples were assessed on the basis of their scores on the Short Marital Adjustment Test, using the same cut-off points as those used by Birchler, Weiss and Vincent (1975). Subjects also filled in the Areas of Change Questionnaire (Weiss & Perry, Note 1) and this data was used as a check on the groupings based on scores on the Marital Adjustment test. Also, many of the dissatisfied couples had already sought clinical help since two agencies offering marital counselling agreed to encourage their clients to participate in the study. The sample used in the studies had 16 couples in each of three groups—high, moderate and low marital adjustment.

Reference Note

1. Weiss, R. L. & Perry, B. A. *Assessment and Treatment of Marital Dysfunction*, Oregon Marital Studies Program. University of Oregon, Eugene, Oregon.

References

AHAMMER, I. M. (1973) Social learning theory as a framework for the study of adult personality development. In BALTES, E. B. & SCHAIE, K. W. (Eds.) *Life-span Developmental Psychology: Personality and Socialization*. New York: Academic Press.

ARGYLE, M., SALTER, V., NICHOLSON, H., WILLIAMS, M. & BURGESS, P. (1970) The communication of inferior and superior attitudes by verbal and nonverbal signals. *British Journal of Social and Clinical Psychology*, 9, 222–31.

BAUMAN, A. & ROMAN, M. (1966) Interaction testing in the study of marital dominance. *Family Process*, 5, 2, 230–42.

BIRCHLER, G. R., WEISS, R. L. & VINCENT, J. P. (1975) Multimethod analysis of social reinforcement exchange between maritally distressed and non-distressed spouse and stranger dyads. *Journal of Personality and Social Psychology*, 31, 349–62.

BRODY, S. A. (1963) Husband-wife communication patterns related to marital adjustment. Unpublished Ph.D thesis, University of Southern California.

BUCK, R. (1977) Nonverbal communication of affect in preschool children: Relationships with personality and skin conductance. *Journal of Personality and Social Psychology*, 35, 225–36.

BUCK, R., MILLER, R. E. & CAUL, W. F. (1974) Sex, personality and physiological variables in the communication of affect via facial expression. *Journal of Personality and Social Psychology*, 30, 587–9.

BUGENTAL, D. E., LOVE, L. R. & GIANETTO, R. M. (1971) Perfidious feminine faces. *Journal of Personality and Social Psychology*, 17, 314–18.

CHAPPLE, E. D. & LINDEMANN, E. (1942) Clinical implications of measurements on interaction rates in psychiatric interviews. *Applied Anthropology*, 1.

CONE, J. D. (1967) Social desirability and marital happiness. *Psychological Reports*, 21, 770–2.

CONE, J. D. (1971) Social desirability, marital satisfaction and concomitant perceptions of self and spouse. *Psychological Reports*, 28, 173–4.

CUNNINGHAM, M. R. (1977) Personality and the structure of the nonverbal communication of emotion. *Journal of Personality*, 45, 564–84.

DAVITZ, J. R. & DAVITZ, L. J. (1959) Correlates of accuracy in the communication of feelings. *Journal of Communication*, 9, 110–17.

DEPAULO, B. M. & ROSENTHAL, R. (1979) Ambivalence, discrepancy and deception in nonverbal communication. In ROSENTHAL, R., *Skill in Nonverbal Communication: Individual Differences*. Cambridge, Mass.: Oelgeschlager, Gunn & Hain.

DITTMAN, A. T. (1972) Interpersonal messages of emotion. New York: Springer.
DIMITROVSKY, L. (1964) The ability to identify the emotional meaning of vocal expressions at successive age levels. In DAVITZ, J. R., *The Communication of Emotional Meaning*. New York: McGraw-Hill, pp. 69–86.
DUCKWORTH, D. (1975) Personality, emotional state and perception of nonverbal communications. *Perceptual and Motor Skills*, 40, 325–6.
EDMONDS, V. M., WITHERS, G. & DIBATISTA, B. (1972) Adjustment, conservatism and marital conventionalization. *Journal of Marriage and the Family*, 34, 96–103.
EISLER, M., HERSEN, M. & AGRAS, W. S. (1973) Videotape: a method for the controlled observation of nonverbal interpersonal behaviour. *Behaviour Therapy*, 4, 420–5.
EKMAN, P. (1966) Communication through nonverbal behaviour: a source of information about an interpersonal relationship. In TOMKINS, S. S. & IZARD, C. E. (Eds.) *Affect, Cognition and Personality*. Tavistock, pp. 390–442.
EKMAN, P. & FRIESEN, W. V. (1967) Head and body cues in the judgment of emotion: a reformulation. *Perceptual and Motor Skills*, 24, 711–24.
EKMAN, P. & FRIESEN, W. V. (1978) *Facial Action Coding System*. Palo Alto, California: Consulting Psychologists Press, Inc.
ENGEL, K. & WEISS, R. L (1976) *Behavioural cues used by marital therapists in discriminating distress*. Paper presented at the Western Psychological Association meeting at Los Angeles, California, April 1976. Distributed by the Oregon Marital Research Institute.
FARINA, A. & HOLZBERG, J. D. (1968) Interaction patterns of parents and hospitalized sons diagnosed as schizophrenic or nonschizophrenic. *Journal of Abnormal Psychology*, 73, 144.
FERREIRA, A. & WINTER, W. D. (1973) Decision-making in normal and abnormal families. *Family Process*, 12, 17–36.
FRIEDMAN, H. S. (1979) The concept of skill in nonverbal communication: implications for understanding social interaction. In ROSENTHAL, R., *Skill in Nonverbal Communication: Individual Differences*. Cambridge, Mass.: Oelgeschlager, Gunn & Hain.
GALLOIS, C. & CALLAN, V. J. (1981) Personality impressions elicited by accented English speech. *Journal of Cross-Cultural Psychology*, 12, 3, 347–59.
GITTER, A. G., BLACK, H. & MOSTOFSKY, D. (1972) Race and sex in the communication of emotion. *Journal of Social Psychology*, 88, 273–6.
GITTER, G. A., KOZEL, N. J. & MOSTOFSKY, D. I. (1972) Perception of emotion: the role of race, sex and presentation mode. *Journal of Social Psychology*, 88, 213–22.
GLICK, B. R. & GROSS, S. J. (1975) Marital interaction and marital conflict: A critical evaluation of current research strategies. *Journal of Marriage and the Family*, 37, 505–12.
GOTTMAN, J. M. (1979) *Marital Interaction: experimental investigations*. New York: Academic Press.
GOTTMAN, J., MARKMAN, H. & NOTARIUS, C. (1977) The topography of marital conflict: a sequential analysis of verbal and nonverbal behaviour. *Journal of Marriage and the Family*, 39, 461–77.
GOTTMAN, J., NOTARIUS, C., MARKMAN, H., BANKS, S., YOPPI, B. & RUBIN, M. E. (1976) Behaviour exchange theory and marital decision making. *Journal of Personality and Social Psychology*, 34, 14–23.
HALL, J. (1979) Gender, gender roles and nonverbal communication skills. In ROSENTHAL, R., *Skill in Nonverbal Communication: Individual Differences*. Cambridge, Mass.: Oelgeschlager, Gunn & Hain.
HARPER, R. G., WIENS, A. N. & MATARAZZO, J. D. (1978) *Nonverbal communication: The State of the Art*. New York: Wiley.
HAWKINS, J. L. (1966) The Locke marital adjustment test and social desirability. *Journal of Marriage and the Family*, 28, 193–5.
HAWKINS, J. L., WEISBERG, C. & RAY, D. C. (1977) Marital communication style and social class. *Journal of Marriage and the Family*, 39, 479–90.
HAYES, A. J. & NOLLER, P. (1982) Problems in the analysis of behaviour: a study of attributions to an infant identified as "normally developing", "intellectually gifted", or "intellectually handicapped". Unpublished study, University of Queensland.

HENLEY, N. M. (1973) Status and sex: Some touching observations. *Bulletin of the Psychonomic Society*, 2, 2, 91–3.

HOPS, H., WILLS, T., WEISS, R. L. & PATTERSON, G. (1971) *Marital Interaction Coding System*. Unpublished manuscript, Department of Psychology, University of Oregon.

KAHN, M. (1969) Nonverbal communication as a factor in marital satisfaction. Doctoral dissertation, Southern Illinois University.

KAHN, M. (1970) Nonverbal communication and marital satisfaction. *Family Process*, 9, 449–56.

KENDON, A. & FERBER, A. (1973) A description of some human greetings. In MICHAEL, R. P. & CROOK, J. H. (Eds.) *Comparative Ethology and Behaviour of Primates*. New York and London: Academic Press.

KRAMER, E. (1963) Judgment of personal characteristics and emotions from nonverbal properties of speech. *Psychological Bulletin*, 60, 408–20.

KRAMER, E. (1964) Elimination of verbal cues in judgments of emotion from voice. *Journal of Abnormal and Social Psychology*, 6, 390–6.

LOCKE, H. J. (1951) *Predicting Adjustment in Marriage: A Comparison of a Divorced and a Happily Married Group*. New York: Henry Holt & Co.

LOCKE, H. J., SABAGH, G. & THOMES, M. (1956) Correlates of primary communication and empathy. *Research Studies of the State College of Washington*, 24, 118.

LOCKE, H. J. & WALLACE, K. M. (1959) Short marital adjustment and prediction tests: their reliability and validity. *Marriage and Family Living*, 21, 251–5.

MACE, D. & MACE, V. (1974) *We Can Have Better Marriages if we Really Want Them*. London: Oliphants.

MARGOLIN, G., CHRISTENSEN, H. & WEISS, R. L. (1975) Contracts, cognition and change: a behavioral approach to marriage therapy. *The Counseling Psychologist*, 5, 15–26.

MCNAMARA, M. L. L. & BAHR, H. M. (1980) The dimensionality of marital role satisfaction. *Journal of Marriage and the Family*, 42, 45–55.

MEHRABIAN, A. (1972) *Nonverbal Communication*, Aldine.

MEHRABIAN, A. & FERRIS, S. R. (1967) Inference of attitudes from nonverbal communication in two channels. *Journal of Consulting Psychology*, 31, 248–52.

MURSTEIN, B. I. & BECK, G. D. (1972) Person perception, marriage adjustment and social desirability. *Journal of Consulting and Clinical Psychology*, 39, 396–403.

NOLLER, P. (1978) Sex differences in the socialization of affectionate expression. *Developmental Psychology*, 14, 317–19.

OLSON, D. H. & RYDER, R. G. (1970) Inventory of marital conflicts: an experimental interaction procedure. *Journal of Marriage and the Family*, 32, 443–8.

OSGOOD, C. E. (1966) The dimensionality of the semantic space for communication via facial expression. *Scandinavian Journal of Psychology*, 7, 1–30.

OWENS, W. J., (1982) A study of bias in television news. Unpublished honours thesis, University of Queensland.

PATTERSON, G. R. & REID, J. B. (1970) Reciprocity and coercion: two facets of social systems. In NEURINGER, C. & MICHAELE, J. L. (Eds.) *Behaviour modification in clinical psychology*. New York: Appleton Century Crofts.

RAUSH, H. L., BARRY, W. A., HERTEL, R. K. & SWAIN, M. E. (1974) *Communication, Conflict and Marriage*. San Francisco: Jossey-Bass.

ROGERS, P. L., SCHERER, K. R. & ROSENTHAL, R. (1971) Content filtering human speech: a simple electronic system. *Behavioral Research Methods and Instrumentation*, 3, 16–18.

ROSENTHAL, R., HALL, J., DIMATTEO, M. R., ROGERS, P. L. & ARCHER, D. (1979) *Sensitivity to Nonverbal Communication: The PONS Test*. The Johns Hopkins University Press.

ROSENTHAL, R., HALL, J. A. & ZUCKERMAN, M. (1978) The relative equivalence of senders in studies of nonverbal encoding and decoding. *Environmental Psychology and Nonverbal Behavior*, 2, 3, 161–6.

ROYCE, W. S. & WEISS, R. L. (1975) Behavioural cues in the judgment of marital satisfaction: a linear regression analysis. *Journal of Consulting and Clinical Psychology*, 43, 816–24.

RUBIN, M. E. Y. (1977) Differences between distressed and nondistressed couples in verbal and nonverbal communication codes. *Dissertation Abstracts International*, 38, 1902.

RYDER, R. G. (1968) Husband-wife dyads versus married strangers. *Family Process*, 7, 233–8.
SCHEFLEN, A. E. (1968) Human communication: Behavioural programs and their integration in interactions. *Behavioural Science*, 13, 1.
SCHERER, K. R. (1971) Randomized splicing: A note on a simple technique for masking speech content. *Journal of Experimental Research in Personality*, 5, 155–9.
SNYDER, D. K. (1979) Multidimensional assessment of marital role satisfaction. *Journal of Marriage and the Family*, 41, 813–23.
SPANIER, G. B. (1973) Whose marital adjustment: a research note. *Sociological Inquiry*, 43, 95–96.
STRODTBECK, F. L. (1951) Husband-wife interaction over revealed differences. *American Sociological Review*, 16, 468–73.
SUMMERFIELD, A. (1975) Errors in decoding tone of voice during dyadic interaction. *British Journal of Social and Clinical Psychology*, 14, 11–17.
VINCENT, J. P., WEISS, R. L. & BIRCHLER, G. (1975) A behavioral analysis of problem-solving in distressed and nondistressed married and stranger dyads. *Behavior Therapy*, 6, 475–87.
WEISGERBER, C. A. (1956) Accuracy in judging emotional expressions as related to college entrance test scores. *Journal of Social Psychology*, 44, 233–9.
WEISS, R. L., HOPS, W. & PATTERSON, G. R. (1973) A framework for conceptualizing marital conflict, a technology for altering it, some data for evaluating it. In CLARKE, F. W. & HAMELYNCK, L. A. (Eds.) *Critical Issues in Research and Practice:* Proceedings of the Fourth Banff International Conference on Behavior Modification. Champaign, Illinois: Research Press.
WEISS, R. L. & MARGOLIN, G. (1975) Marital conflict and accord. In CIMINERO, A. R., CALHOUN, K. S. & ADAMS, H. E., *Handbook for Behavioral Assessment*. New York: John Wiley and Sons.
WHITE, S. J. (1982) Communication accuracy and the structure of social perception in face-to-face interaction. Unpublished Honours Thesis, University of Queensland.
WILLS, T. A., WEISS, R. L. & PATTERSON, G. R. (1974) A behavioral analysis of the determinants of marital satisfaction. *Journal of Consulting and Clinical Psychology*, 42, 6, 802–11.
WINTER, W. D., FERREIRA, A. J. & BOWERS, N. (1973) Decision-making in married and unrelated couples, *Family Process*, 12, 83–94.
ZUCKERMAN, M. & LARRANCE, D. T. (1979) Individual differences in perceived encoding and decoding abilities. In ROSENTHAL, R., *Skill in Nonverbal Communication: Individual Differences*. Cambridge, Mass.: Oelgeschlager, Gunn & Hain.
ZUCKERMAN, M. & PRZEWUZMAN, S. J. (1979) Decoding and encoding facial expressions in pre-school age children. *Environmental Psychology and Nonverbal Behavior*, 3, 147–63.

5

Nonverbal Accuracy and the Marital Relationship

Bach and Wyden (1969) have claimed that married couples are especially prone to misunderstanding one another's communications, and that this particularly applies to couples where there is a history of hostility and negative expectations. It is also probable that nonverbal communication, which is so often crucial to the understanding of a message, may be more easily misunderstood. This is likely since the rules for nonverbal communication are not stated as explicitly as are the rules for verbal communication (Hall *et al.*, 1978).

Factors Affecting Encoding

Misunderstandings, or inaccuracies in communication can be logically divided into those related to the encoding process, and those related to the decoding process. Errors related to the encoding process occur where the encoder is unable to send the message in such a way that his/ her intention is clearly recognizable in the message. In Chapter 1 we discussed the situation of the husband who was trying to let his wife know that he wanted her to be an equal in their relationship, but who for various reasons, such as lack of social skill, lack of expressivity, or ambivalence was unable to get this message across to her.

Nonverbal "leakage" (Ekman & Friesen, 1969), as has been suggested earlier, may also cause problems in encoding. The idea is that attitudes and affect that people manage to conceal in the verbal channel (or even deny to themselves) may be revealed in the nonverbal channels (usually the voice or the body, which are not so readily controlled as the face) (Rosenthal & DePaulo, 1979a; 1979b). The implication for the marital situation is that underlying hostility, deception, or desire to dominate (for example) may be "leaked", perhaps consciously, perhaps unconsciously, even when one is trying to send a positive message.

TABLE 5.1. *Examples of Marital Communication Scale Items for Husbands and Wives*

Wife Item	
Situation	You and your husband are sitting alone in your living room on a winter evening. You feel cold.
Alternative intentions	(a) You wonder if he is also cold or it is only you who are cold.
	(b) You want him to warm you with physical affection.
	(c) You want him to turn up the heat.
Statement	I'm cold, aren't you.
Husband Item	
Situation	You come to the dinner table as your wife begins to serve chicken, a main course you recall having had 4 days ago for dinner.
Alternative intentions	(a) You are irritated with her for preparing the same meal again and are warning her that she had better not make the same mistake in the future of a closely repeated meal.
	(b) You do not mind but are curious to see if your memory for meals is accurate.
	(c) You are elated because chicken is one of your favourites and you are not accustomed to her graciousness of serving it so often for you.

Factors Affecting the Decoding Process

Errors related to the decoding process occur when the receiver of the message is unable to recognize accurately the cues present in a message or situation. Remember the wife who believed that her husband would be unwilling to spend money on a trip, and who, as a result could not recognize any evidence of a more positive attitude in his messages! Decoding can be affected by such factors as the attitude one has to the partner (Fraser, 1976; Newcomb, Turner & Converse, 1965), preconceived prejudices (Williams, 1969), mood or the past history of the relationship (Ahammer, 1973; Glick & Gross, 1975), and the attitude one has to the topic being discussed (Raush *et al.*, 1974), all of which can result in the message being misunderstood.

Kahn's Study using the Marital Communication Scale

As has been discussed earlier, Kahn (1969, 1970) developed a method for testing the effectiveness (or accuracy) of nonverbal communication between spouses, using an instrument which he called the Marital Communication Scale (M.C.S.). This scale is based on the standard content method described in Chapter 4, and is basically a set of ambiguous messages which may be sent by spouses to one another in a standardized situation. Each of the messages is capable of conveying three meanings, depending on the nonverbal behaviour accompanying that message. Table 5.1 gives examples of both husband messages and wife messages used by Kahn, including the situation in which the couple were to imagine themselves, the words they were to use, and three possible intentions to be conveyed.

TABLE 5.2. *Sample Encoder's Card*

Situation	You and your husband are sitting alone on a winter evening. You feel cold.
Intention	(a) You wonder if it's only you who are cold or if he is cold, too.
Statement	I'M COLD, AREN'T YOU.

TABLE 5.3. *Sample Decoder's Card*

Situation	You and your husband are sitting alone on a winter evening. You feel cold.
Alternatives	(a) You wonder if it's only you who are cold or if he is cold, too.
	(b) You want him to warm you with physical affection.
	(c) You're feeling that he is being inconsiderate in not having turned up the heat by now and you want him to turn it up straight away.

(Noller, 1980, p. 1136)

The Marital Communication Scale used by Kahn (1970) contained eight items for the husbands to send and eight items for the wives to send. Each spouse sent one version of each message (randomly assigned). Table 5.2 shows the information that was on the encoder's card, while Table 5.3 shows the information on the decoder's card.

Each couple was given a score which equalled the number of items correctly decoded by the husband when the wife was the encoder, plus the number of items correctly decoded by the wife when the husband was the encoder (a score out of 16 for each couple). Kahn added these scores together on the assumption that each member of the dyad contributed equally to each score. He found that happy couples had significantly higher scores than did unhappy couples.

Problems with the Kahn study

Unfortunately, Kahn left many questions unanswered. Because of the methodology which he used he was unable to sift out the separate contribution of each member of the dyad—and so he was unable to look for sex differences. Yet, in the general nonverbal literature there is considerable evidence for sex differences in both the encoding and decoding of nonverbal communication. Hall (1978) summarized the data on sex differences in decoding nonverbal behaviour. In a meta-analysis involving 75 separate studies, she showed that while some studies found no differences between the sexes (e.g. Zuckerman *et al.*, 1976) and some found males to be better than females (Levitt, 1964), more of these studies than would be expected by chance demonstrated female superiority in decoding nonverbal communication. Hall (1979) also reviewed the literature on sex differences in encoding. Here she analysed the results of 26 studies and showed that females were more accurate senders of nonverbal cues, especially visual cues.

Kahn's (1970) methodology also did not enable him to test whether the inaccuracies in communication of the unhappy couples were related to the encoding process or the decoding process, nor was he able to check whether some types of messages were more frequently misunderstood than others.

Gottman and Porterfield's Study using M.C.S.II

Gottman and Porterfield (1981) revised the Marital Communication Scale by rewriting many of the items to ensure that the verbal content of each item was unbiased, and was not more likely to be interpreted in one way rather than another. The revised instrument was named M.C.S.II. These researchers aimed to repeat Kahn's (1970) experiment (using the revised instrument), and at the same time to test whether the communication deficits found by Kahn were sender or receiver deficits. In order to be able to do this, they included two groups of married couples in their design, one which encoded and decoded M.C.S.II messages from each other, and another group which were used as additional receivers of each message. "Hence, each message was received by both a sender's spouse and an opposite-sexed married stranger" (Gottman and Porterfield, 1981, p. 818).

Method

Gottman and Porterfield (1981) had 21 couples in their study who carried out both the encoding and the decoding tasks of the M.C.S.II, and 21 couples who constituted the stranger group and decoded messages sent by the spouse group. The Marital Relationship Inventory (Burgess *et al.*, 1971) was used to assess marital satisfaction and scores on this test were used in the correlation analyses.

The encoder sent all three of the alternatives for a particular M.C.S.II message consecutively, but in an order determined by the experimenter. The task of the decoder was to decide in which order the alternatives were actually presented. Messages were sent without the decoder present, and were transmitted to the decoder on a video monitor. This procedure was followed in order to ensure that both spouse and stranger decoders performed their task under the same conditions.

Results

There was a high correlation between the wife's marital satisfaction and her husband's score on M.C.S.II ($r = 0.68$, $p < .001$), but there was no correlation between the husband's marital satisfaction and the wife's M.C.S.II score. Also, there was no correlation between the wife's marital satisfaction and the stranger's M.C.S.II score. Gottman and Porterfield

(1981) argued that these results support a communication deficit located in the husband's decoding since strangers decoded equally well regardless of the sender's marital satisfaction, while spouses did not. As well, the correlation between marital satisfaction and decoding skill of the partner was found for husbands as decoders but not wives.

The results obtained by these researchers also indicated that for the satisfied couples, husbands were better receivers than strangers, while for the dissatisfied couples strangers were better receivers than spouses. This issue of the relationship between the decoding of one's spouse, and the decoding of opposite-sexed strangers will be taken up again in Chapter 6.

Noller's Study using the Marital Communication Scale (Revised)

Noller (1980) also conducted an experiment using the standard content method used by Kahn (1970), but she used a different experimental design from those used by Kahn (1970) or Gottman and Porterfield (1981).

Revising the Marital Communication Scale

Noller (1980) restructured the Marital Communication Scale devised by Kahn (1970) to ensure that each item had a positive, a neutral and a negative intention included in its set of alternatives. She also added a ninth item to each set as used by Duckworth (1975). The items were validated by having the verbal forms of the intentions rated by 40 married people. This rating was on the basis of a 5-point scale from very negative (1) to very positive (5). Mean ratings for each group of intentions were:

Wife items	positive = 3.97 (SD = .368)
	neutral = 3.16 (SD = .184)
	negative = 2.06 (SD = .416)
Husband items	positive = 3.89 (SD = .230)
	neutral = 3.14 (SD = .230)
	negative = 2.02 (SD = .203)

It was considered important to design the alternatives so that they were, at least reasonably clearly, positive, neutral and negative so that the study could explore whether accuracy is related to type of message, and also whether inaccuracy in some types of messages is more related to marital satisfaction than is inaccuracy in other messages. Previous research in the general area of nonverbal communication has shown accuracy of communication to be related to the particular feeling being transmitted (Mehrabian & Wiener, 1967; Osgood, 1966; Zuckerman et al., 1976) but there is little evidence about what such effects mean in the context of the marital relationship. Designing the scale on this single dimension of positivity/ negativity should enable some questions to be answered about the effects of message-type, but it should be kept in mind that this oversimplifies the true situation since other dimensions, such as the dominance dimension, are likely to be relevant as well. Using a variety of situations allows some of these factors to be taken into account, since in some of the situations items are likely to be seen as negative because they are interpreted as attempts to dominate. For example, the negative forms of "What are you doing?", "Did you do that?" and "Didn't we have chicken for dinner a few nights ago?" would be highly likely to be seen as attempts by one partner to dominate the other.

Method

Husbands and wives each sent their partner 27 messages (nine messages, each with three alternatives) arranged in a randomized order. Husbands and wives faced each other across a table and communicated the messages directly to one another, using cards similar to those shown in Tables 5.2 and 5.3. In half the couples the wife acted as encoder first, while in the other half of the couples the husband acted as encoder first.

As each message was sent, it was recorded on video for use in a later part of the experiment, when the items were shown to groups of judges. These judges performed the same decoding task as the spouses, in order to help us decide whether items were sent clearly or not. These videotapes were also played to the spouses later in the experimental session so that they could repeat the decoding task using information obtained from the visual channel only (sound turned down), or the vocal channel only (picture turned off).

Scoring

When both the husband and wife had encoded all their messages the items were scored. An item was marked as correct when the intention chosen by the decoder was the same as the alternative the encoder had been instructed to send. Each couple was given three scores at this stage:

1. a husband-to-wife score (the number of items out of 27 correctly decoded by the wife when the husband was the encoder).

2. a wife-to-husband score (the number of items out of 27 correctly decoded by the husband when the wife was the encoder).

3. a combined Marital Communication Scale score (the sum of the other two scores).

TABLE 5.4. *Mean Number of Correct Responses on Marital Communication Scale Items*

Marital adjustment level	Husbands to wives*	Wives to husbands*	Combined†
High‡	17.4	19.5	39.9
Moderate‡	16.2	18.7	34.9
Low‡	16.2	16.3	32.5

* Each of these scores is out of 27.
† This score is out of 54.
‡ $n = 16$ for each group.
(Noller, 1980, p. 1141)

Results

Analysis of these three sets of scores showed that there was a difference in combined score between couples (16) in the high marital adjustment group and couples (16) in the low marital adjustment group, $t(31) = 2.15$, $p < .025$. This result replicates the finding of Kahn (1970), although a little more convincingly. This may be, as Gottman and Porterfield (1981) have suggested, because of the rewriting of the items. Mean scores for each group are in Table 5.4.

An analysis of variance was performed using the number of M.C.S. items correctly decoded by each member of the dyad as the dependent variable, and using marital adjustment level and direction of sending (husband sending to wife or wife sending to husband), as the independent variables. Higher scores were obtained when wives were the message-senders than when husbands were, $F(1, 45) = 5.517$, $p < .02$, $d = .7003$. While there was no main effect for marital adjustment level, t-tests (*a priori*) showed that when wives were the encoders and husbands were the decoders, couples in the high marital adjustment group had significantly higher scores than couples in the low marital adjustment group, $t(31) = 2.51$, $p < .01$, $d = .9016$. This finding is very similar to that of Gottman and Porterfield (1981) who showed that the marital satisfaction of the wife was related to the decoding score of the husband. What we have here is that the marital adjustment level of the couple is related to the decoding score of the husband. However, at this point we have no confirmation that this is because of a decoding deficit in the husband.

Separating the effects of encoding and decoding

In order to separate the encoding and decoding effects in this study, it was decided to evaluate the items by showing the videotapes to groups of judges. Groups of 8 to 12 psychology students were used as judges and they were asked to perform the same task as the spouses, that is, to decide which of the three possible alternatives they thought the spouse was sending. Twenty-eight of these sessions were held, each of two hours duration, with the tapes of 5 couples being shown in any 2-hour period. Each videotape (set of messages) was shown on three different occasions to three different groups of students.

Classification of items

A separate score was calculated for each item for each subject. If two-thirds of the judges who viewed an item was able to code that item correctly (that is, the response they chose corresponded to the alternative the encoder was instructed by the experimenter to send), then that item was classified as a "good communication" (an item that had been clearly sent). Thus the successfulness of a communication was judged by how well the intention was communicated to the group of students.

This technique allowed items to be evaluated independently of whether the spouse decoded the item correctly, and thus recognition was given to the fact that an error could occur either because the item was not clearly sent in the first place, or because, even though the message was clearly sent, the decoder misunderstood the cues. On the basis of these scores (the percentage of students who correctly decoded the item) messages were classified as "good communications" (two-thirds or more of the judges decoded the item correctly), or as "bad communications" (fewer than two-thirds of judges decoded it correctly). All errors made by spouses were then classified as either encoding errors or decoding errors.

An item was classified as an encoding error if the spouse decoded it incorrectly, and more than one-third of the judges also decoded it incorrectly—in other words, the item was a bad communication incorrectly decoded by the spouse. The argument here is that if neither the spouse nor the judges can decode the item correctly, then it is likely that there is a problem in the way the message was sent.

An item was classified as a decoding error if two-thirds or more of the judges decoded the item correctly, but the spouse failed to decode the item correctly—in other words, the item was a good communication incorrectly decoded by the spouse. The argument here is that since we have established that the item was sent clearly enough for most of the judges to decode it correctly, then an error is likely to be related to the decoding rather than the encoding.

A further classification of items was as idiosyncratic communications. An idiosyncratic communication was a bad communication correctly decoded by the spouse. Such an item was seen as evidence for a private message system, where spouses could correctly decode items which the judges found difficult to decode. Table 5.5 summarizes the five classifications of messages.

TABLE 5.5. *Summary of Item Classifications*

Classification	Criterion
Good communication	An item decoded correctly by 2/3 judges
Bad communication	An item decoded correctly by fewer than 2/3 judges
Encoding error	A bad communication incorrectly decoded by the spouse
Decoding error	A good communication incorrectly decoded by the spouse
Idiosyncratic communication	A bad communication correctly decoded by the spouse.

TABLE 5.6. *Mean Percentages of Good Communications*

Marital adjustment level		Type of message		
		Positive	Neutral	Negative
High*	Males	38.2	50.7	56.9
	Females	52.1	42.4	59.7
Moderate†	Males	32.6	47.2	50.0
	Females	60.4	52.1	61.8
Low†	Males	25.4	36.5	50.0
	Females	51.6	40.5	58.7

* $n - 16$.
† $n = 14$.
(Adapted from Noller, 1980, p. 1141)

Analysis of good communications

An analysis of good communications revealed that females had significantly more good communications than males, that more negative messages were rated as good communications than other types, and that the difference between males and females was particularly on the number of positive messages which were rated as good. Table 5.6 presents the percentages of communications rated as good for each marital adjustment level, sex and type of message and Figure 5.1 shows the relationship between sex and type of message.

Although there was no main effect for marital adjustment level, *a priori* t-tests showed that those with low marital adjustment had fewer good communications than those with high marital adjustment, and this was particularly true for males.

Analysis of encoding errors

An analysis of encoding errors showed a very similar pattern. Encoding errors were made more by males than by females, and on positive messages more than on other types. Also, it was mainly male subjects who made

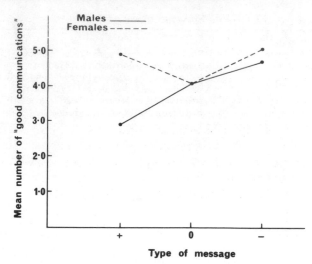

FIG 5.1. Interaction of sex and type of message for "good communications".
(Noller, 1980, p. 1142)

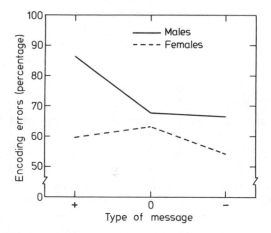

FIG 5.2. Interaction of sex and type of message for encoding errors.

encoding errors on their positive messages (see Figure 5.2). Table 5.7 presents the mean percentages of errors related to encoding for each group. Figure 5.2 illustrates the interaction of sex and type of message for encoding errors.

Analysis of decoding errors

Decoding errors (the percentage of good communications incorrectly decoded by the spouse) were also analysed, with subjects making more

TABLE 5.7. *Encoding Errors as a Percentage of the Total Errors on a Subject's Messages*

		Type of message		
Marital adjustment level		Positive	Neutral	Negative
High*	Males	82.7	63.2	69.9
	Females	70.3	58.3	51.0
Moderate*	Males	83.3	68.3	70.9
	Females	44.4	62.3	54.2
Low†	Males	94.2	71.9	58.7
	Females	64.0	69.8	57.1

* $n = 16$.
† $n = 14$.
(Noller, 1980, p. 1142)

TABLE 5.8. *Decoding Errors as a Percentage of the Spouse's Good Communications*

		Type of message		
Marital adjustment level		Positive	Neutral	Negative
High*	Males	9.9	14.6	16.8
	Females	25.5	27.9	9.3
Moderate†	Males	21.9	22.7	12.8
	Females	13.2	22.5	20.3
Low†	Males	24.6	27.8	24.2
	Females	23.8	17.4	20.2

* $n = 16$.
† $n = 14$.
(Noller, 1980, p. 1142)

errors on neutral messages than on positive or negative messages. Although there was no main effect for marital adjustment, and no sex by marital adjustment interaction, *a priori* t-tests showed that subjects in the low marital adjustment group made a greater percentage of decoding errors than did subjects in the high marital adjustment group, and that this result was largely due to the differences between the males in the two groups. Table 5.8 presents mean percentages for each group.

Discussion of results related to encoding and decoding

These findings, then, support Gottman and Porterfield's (1981) finding of a decoding problem in husbands in low marital adjustment couples, but they also show that encoding, particularly that of the husband is very important to marital satisfaction. As well, the encoding problem seems to be particularly related to the sending of positive messages.

These findings with regard to positivity would seem relevant to the Talk Table studies of Gottman *et al.* (1976), where it was found that messages between unhappy spouses had a more negative impact on the spouse receiving them than did messages between happy spouses, even when intent did not differ. Taking into account the present finding, the most likely reason for the negative effect is that those sending them had difficulty sending the more positive messages they wanted to send, and these messages "came out sounding negative". This would seem to be particularly likely for the low marital adjustment husbands.

A number of writers have noted the problem of male inexpressiveness (Balswick, 1979; Balswick & Avertt, 1977; Balswick & Peek, 1971), particularly in the case of expressing love and happiness. Wills, Weiss and Patterson (1974) emphasized the importance of positive expressions of affection on the part of the husbands, to the wives' general satisfaction with the marriage.

The finding that both both males and females had little difficulty communicating their negative messages fits with much of the discussion in Chapter 2 of the behaviours that unhappy married couples complain about, such as criticism, nagging etc. Since all couples seem about equally adept at sending such messages, it seems likely that the frequency of their occurrence, rather than accuracy at sending or receiving is what distinguishes happy and unhappy couples. This issue will be raised in Chapter 7, when a study bearing on this issue will be reported.

While some early studies found that female superiority at encoding was due mainly to their superiority at sending negative messages, this finding was not supported here. Although females were slightly better at sending negative messages than were males, their real superiority was at sending positive messages. The differences in results between this study and other studies may be due to the fact that messages in the present study were all sent to the spouse and related specifically to the marriage relationship.

It is also interesting that no sex difference was found in the present study with regard to decoding errors. This supports the findings of Zuckerman and his colleagues (Zuckerman *et al.*, 1975) that when males know the sender, their decoding is as accurate as that of females. The whole issue of sex differences in nonverbal communication, and their impact on the marital relationship will be taken up in Chapter 11.

Idiosyncratic communication

Bad communications correctly decoded by the spouse were also analysed, and a sex difference was found, with wives having a larger percentage of these communications correctly decoded by the spouse than did husbands. This finding, together with the finding for the importance of encoding, would seem to imply that more idiosyncratic communication (understood by the spouse but not others) occurred when wives were the message-senders. So these present data support Gottman and Porterfield's (1981) finding that private message systems between couples particularly seem to operate when wives are the message senders, but does not support the finding that such a system is exclusive to nonclinic couples. Of course, care needs to be taken with both these studies, because of the assumptions underlying each of their methodologies. Gottman and Porterfield use only one other decoder as a check on the spouse's decoding and individual differences in decoding ability could well be having an impact. Noller (1980), on the other hand, uses a number of decoders, which should provide a more stringent check on the spouse's decoding, but at the same time assumes that a good communication in the marital situation is one which can be decoded by both the spouse and others. Gottman and Porterfield's (1981) assumption, on the other hand, is that as long as there is low agreement between the stranger's decoding and the spouse's decoding this indicates the existence of a private message system, whether the spouses are decoding each other accurately or not. This point will be taken up again in Chapter 6 where the relationship between skill at decoding the spouse and skill at decoding strangers will be discussed.

Bias in decoding

As mentioned earlier, a number of writers have commented on the factors that can influence the decoding process (Ahammer, 1973; Glick & Gross, 1975; Raush et al., 1974). As well, it makes intuitive sense that unhappy spouses distort the partner's message in a negative direction. Kahn (1970) maintained that husbands in happy marriages distort their wives' emotional messages toward the negative. However, as Gottman and Porterfield (1981) point out, "Kahn presented no data to support his conclusion about affective distortion, and, what is perhaps even more unfortunate, other writers have assumed that he did" (p. 823). In fact, as has already been discussed, Kahn (1970) was in no position to present these data since the methodology he used did not enable him to separate sender and receiver effects, nor husband and wife effects.

In the present situation, it was decided to examine the data to see whether spouses had a tendency to make errors in decoding in a particular direction, that is, in a positive direction or a negative direction. It was expected that unhappy couples would show a bias in a negative direction, while happy couples would show no such bias, or perhaps even a bias in a positive direction.

For this analysis, if a spouse decoded an item incorrectly, and made the error in a negative direction (that is, decoded a neutral item as negative or a positive item as neutral or negative) he or she received a negative score, -1 for responding to a positive item as neutral or a neutral item as negative, and -2 for responding to a positive item as negative. On the other hand, if he or she decoded an item incorrectly, but made the error in a positive direction (that is, neutral as positive, or negative as neutral or positive) then he or she

TABLE 5.9. *Scoring of Errors for Response Bias*

Type of Message How decoded	Positive	Neutral	Negative
Positive	0	−1	−2
Neutral	+1	0	−1
Negative	+2	+1	0

TABLE 5.10. *Mean Bias Scores*

	Direction of sending	
Marital adjustment level	Husband to wife	Wife to husband
High*	0.127	−0.194
Moderate*	0.341	−0.199
Low†	0.220	−0.107

* $n = 16$.
† $n = 14$.
(Noller, 1980, p. 1143)

received a positive score, +1 for responding to a negative item as neutral, or a neutral item as positive, and +2 for responding to a negative item as positive. See Table 5.9 for a summary. For this analysis, only decoding errors (that is, good communications incorrectly decoded) were used. This procedure helped to ensure that any bias was in the decoding and not in the encoding. These bias scores were totalled over all decoding errors, and then averaged. The size and direction of a subject's total score indicated the size and direction of his or her tendency to respond either positively or negatively—that is, his or her response bias.

There was no effect for marital adjustment level, but there was an effect for sex, with females tending to make errors in a positive direction, and males tending to respond in a negative direction, $F(1,78) = 4.73$, $p < .05$, $d = .2463$. Mean scores are presented in Table 5.10.

This finding makes it likely that decoding errors for the males were in a negative direction at all levels of marital adjustment, but presumably the negative effects would be greater for the unhappy husbands who made more such errors. Care needs to be taken, however, since the effects are slight. This finding fits with that of Bugental and her colleagues (1970), who found that the positive components of women's messages tended to be discounted. In the present study, where only good communications were used, it becomes even more clear that this tendency is related to the decoding process, rather than the encoding process.

The fact that females showed a positive bias, suggests a tendency on the part of wives to see even slight positivity as an indication of a positive

TABLE 5.11. *Mean Accuracy Scores for Single Channel Decoding Task*

		Channel	
Marital adjustment level		Visual	Auditory
High	Husband to wife	5.44	5.19
	Wife to husband	4.63	6.06
Moderate	Husband to wife	5.38	5.50
	Wife to husband	5.81	6.06
Low	Husband to wife	4.57	5.14
	Wife to husband	5.21	6.00

(Noller, 1980, p. 1144)

message. Venardos (1982) carried out a study using the standard content methodology of the Marital Communication Scale, but without videotaping the messages and having them rated by judges. She had subjects indicate how confident they were about their decoding. She found that females were more confident on incorrect negative messages than they were when they decoded other types of message incorrectly. This finding implies that females tend not to realize when they have misunderstood a negative message (which means, of course, making a decoding error in a positive direction). What we do not know is whether these positive errors have a good or bad effect on marital relationships. It could be that such a practice avoids a lot of unnecessary argument, on the other hand it could mean that important issues are ignored and not resolved.

Channels analysis

As mentioned previously, subjects were also asked to repeat the decoding task using:

(a) The visual channel only.
(b) The vocal channel only.

Ten items were decoded in each mode, that is 10 with only auditory cues, and 10 with only visual cues available. A counterbalanced design was used with the husbands decoding first in half the couples, and the wives decoding first in the other half. As well, within each of these groups, half decoded using the visual channel first, while the other half decoded using the vocal channel first.

For husband-to-wife communication the accuracy was similar whichever channel was employed. However, in the case of wife-to-husband communications, there was greater accuracy when only the auditory channel was used, $F(1, 43) = 5.05$, $p < .03$, $d = .6854$. See Table 5.11 for mean scores for each channel. This finding indicates that when wives were the message-senders, greater accuracy was achieved by focusing on the tone of voice than

TABLE 5.12. *Correlations between Single Channel Scores and Total Scores*

Group	Channel	Total
Husbands decoding wives		
Combined	Vocal	.45†
	Visual	.34*
High marital adjustment	Vocal	.37
	Visual	.1
Moderate marital adjustment	Vocal	.67†
	Visual	.43
Low marital adjustment	Vocal	.36
	Visual	.64†
Wives decoding husbands		
Combined	Vocal	.32
	Visual	.49†
High marital adjustment	Vocal	.38
	Visual	.65*
Moderate marital adjustment	Vocal	.32
	Visual	.53*
Low marital adjustment	Vocal	.27
	Visual	.41

* $p < .05$.
† $p < .01$.
(Noller, 1980, p. 1144)

on facial expression (the largest component of the visual channel in this situation). Such a finding could also imply that the greater amount of idiosyncratic communication found when wives were the message-senders was related to tone of voice.

Correlational analyses were also carried out in order to:

(a) Test for relationships between skill at decoding the visual channel, and skill at decoding the vocal channel.

(b) Test for relationships between single channel decoding, and decoding when the total information was available—that is, the original task for the same items.

No significant relationships were found between the single channel scores for any group. However, there were significant correlations between both single channel scores and total scores for the combined group on wife-to-husband communication, with the strongest effects between the vocal and total for the moderate marital adjustment group, and the visual and total for the low marital adjustment group. This finding seems to indicate that low satisfaction husbands relied on the visual channel when decoding, a procedure that should decrease accuracy, given the earlier finding that greater accuracy was achieved by focusing on the tone of voice when wives were the message-senders. This decoding behaviour could be an important component of the decoding deficit in low satisfaction husbands which was discussed earlier.

For husband-to-wife communications, there was a significant correlation between scores on the visual channel and the total channel for the combined group, with the strongest effect being for the high and moderate marital adjustment groups. The finding suggests that when husbands were the encoders, the vocal channel was relied on most, except by the unhappy couples. See Table 5.12 for correlations between single channel scores and total scores.

The use of the different communication channels for both encoding and decoding will be discussed in greater detail in Chapter 8..

Summary of findings on accuracy

Accuracy in nonverbal communication in the marital situation seems to be related to a number of variables. The main findings of the experiments described here are:

1. Couples low in marital adjustment misunderstand one another's messages more than to other couples.

2. More misunderstandings seem to be related to encoding (or sending) than to decoding (or receiving).

3. The nonverbal sending and receiving of husbands is more strongly related to marital adjustment than is that of wives, with low marital adjustment husbands making more errors in both sending and receiving than high marital adjustment husbands.

4. Wives are better message-senders than husbands (over all groups), but particularly at sending positive messages.

5. Neutral messages are more often incorrectly decoded than other messages.

6. More idiosyncratic communication occurs on wife-to-husband communications than on husband-to-wife communications.

7. Wives have a tendency to make decoding errors in a positive direction, while husbands are more likely to make such errors in a negative direction.

8. For wife-to-husband communications, greater accuracy is achieved with the vocal channel only than the visual channel only. For husband-to-wife communications, on the other hand, accuracy is similar whichever channel is used.

9. Husbands in the high and moderate marital adjustment groups rely more on the vocal channel (leading to greater accuracy) while husbands in the low marital adjustment group rely on the visual channel (leading to less accuracy), a factor likely to be relevant to the husband decoding deficit already discussed.

References

AHAMMER, I. M. (1973) Social learning theory as a framework for the study of adult personality development. In BALTES, E. B. & SCHAIE, K. W. (Eds.) *Life-span Developmental Psychology: Personality and Socialization.* New York: Academic Press.

BACH, G. R. & WYDEN, P. (1969) Marital fighting: A guide to love. In ARD, B. N. & ARD, C. C. (Eds.) *Handbook of Marriage Counseling.* Palo Alto: Science and Behavior Books, pp. 313–21.

BALSWICK, J. (1979) The inexpressive male: Functional conflict and role theory as contrasting explanations. *The Family Coordinator*, **28**, 3, 331–6.

BALSWICK, J. & AVERTT, C. P. (1977) Differences in expressiveness: Gender, interpersonal orientation and perceived parental expressiveness as contributing factors. *Journal of Marriage and the Family*, **26**, 1, 121–7.

BALSWICK, J. & PEEK, C. (1971) The inexpressive male: A tragedy of American society. *The Family Coordinator*, **20**, 4, 363–8.

BUGENTAL, D. E., KASWAN, J. M. & LOVE, L. R. (1970) Perception of contradictory meanings conveyed by verbal and nonverbal channels. *Journal of Personality and Social Psychology*, **16**, 647–55.

BURGESS, E. W., LOCKE, H. J. & TOMES, M. M. (1971) *The Family.* New York: Van Nostrand Reinhold.

DUCKWORTH, D. (1975) Personality, emotional state and perception of nonverbal communications. *Perceptual and Motor Skills*, **40**, 325–6.

EKMAN, P. & FRIESEN, W. V. (1969) Nonverbal leakage and cues to deception. *Psychiatry*, **32**, 88–106 (a).

FRASER, C. (1976) An analysis of face to face communication. In BENNETT, A. E. (Ed.) *Communication between Doctors and Patients.* Oxford University Press for Nuffield Provincial Hospitals Trust, pp. 7–28.

GLICK, B. R. & GROSS, S. J. (1975) Marital interaction and marital conflict: A critical evaluation of current research strategies. *Journal of Marriage and the Family*, **37**, 505–12.

GOTTMAN, J., NOTARIUS, C., MARKMAN, H., BANKS, S., YOPPI, B. & RUBIN, M. E. (1976) Behaviour exchange theory and marital decision making. *Journal of Personality and Social Psychology*, **34**, 14–23.

GOTTMAN, J. M. & PORTERFIELD, A. L. (1981) Communicative competence in the nonverbal behaviour of married couples. *Journal of Marriage and the Family*, **4**, 817–24.

HALL, J. (1978) Gender effects in decoding nonverbal cues. *Psychological Bulletin*, **85**, 845–57.

HALL, J. A. (1979) Gender, gender roles and nonverbal communication skills. In ROSENTHAL, R. (Ed.) *Skill in Nonverbal Communication.*

HALL, J., ROSENTHAL, R., ARCHER, D., DIMATTEO, M. R. & ROGERS, P. L. (1978) Profile of nonverbal sensitivity. In MCREYNOLDS, PAUL (Ed.) *Advances in Psychological Assessment*, Vol. 4. Palo Alto, Calif: Jossey-Bass.

KAHN, M. (1969) Nonverbal communication as a factor in marital satisfaction. Doctoral dissertation, Southern Illinois University.

KAHN, M. (1970) Nonverbal communication and marital satisfaction. *Family Process*, **9**, 449–56.

LEVITT, E. A. (1964) The relationship between abilities to express emotional meanings vocally and facially. In DAVITZ, J. R., *The Communication of Emotional Meaning.* New York: McGraw-Hill, pp. 43–55.

MEHRABIAN, A. & WIENER, M. (1967) Decoding of inconsistent communications. *Journal of Personality and Social Psychology*, **6**, 109–14.

NEWCOMB, T. M., TURNER, L. H. & CONVERSE, P. E. (1965) *Social psychology: The study of human interaction.* New York: Holt, Rinehart & Winston.

NOLLER, P. (1980) Misunderstandings in marital communication: A study of couples' nonverbal communication. *Journal of Personality and Social Psychology*, **39**, 1135–48.

OSGOOD, C. E. (1966) The dimensionality of the semantic space for communication via facial expression. *Scandinavian Journal of Psychology*, **7**, 1–30.

RAUSH, H. L., BARRY, W. A., HERTEL, R. K. & SWAIN, M. E. (1974) *Communication, Conflict and Marriage.* San Francisco: Jossey-Bass.

Rosenthal, R.& DePaulo, B. M. (1979) Sex differences in eavesdropping on nonverbal cues. *Journal of Personality and Social Psychology*, **37**, 273–85 (a).

Rosenthal, R. & DePaulo, B. M. (1979) Ambivalence, discrepancy and deception in nonverbal communication. In Rosenthal, R. (Ed.) *Skill in Nonverbal Communication*.

Venardos, C. (1982) Communication awareness in married couples. Unpublished Honours Thesis, University of Queensland.

Williams, J. (1969) Feedback techniques in marriage counseling. In Ard, B. N. & Ard, C. C. (Eds.) *Handbook of Marriage Counseling*. Palo Alto: Science and Behavior Books.

Wills, T. A., Weiss, R. L. & Patterson, G. R. (1974) A behavioral analysis of the determinants of marital satisfaction. *Journal of Consulting and Clinical Psychology*, **42**, 6, 802–11.

Zuckerman, M., Hall, J., DeFrank, R. S. & Rosenthal, R. (1976) Encoding and decoding of spontaneous and posed facial expressions. *Journal of Personality and Social Psychology*, **34**, 966–77.

Zuckerman, M., Lipets, M., Koivumaki, J. & Rosenthal, R. (1975) Encoding and decoding nonverbal cues of emotion. *Journal of Personality and Social Psychology*, **32**, 1068–76.

6

Relationship Between Communication with the Spouse and Communication with Strangers

A number of researchers have sought to compare interactions with the spouse with interactions with strangers. Generally, studies have compared spouse and stranger couples with regard to the amount of positivity and negativity in the interaction. The results have tended to show that strangers are treated more gently and politely than spouses (Birchler, Weiss & Vincent, 1973; Ryder, 1968; Winter, Ferreira & Bowers, 1973).

Ryder (1968) used the Color Matching Test with dyads being involved in resolving discrepancies about the name of various patches of colour (when the experimenter had given one of them misleading information). While this is the kind of situation that husbands and wives would be likely to argue about, the differences between spouses and strangers in such interactions are related to the fact that spouse interactions have both a past and a future:

A *past* which may include similar arguments and unresolved feelings related to such questions as the colour that the bedroom walls should be painted;

A *future* which may include similar decisions to be made at some later date and the possibility that the present interaction may affect the outcome of such future discussions.

Winter *et al.* (1973) had subjects list some preferences on such questions as a country to visit for a year, the colour of the next car etc. and then had dyads (either spouses or strangers) discuss any discrepancies between them. This task has similar effects as the task discussed earlier, with spouses again being different in the ways already discussed. While each of these studies compared spouse–spouse interactions with interactions with strangers, neither sought to discriminate between couples who were happy or unhappy in their marriages. Birchler and his colleagues (1975) have, however, made this comparison in order to see:

(a) Whether individuals who are negative in their interaction with their spouses are also negative in their interactions with strangers.

(b) Whether there is consistency in behaviour to two strangers. This study will be described in considerable detail.

The Birchler *et al.* Study

Birchler, Weiss and Vincent (1975) videotaped three interactions for each subject:

(a) the subject interacting with his/her own spouse.

(b) The subject interacting with an opposite-sex stranger from a distressed marriage.

(c) The subject interacting with an opposite-sex stranger from a non-distressed marriage.

A modification of Olson and Ryder's (1970) Inventory of Marital Conflicts was used and dyads had to come to some resolution about vignettes on which they disagreed.

The videotapes were coded using the major summary categories of the Marital Interaction Coding System (see Table 6.1), with rate per minute for each type of behaviour being used as the dependent variable. Distressed married couples used more negative social reinforcement both in the problem-solving situation and in general conversation and less positive social reinforcement than nondistressed spouses, particularly in the problem-solving situation.

When interaction with spouses was compared with interaction with strangers (averaged across distressed and nondistressed) it was found that:

"Married individuals observed interacting in a laboratory setting emitted more negative and less positive social reinforcement toward spouses than they did toward strangers. This pattern was consistent for individuals from either distressed or nondistressed marriages" (p. 353).

TABLE 6.1. *Major Summary Categories of the Marital Interaction Coding System*

Measure	Code
Positive social reinforcement (SR+)	
Verbal	Agreement, approval, humour
Nonverbal	Assert, laugh, positive physical contact, smile
Negative social reinforcement (SR−)	
Verbal	Complain, criticize, deny responsibility, excuse, put down, interrupt, disagree.
Nonverbal	No response (ignore), not tracking (inattention), turn off.
Problem solving	
Verbal	Problem solution, accept responsibility, compromise.

From Birchler, Weiss & Vincent, 1975, p. 352.

TABLE 6.2. *Mean Rate per Minute for Positive and Negative Social Reinforcement for Distressed and Nondistressed Couples*

Group	Type of social reinforcement	
	Positive	Negative
Nondistressed		
Conversation	2.77	.73
Problem solving	1.93	.74
Distressed		
Conversation	2.10	1.07
Problem solving	1.49	1.10

Adapted from Birchler *et al.*, 1975.

Table 6.2 presents mean rates per minute for each group in each situation, as well as t-test results.

Overall, in the problem-solving situation there were some differences.

1. Stranger dyads engaged in the most positive social reinforcement and the least negative social reinforcement.

2. Married couples from distressed marriages engaged in the most negative social reinforcement and the least positive reinforcement.

3. Nondistressed married couples engaged in less positivity and more negativity than stranger dyads, and more positivity and less negativity than distressed spouses.

Analyses were also carried out to look for consistencies in behaviour:

(a) Consistency between behaviour to the spouse and behaviour to each of two strangers.

(b) Consistency between behaviour to each of two strangers.

The results showed that there were consistencies in positive behaviours to strangers, but spouse to stranger consistencies were rare.

For negative behaviours spouse–stranger correlations were not different from chance:

> "Only for individuals from distressed marriages was there evidence of trait-like negative behavioural output. This would suggest that individuals from distressed relationships may be more likely to respond similarly from person to person with regard to output of negative behaviours" (p. 355).

So while there is some evidence for trait-like communication patterns, and then only in the one group, the overall finding is that the two sets of relationships are independent, with response to one's spouse being unrelated to one's response to strangers. As Birchler and his colleagues (1975) say:

"It appears that individuals learn to relate in an ineffective manner, specifically with their spouses, while retaining social competency in other areas" (p. 359).

The Honeycutt *et al.* Study

Honeycutt and his colleagues (Honeycutt, Wilson & Parker, 1982) explored the question of perceived styles of communication in and out of the marital relationship to see whether those who saw themselves as good communicators in the marital relationship, and those who saw themselves as good communicators outside the relationship in more general situations, saw themselves as using similar or different styles of communicating. These researchers used the definition of communicator style supplied by Norton (1978):

"the way one verbally and paraverbally interacts to signal how literal meaning should be taken, interpreted, filtered or understood" (p. 99).

Clearly communicator style, by this definition is very closely related to nonverbal communication, or at least to nonverbal style, and fits with definitions of nonverbal communication by such theorists as Watzlawick (Watzlawick *et al.*, 1967), Argyle (1975) and Mehrabian (1971).

Honeycutt *et al.* (1982) also used Norton's (Norton, 1978; Norton & Montgomery, 1979) definitions of the style variables which are part of communicator style. The salient points of these styles will be summarized below, but readers should see the earlier references if they need more detail.

Dominance—including frequent interruptions, frequent simultaneous talk, large amount of talk.

Relaxed—calm and free of tension.

Friendly—generally loosely defined—from not hostile to deeply intimate, showing liking.

Open—disclosing of true feelings, beliefs and opinions.

Contentious—characterized by argument and conflict.

Dramatic—engaging in theatrics in order to accent the verbal message.

Animated or expressive—using gestures, postures etc. to emphasize or exaggerate the verbal message.

Attentive—listening to the other and signalling that attentiveness.

Impression-leaving—making an impression on the other, nonverbally.

Precise—concerned with accuracy and proof.

Flexible—using a variety of means of communication.

A self-report questionnaire was used to assess the tendencies for couples to use the various styles, both in the marital relationship, and in general interaction situations:

"A questionnaire was administered to spouses which asked them to indicate if the word description of the various communicator styles described the way they communicated (a) in general with other people and (b) with the marriage partner. A series of five-point Likert-type scales ranging from 'does not describe me well' to 'describes me well' was used for each style" (Honeycutt *et al.*, 1982, p. 398).

Analyses compared styles used by good communicators in the marital relationship, with those used by good communicators in general. Table 6.3 summarizes the variables important in predicting a good communicator in general situations (dominant, relaxed, attentive and impression-leaving) and in the marital situation (friendly, attentive, precise and expressive).

There were also differences in style related to gender, and level of happiness in the marriage, and these are summarized in Table 6.4. "Friendly" was the best predictor of a good communicator in the marital relationship, while dominant and impression-leaving were generally indicative of good communicators in general situations. The finding that "friendly" was so important in the marital relationship doesn't fit with the findings of Winter *et al.* (1973) and Birchler *et al.* (1975) that strangers (those outside the marital relationship) are treated more gently and politely than spouses. A number of explanations are possible for this result:

1. The different methodologies—perhaps people think (and therefore report) that they are more friendly with spouses, while behavioural measures indicate that they are not.

2. The vague definition of "friendly"—perhaps degree of friendliness would be more useful, rather than just a measure of the extent to which a friendly style is characteristic.

3. Style being defined differently in the different situations—perhaps friendliness is expressed differently in marital relationships, and is not necessarily characterized by politeness and gentleness.

The finding that "expressive" was an important variable for husbands in

TABLE 6.3. *Styles of Interaction Important in Predicting a Good Relationship in Marital and General Situations*

In general situations			In marital relationship		
Style of interaction	γ^2	Regression weight	Style of interaction	γ^2	Regression weight
Impression-leaving	.24	.25	Friendly	.58	.41
Dominant	.35	.32	Attentive	.68	.19
Relaxed	.41	.16	Precise	.71	.19
Attentive	.44	.12	Expressive	.73	.21

Adapted from Honeycutt *et al.*, 1982.

TABLE 6.4. *Style Differences inside and outside the Marital Relationship for Males and Females high and low in Marital Happiness in Marital Relationships in General*

	Inside marital relationship	Outside marital relationship
Higher happily married		
Spouses	Friendly, impression-leaving, precise, expressive	Dominant, impression-leaving open
Males	Expressive, open, precise	Dominant, open
Females	Friendly	Impression-leaving
Lower happily married		
Spouses	Friendly, relaxed	Relaxed
Males	Friendly, impression-leaving	No predictors
Females	Attentive	Impression-leaving

From Honeycutt *et al.*, 1982.

the high happiness group is interesting given the findings reported earlier (Chapter 5) that the husband's skill at encoding is important to marital satisfaction, and the more general findings of male inexpressiveness (Balswick & Peek, 1971).

The Question of Accuracy

Thus, while there is considerable evidence that strangers are treated differently from spouses, a further important question is whether people are more accurate with their spouses than they are with strangers. We have already shown in Chapter 5 that happy couples are more accurate than unhappy couples, and that it is the message-sending and message-receiving of the husband which seems to be crucial. But, for example, is the problem in decoding which was evident for low marital adjustment husbands in the study described in Chapter 5 (Noller, 1980) also evident in their decoding of strangers? Or, on the other hand, is the decoding deficit specific to the marital relationship?

Gottman and Porterfield (1981) have explored this question in their study of communicative competence in the nonverbal behaviour of married couples. In this study (already described in some detail in Chapter 5) subjects were decoded by both spouses and strangers. These researchers correlated the number of items the spouse correctly decoded with the number of items correctly decoded by a stranger and found a significant correlation (.68, p < .001) between the wife's marital satisfaction and her husband's score on the decoding task, but no such relationship between the husband's marital satisfaction and his wife's score on the decoding task. (These correlation analyses are summarized in Table 6.5.) As well, the correlation between the wife's marital satisfaction and the male stranger's score on the decoding task was very low (.31, n.s.). Thus, while the wife's

TABLE 6.5. *Summary of Correlational Results from Gottman and Porterfield (1981)*

Wife	High correlation between marital satisfaction and husband's decoding score. Low (nonsignificant) correlation between marital satisfaction and male stranger's decoding score.
Husband	No correlation between marital satisfaction and wife's decoding score.
Male stranger	No correlation between own marital satisfaction and score obtained decoding a woman in the spouse group (not his wife).

marital satisfaction accounted for 46 per cent of the variance in her husband's score, it only accounted for about 10 per cent in the stranger's score, implying that "in distressed marriages, husbands but not male strangers are poor receivers of wives' nonverbal messages" Gottman & Porterfield, 1981, p. 821).

Also, since there was no difference between the mean for husbands on the decoding task and that for strangers, it seems likely that strangers were better receivers than husbands for dissatisfied wives but worse receivers than husbands for satisfied wives. In fact, Gottman and Porterfield present a scatterplot of scores (p. 823) which shows that strangers' scores were higher than husbands' scores for dissatisfied wives and lower than the husbands' scores for satisfied wives.

Gottman and Porterfield also discuss the issue of across-sender consistencies in accuracy. The question of importance is whether the husband receiver deficit found in this study is also likely to affect his decoding of people other than the wife. Unfortunately no direct test of this question was possible from their study, although they do report that there was no relationship between a male stranger's marital satisfaction and the score he obtained when decoding a woman other than his wife ($-.14$, n.s.). Such a finding implies that the decoding deficits found in dissatisfied husbands' are specific to their relationships with their wives. What is needed for a direct test of such a hypothesis is data for the same subjects decoding their wives, and decoding opposite-sex strangers.

Noller (1981) obtained decoding stranger data for the same couples who encoded and decoded messages to their spouses in the study described already in Chapter 5, and was able to examine the pattern of sex and message-type differences for decoding strangers, and to make a direct comparison between a subject's score when decoding the spouse and score when decoding strangers of the opposite sex. This study will now be described in detail.

Accuracy with the spouse and strangers—a within subjects study

Since the aim was to compare the subjects' ability to decode the spouse with their ability to decode strangers of the opposite sex, it was decided to have subjects decode the same items as they had decoded in the earlier experiment with their spouses. Also, because it was important to be able to compare between subjects (for example, the marital adjustment groups) a standard videotape was made which could be shown to all subjects.

Making the videotape

Husbands and wives from five married couples were videotaped while sending each other, in random order, the messages from the Marital Communication Scale (as revised by Noller, 1980). Each husband sent 27 messages (nine different items each with three alternatives) and each wife also sent 27 messages. The couples sent the messages in exactly the same way as did the couples in the earlier experiment:

1. They sent the messages directly to one another while facing each other across a table.

2. The encoder noted down the intention he/she was trying to send, while the decoder noted down the intention which he/she thought the spouse was sending.

3. Each message was videotaped.

When all the couples had participated there were five videotaped versions of each of the husband communications and each of the wife communications.

These messages were then shown to several groups of subjects who received a score for the number of items they correctly decoded. The "best" version of each item was selected by choosing the version of each item which correlated best with the total—that is, the version of each item which good decoders tended to get right, while poor decoders tended to get wrong. The 27 "best" husband items and 27 "best" wife items were made into a single test video which could be decoded by all the couples who took part in the experiment (Noller, 1980) described in Chapter 5. Two practice items were also included on the videotape.

The videotape was then shown to each of the couples during the experimental session, always after they had completed the earlier task with their spouses. Subjects were asked to decide, as they did with their spouses, which of the three possible alternatives they thought was being encoded. Both members of the couple decoded the video at the same time but they were asked not to consult one another, or to comment about how they were answering the items. Both husbands and wives decoded all 54 items (that is, husband items and wife items) and answers were filled in on a specially prepared sheet. Subjects were each given a score for decoding the opposite sex and a score for decoding the same sex for each type of message.

Sex and message-type effects. The major findings with regard to sex and message type included:

1. Females obtained higher scores on the decoding task than the males, $F(2,84) = 13.21$, p < .001, $\eta = 489$. This finding is different from that in the earlier study (Chapter 5) and is almost certainly related to the fact that in the present study strangers are being decoded, while in the earlier study spouses were being decoded. Zuckerman and his colleagues (1975) showed that females are better than males at decoding strangers but lose this advantage in situations where the decoders are acquainted with the sender.

2. *Both sexes* obtained higher scores when decoding the females than when decoding males, particularly on positive and negative messages, implying that the females are better *encoders* for these messages.

3. Whichever sex was decoding the males similar scores were obtained for each message type, while whichever sex was decoding the females, higher scores were obtained for positive and negative messages than for neutral messages. (See Figure 6.1 and Table 6.6.)

4. Lower scores were obtained on neutral messages than other messages, just as in the earlier study with spouses. (See Chapter 5.)

Differences related to marital adjustment level. Low marital adjustment subjects scored higher than moderate marital adjustment subjects, but not higher than the high marital adjustment subjects, $F(2,84) = 3.367$, p = .04, $\eta = .27$. Such a result argues against the idea of a trait-like decoding deficit

TABLE 6.6. *Mean Scores on Decoding Videotaped Messages of Same and Opposite Sex Others*

Group*	Message type		
	Positive	Neutral	Negative
High marital adjustment			
Males: Same sex	5.5	5.1	5.3
Opposite sex	6.9	4.9	6.6
Females: Same sex	6.9	5.1	7.7
Opposite sex	6.1	5.9	6.2
Moderate marital adjustment			
Males: Same sex	5.9	5.3	5.6
Opposite sex	6.5	4.7	6.0
Females: Same sex	7.3	5.1	7.2
Opposite sex	6.1	6.1	5.7
Low marital adjustment			
Males: Same sex	6.1	5.8	5.4
Opposite sex	6.6	6.1	6.7
Females: Same sex	7.2	5.8	7.2
Opposite sex	6.3	6.6	6.2

Note: Maximum score = 9.
* 15 subjects in each group.
(Noller, 1981, p. 275)

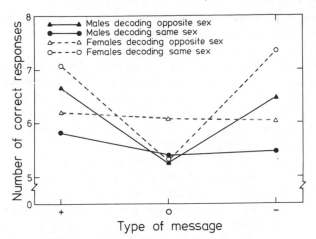

FIG 6.1. Graph showing the interaction of sex of decoder, sex of encoder, and type of message, with scores decoding the videotape as the dependent variable.
(Noller, 1981, p. 275)

in low marital adjustment subjects. This result is also different from the results found with spouses, since low marital adjustment subjects obtained lower scores overall, and low marital adjustment husbands made more decoding errors than other husbands.

Since spouses were decoding similar messages from strangers as from spouses it was possible to make a direct comparison between scores obtained when decoding the spouse and scores obtained when decoding strangers. A difference score was calculated by subtracting the score obtained when decoding strangers of the opposite sex from the score obtained when decoding the spouse. Means for this decoding difference score are presented in Table 6.7.

TABLE 6.7. *Mean Scores* for the Difference between Decoding Spouse Scores and Scores for Decoding Opposite Sex Others*

Marital adjusment level†	Sex	
	Males	Females
High	+1.33	−0.73
Moderate	+1.33	−0.60
Low	−2.67	−2.87

*The scores on which this difference score was based were out of 27.
X̄ = 17.5 for decoding spouse, 18.3 for decoding others.
†15 subjects in each group.
(Noller, 1981, p. 276)

Low marital adjustment subjects had a significantly larger difference between these two scores than did other subjects, $F(2,84) = 4.93$, $p < .01$. This difference was also negative for subjects in this group, indicating that their scores were higher for decoding strangers than for decoding the spouse.

Interestingly, although there was no sex difference, females showed a general tendency to score better with strangers than with the spouse. If we relate this finding to the sex difference found with strangers, it is possible to conclude that at least part of the reason for this sex difference is that females actually score better with people they don't know. Perhaps when women know the person they are decoding they rely on factors other than the nonverbal behaviour (past history etc.) and don't make use of their superior decoding ability. Since it is particularly the low satisfaction wives who make more errors with their spouses, it could be that these wives, in particular, rely on factors other than nonverbal behaviour and assume they know what the spouse means. This issue will be taken up again in the chapter on awareness of communication.

The case of the low marital adjustment husbands, who, like their wives decode strangers better than they decode their spouses is particularly interesting in the light of the general finding (Zuckerman et al., 1975) that males are better at decoding people they know than people they don't know. In that case it is noteworthy that low marital adjustment husbands decode their wives so much worse than they decode opposite sex strangers. Since the means for the other two groups of husbands are positive, the husbands in the other groups seem to be following the pattern found by Zuckerman et al. (1975).

The overall finding that spouses in unhappy couples actually decode their spouses less accurately than they decode strangers underlines the claims of writers such as Raush and his colleagues (1974) that factors such as the history of the relationship between the members of a dyad affect the accuracy with which communications between the members of that dyad are decoded. One would expect that a pre-existing negative attitude would lead to misunderstanding. As well, the finding fits with those of Gottman and Porterfield (1981) who showed that husbands decoded better than strangers for satisfied spouses and worse than strangers for dissatisfied couples.

The finding also lends support to the contention that decoding ability is not trait-like, but is, in fact, specific to particular relationships. Other studies discussed in this chapter have also supported this view that behaviour in marital relationships is generally independent of behaviour in other relationships. Birchler et al. (1975) showed that there was little relationship between interactions with the spouse and interactions with a stranger. Gottman and Porterfield (1981) also reported data indicating that the decoding deficits which they found for dissatisfied married couples were specific to those marital relationships, and did not carry over to other relationships.

Discussion

The general pattern of sex and message-type differences found when subjects were decoding strangers is essentially the same as that found when the same subjects were decoding the spouse. The main difference was that females were better than males at decoding for the task with strangers, although there were no sex differences in decoding errors for spouses.

The comparison between males and females both decoding the opposite sex is the one that relates best to the marital situation, and hence to the earlier study (Noller, 1980) where spouses were being decoded. For the stranger task, males had higher scores than females on positive messages, females had higher scores than males on neutral messages, and there were no differences on negative messages.

These results almost certainly reflect sex differences in encoding as well as decoding, and this is confirmed by the finding that decoding scores were spread in much the same way across message-types for each sex of encoder, irrespective of which sex was doing the decoding. However, while such confoundings are problematical for researchers trying to understand the relative effects of encoding and decoding in communication, it must be admitted that these confoundings actually occur in interaction situations, marital or otherwise. Several points are clear:

1. Males are likely to be better at decoding positive messages from their spouses because they are decoding females who are superior encoders of positive messages (a finding common to both the spouse and stranger studies).

2. Males and females score equally well on negative messages from the opposite sex because the males (who are less skilled at decoding) are receiving messages from the females (the superior encoders), while the females (the superior decoders) are receiving messages from the males (the inferior encoders).

3. The finding that females score better than males on neutral messages is likely to be related to the superior decoding of the females—although this result is not as clear as the other findings.

In general then, males would seem to have an advantage in marital exchanges because they are more likely to be able to understand their spouses, and also more likely to be understood by them.

The findings with regard to marital adjustment confirm that being a poor decoder of the spouse does not necessarily mean that one will be a poor decoder of strangers. Low marital adjustment subjects had more skill at decoding than was evident in their interactions with their spouses. Such a finding raises the question of whether general communication training is likely to generalize to the marital relationship. If, as Birchler *et al.* (1975) have suggested, "individuals learn to relate in an ineffective manner specifically with their spouses", it seems likely that any training to improve communication skills for married couples should also take place in the context of the marital relationship.

References

ARGYLE, M. (1975) *Bodily Communication*. London: Methuen.
BIRCHLER, G. R., WEISS, R. L. & VINCENT, J. P. (1975) Multimethod analysis of social reinforcement exchange between maritally distressed and non-distressed spouse and stranger dyads. *Journal of Personality and Social Psychology*, 31, 349–62.
GOTTMAN, J. M. & PORTERFIELD, A. L. (1981) Communicative competence in the nonverbal behaviour of married couples. *Journal of Marriage and the Family*, 4, 817–24.
HALL, J. (1978) Gender effects in decoding nonverbal cues. *Psychological Bulletin* 85, 845–57.
HONEYCUTT, J. M., WILSON, C. & PARKER, C. (1982) Effects of sex and degrees of happiness on perceived styles of communicating in and out of the marital relationship. *Journal of Marriage and the Family*, 44, 2, 395–406.
MEHRABIAN, A. (1971) *Silent Messages*. Belmont, California: Wadsworth Publishing Company.
NOLLER, P. (1980) Misunderstandings in marital communication: A study of couples' nonverbal communication. *Journal of Personality and Social Psychology*, 39, 1135–48.
NOLLER, P. (1981) Gender and marital adjustment level differences in decoding messages from spouses and strangers. *Journal of Personality and Social Psychology*, 41, 272–8.
NORTON, R. (1978) A foundation of a communicator style construct. *Human Communication Research*, 4, 99–112.
NORTON, R. & MONTGOMERY, B. (1979) An integration of style, content, and target in defining openness. Paper presented at the International Communication Association Convention, Philadelphia, May 1979.
RAUSH, H. L., BARRY, W. A., HERTEL, R. K. & SWAIN, M. E. (1974) *Communication, Conflict and Marriage*. San Francisco: Jossey-Bass.
RYDER, R. G. (1968) Husband-wife dyads versus married strangers. *Family Process*, 7, 233–8.
WATZLAWICK, P., BEAVIN, J. H. & JACKSON, D. (1967) *Pragmatics of Human Communication*. New York: Norton.
WINTER, W. D., FERREIRA, A. J. & BOWERS, N. (1973) Decision-making in married and unrelated couples. *Family Process*, 12, 83–94.
ZUCKERMAN, M., LIPETS, M., KOIVUMAKI, J. & ROSENTHAL, R. (1975) Encoding and decoding nonverbal cues of emotion. *Journal of Personality and Social Psychology*, 32, 1068–76.

7

Communication Awareness in Married Couples

It seems clear from the evidence already reviewed that communication accuracy is important to marital adjustment, with more misunderstandings occurring between unhappy couples than happy couples. Some writers, however, have raised a further issue—the extent to which, in an ongoing interaction, spouses are conscious of the possibility of misunderstanding or being misunderstood.

Watzlawick, Beavin and Jackson (1967) have emphasized that communication is not just a matter of a person being an accurate or inaccurate encoder, but being aware when the message fails to communicate, or is misinterpreted. As we have noted earlier (Chapter 2), these authors describe the communication process in terms of levels, with communication failing at one level when the communicator doesn't get across the message intended, and at a second level when he/she doesn't realize the message has not been understood, or has been misunderstood.

Of course, the decoder may have similar problems. The person receiving the message may not realize that he/she has not understood the message or has misunderstood it. In marriage, one would expect that problems would be created by:

1. Thinking that one's message has been communicated clearly when it has not, with the spouse being left confused.

2. Thinking a particular message has been communicated clearly, when a different message has been communicated.

3. Thinking one has understood the spouse's message, when one has misunderstood the message and received a different message from the one intended.

While all of these situations have the potential to lead to quarrelling and arguments, the seriousness of the effect will depend on how willing the interactants are to accept the responsibility for misunderstandings: the encoder to accept the possibility that the message was not sent clearly, the decoder to accept the possibility that he/she has not accurately interpreted the message.

Where spouses hold adamantly to their interpretations despite the protests of the encoding partner that the message has been misunderstood, or where encoders fail to recognize that the message may not have been clear to the spouse, or may have conveyed something other than what was intended, one would expect greater problems. Workers in the area of marital communication have emphasized the need for couples to clarify meanings (Mace & Mace, 1974; Miller, Nunnally & Wackman, 1975) and to ensure that the message intended by the encoder and the one received by the decoder are, in fact, the same message.

There seem to be three main sets of questions which need to be answered if we are to gain understanding of the importance of awareness of communication to the marital relationship.

1. How aware are people of their own encoding? Do they know whether the message they have sent has adequately expressed their intention?

2. How aware are people of their own decoding? Do they sometimes feel confident about their decoding, and sometimes feel unsure—and do they respond differently in the two situations?

3. How accurately can encoders predict whether their marriage partners will correctly decode messages sent to them?

Venardos (1982) carried out research under the supervision of the author which was designed to answer these questions. The same standard content task used in earlier research on accuracy (Gottman and Porterfield, 1981; Kahn, 1970; Noller, 1980a; 1981) was used for this research into communication awareness. Husbands and wives each sent 27 messages to the spouse (nine messages each with three alternatives) and decoded 27 messages from the spouse, just as in the earlier study (Noller, 1980a). Each message was marked as correct or incorrect depending on whether it was accurately decoded by the spouse or not.

However, as well as performing the tasks of encoding and decoding, subjects were also asked to make a number of other ratings (as in Gottman and Porterfield's 1981 study).

1. The encoder was asked to rate how clearly he/she thought the message was sent. This rating was on a 6-point scale from 1: not at all clear, to 6: very clear.

2. The decoder was asked to rate how confident he/she was of the interpretation they had made of the message sent by the encoder. This rating was again on a 6-point scale from 1: not at all confident to 6: very confident.

3. Encoders were asked to predict whether the spouse would accurately decode the message.

Using these sets of ratings it was possible to calculate a set of nine scores for each subject. It should be noted here that only one measure of accuracy was available for each message—whether it was correctly decoded by the spouse or not. This situation is different from that in the earlier study where separate measures of encoding and decoding could be made. Since the items were not videotaped and shown to judges, no actual measure of encoding could be made—items were judged as both well encoded and well decoded if they were correctly decoded by the spouse. Nine scores were calculated for each subject using as a basis the ratings of confidence and clarity, and the predictions as to whether the spouse would decode correctly or not. The nine scores were:

1. Accuracy score—the number of items correctly decoded by the subject when the spouse was the encoder—as noted before, this was the only measure of accuracy available.

2. Decoding confidence scores:

(a) The mean confidence score for items correctly decoded by the subject when the spouse was the encoder.

(b) The mean confidence score for items incorrectly decoded by the subject when the spouse was the encoder.

3. Encoding clarity scores:

(a) The mean clarity rating for items correctly decoded by the spouse when the subject was the encoder.

(b) The mean clarity rating for items incorrectly decoded by the spouse when the subject was the encoder.

4. Prediction scores:

(a) Number of correct predictions yes/total number of predictions yes (that is, predictions that the spouse would correctly decode the subject's message).

(b) Number of correct predictions no/total number of predictions no (that is, predictions that the spouse would incorrectly decode the subject's message).

5. Relationship between clarity and prediction:

(a) Mean clarity rating for items where predicted the spouse would correctly decode the message encoded by the subject.

(b) Mean clarity rating for items where predicted the spouse would incorrectly decode the message encoded by the subject.

As well, the Primary Communication Inventory (Locke, Sabagh & Tomes, 1956) was administered to all subjects and each received a further two scores: a verbal P.C.I. score and a nonverbal P.C.I. score. See Chapter 3 for more detail about this instrument. Thus eleven scores were obtained for each subject.

One would expect that subjects who were aware of their own communication, and of the possibility of misunderstandings, would behave in the following ways:

1. Have higher confidence ratings for items correctly decoded than for items incorrectly decoded.

2. Have higher clarity ratings for items correctly decoded by the spouse than for items incorrectly decoded by the spouse.

3. Have higher clarity ratings for items where they predicted that their

spouse would decode correctly than for items where they predicted that their spouse would decode incorrectly.

4. Have a higher percentage of correct predictions, for both yes and no than other subjects.

On the other hand, subjects who were generally unaware of their communication would be expected to behave in the following ways:

1. Have confidence scores as high when they were decoding incorrectly as when they were decoding correctly.

2. Have clarity ratings as high when the item was decoded incorrectly by the spouse as when it was decoded correctly by the spouse.

3. Have clarity ratings as high when predicting that their spouse would decode the item incorrectly as when predicting that they would decode the item incorrectly—indicating that the responsibility for the communication process is being put on the decoder.

4. Have a lower percentage of correct predictions than other subjects.

Analyses and Results

Analysis was carried out for each sex which enabled the isolation of a group of variables from the 11 included in the analysis which discriminated between those high, moderate and low in marital adjustment.

The analyses indicate that the low marital adjustment wives were significantly different from other wives in the following ways:

1. Low marital adjustment wives were more confident than other wives on items which they decoded incorrectly.

2. Low marital adjustment wives had a lower percentage of correct predictions yes than high marital adjustment wives.

3. Low marital adjustment wives had lower scores on the verbal P.C.I. than high marital adjustment wives.

These findings would seem to indicate that low marital adjustment wives are, in fact, less aware of their own and their spouses' communication than are other wives. Table 7.1 presents group means for each of these variables. Results indicated that it was the combined scores on three variables which discriminated between the groups. Further, the results indicated that it was the males in the moderate marital adjustment group who had the lowest scores on these variables.

The only other variable discriminating between the groups was variable 7 (Accuracy score), $F(2,43) = 2.19$, $p < .05$, with high marital adjustment males having higher scores than low marital adjustment males ($p < .05$). This finding is, of course, a further replication of the studies by Noller (1980a) and Gottman and Porterfield (1981) that low marital adjustment husbands were less accurate decoders of their wives' messages than other husbands.

TABLE 7.1. *Group Means for Discriminating Variables for Females*

No.	Variable	Group 1*	Group 2†	Group 3‡
		Group means		
1	Confidence when decoded incorrectly	4.38	3.88	3.62
8	Verbal P.C.I.	68.54	72.81	77.33
10	Correct predictions "Yes"/total predictions "No" (%)	62.46	71.43	79.08

* Group 1: Low marital adjustment group.
† Group 2: Moderate marital adjustment group.
‡ Group 3: High marital adjustment group.

To summarize then, high marital adjustment husbands were different from other husbands in three ways:

1. High marital adjustment husbands were better decoders of their wives' messages than low marital adjustment husbands.

2. High marital adjustment husbands were better than moderate marital adjustment husbands at predicting their wives' responses—that is, whether the wives would decode their messages accurately or not.

3. High marital adjustment husbands were more confident than the moderate marital adjustment husbands when they were correctly interpreting their spouses' messages.

Analyses related to message-type

Further analyses were carried out to check whether awareness of communication varied with message-type, and correct or incorrect decoding of the message by the spouse. Confidence results for females showed that females were more confident when decoding correctly than incorrectly $F(1,43) = 14.52$, $p < .001$. For incorrect messages, females were more confident on negative messages and less confident on positive and neutral messages, $F(2,86) = 3.3$, $p < .05$, implying that females were less aware for negative messages than other messages. There were no other effects for message type for the females.

For males confidence ratings were higher for messages decoded correctly than for messages decoded incorrectly, $F(1,43) = 47.17$, $p < .001$, and the difference between confidence ratings when correct, and confidence ratings when incorrect were greater for negative messages, $F(2,86) = 3.9$, $p < .02$, indicating that males were more aware for negative messages than other messages. Results for males and females for the analyses of confidence ratings are summarized in Table 7.2, while mean confidence ratings for each group on each message-type are presented in Table 7.3.

TABLE 7.2. *Summary of Results Related to Confidence Ratings by Decoders*

Males	Females
Husbands more confident when decoding correctly than when decoding incorrectly	Wives more confident when decoding correctly than when decoding incorrectly
Moderate marital adjustment husbands less confident than other husbands when correctly decoding their spouse's messages	Low marital adjustment wives more confident when decoding incorrectly than other wives
For husbands difference between confidence ratings when correct and incorrect greater for negative messages—that is, husbands *more* aware of decoding for negative messages	Wives more confident on incorrect negative message than for other message types— that is, wives *less* aware of decoding for negative messages

TABLE 7.3. *Mean Confidence Ratings for Males and Females at Three Levels of Marital Adjustment*

	Confidence when correct	Confidence when incorrect
High marital adjustment		
Males	4.9	4.2
Females	4.5	3.6
Moderate marital adjustment		
Males	4.4	3.5
Females	4.4	3.9
Low marital adjustment		
Males	4.6	3.9
Females	4.35	4.4

Clarity

With regard to clarity, females had higher clarity ratings for those messages which their spouses decoded correctly, $F(1,43) = 34.95$, $p < .001$, and as well there were greater differences between clarity ratings of correct and incorrect negative messages, than for other message types.

Results for males for clarity revealed that they could discriminate their clearly sent and poorly sent messages since they rated their clarity higher for messages correctly decoded by the spouse, $F(1,43) = 35.9, p < .0001$, and high marital adjustment males were particularly able to make this discrimination, $F(2,43) = 4.9, p < .01$. Results for males and females on clarity are summarized in Table 7.4 while mean clarity ratings are presented in Table 7.5.

TABLE 7.4. *Summary of Results Related to Clarity Ratings by Encoders*

Males	Females
Higher clarity ratings for messages correctly decoded by the spouse than for messages incorrectly decoded by the spouse	Higher clarity ratings for messages correctly decoded by the spouse than for messages incorrectly decoded by the spouse
High marital adjustment males discriminated more between their clearly sent and poorly sent messages than did other males	No differences related to marital adjustment
No differences related to message type	Greater differences between clarity ratings when correct and clarity ratings when incorrect for negative messages than other message types

TABLE 7.5. *Mean Clarity Ratings for Males and Females at Three Levels of Marital Adjustment*

	Clarity when decoded correctly	Clarity when decoded incorrectly
High marital adjustment		
Males	4.6	3.8
Females	4.5	3.9
Moderate marital adjustment		
Males	4.3	4.05
Females	4.3	3.7
Low marital adjustment		
Males	4.4	3.8
Females	4.4	3.9

Predictions

Results for females indicated that wives were better at predicting whether their spouses would correctly decode their negative messages than they were at predicting their spouses' responses on positive or neutral messages. Such a finding suggests that wives are more aware for negative messages—either of their own encoding, their spouse's decoding, or both. Results for the clarity ratings support the proposition that the wives are more aware of their own encoding for negative messages. On the other hand, correct prediction would still seem to involve some awareness of the decoding abilities of the spouse.

For males, the results indicated that moderate marital adjustment husbands were worse than other husbands at predicting their spouse's decoding,

TABLE 7.6. *Summary of Results Related to Prediction of Spouse's Decoding*

Males	Females
Moderate marital adjustment husbands less able to predict when spouses would decode correctly than other husbands. Highs and lows equally able to predict correctly	Low marital adjustment wives less able to predict when their spouses would decode correctly than other wives
Husbands more able to predict when spouses would correctly decode for negative messages than for other message types	Wives better able to predict when spouses would correctly decode for negative messages than for other messages

TABLE 7.7. *Mean Percentage of Correct Predictions for Males and Females at Three Levels of Marital Adjustment*

Marital adjustment level	Type of Messages		
	Positive	Neutral	Negative
High			
Males	69.16	63.78	80.89
Females	79.0	80.17	84.17
Moderate			
Males	54.81	56.82	67.12
Females	66.29	70.2	79.1
Low			
Males	71.57	63.97	76.93
Females	57.54	49.2	77.38

$F(2,44) = 3.6$, $p < .05$, while there was little difference between the high marital adjustment husbands and the low marital adjustment husbands. As well, husbands were better at predicting their spouse's responses for negative messages, $F(2,88) = 7.4$, $p < .001$. Thus, like the wives, the husbands would seem to be more aware for negative messages than for other messages. However, the results for the clarity analyses showed that the husbands (unlike the wives) were not more aware of their encoding for negative messages than other messages. Such a finding would imply that they must be more aware of their spouse's decoding for negative messages than other messages, and that their greater accuracy of prediction is related to this. Since females were, in fact, less aware of their own decoding for negative messages, it is possible that the husbands are more aware than the wives themselves of how these wives decode negative messages. A summary of results for prediction analyses for both males and females are presented in

Table 7.6, while mean percentages of correct predictions are presented in Table 7.7.

General implications

Results show that generally people were aware of their encoding and decoding, and ratings for both confidence and clarity were higher for accurately encoded or decoded items. Also, people seemed to be more aware of their negative messages, and seemed better able to discriminate between correct and incorrect for negative messages than for other messages. Low marital adjustment females were more confident on incorrectly decoded messages than other subjects were, indicating that they had problems recognizing when their decoding was incorrect. As well, these low marital adjustment wives had greater trouble predicting whether their husbands would correctly decode their messages. On the other hand, for males it was clarity ratings which discriminated between marital adjustment groups—high marital adjustment husbands were more aware than other husbands of when their messages were clearly encoded.

It would seem then that both males and females are better at predicting their spouses' responses on negative messages than other messages, but the reasons would seem to be different for the two sexes. The females would seem to be better predictors of their spouses' responses on negative messages mainly because of their greater awareness of their own clarity for negative messages. The males, on the other hand, would seem to be relying on knowledge of their spouses' decoding skills, about which they would seem to be more aware than are the wives themselves.

The fact that there were clear differences in ratings for both clarity and confidence between correct and incorrect items shows that generally subjects were aware of their communication ability—and could discriminate items they were sure about from items they were not sure about. Also, they tended to be more sure about items which they sent clearly or interpreted accurately, and less sure about items which were not sent clearly (did not communicate adequately to the spouse) or which they misinterpreted. Both husbands and wives were more confident when decoding correctly than when decoding incorrectly, and rated their clarity as higher on items correctly decoded by the spouse than on items incorrectly decoded by the spouse. However, it should be kept in mind that ratings for incorrect messages were still fairly high (mostly about 3.5), so while the differences in ratings between correct and incorrect messages were highly statistically significant, they may not have had much effect on the actual communication process, and may not have resulted in the spouses clarifying their communication and checking that each understood the other.

Relationship between marital adjustment and communication awareness

It would seem that there is some relationship between marital adjustment level and awareness of communication, with different types of awareness being important for each of the sexes. For females, confidence when decoding incorrectly and ability to predict the spouse's response were important to marital satisfaction. Low marital adjustment wives were more confident than other wives when they were decoding incorrectly and were less able to predict their spouses responses. It would seem, then, that it is these wives who could be more likely to hold onto their interpretations, and be less conscious of the possibility of decoding incorrectly. Several writers have contended that couples low in marital adjustment do not really know or understand each other, although they may frequently wrongly assume that they do (Dymond, 1954; Tiggle *et al.*, 1982). The fact that these wives also had problems predicting the responses of their spouses would suggest that they are also less aware than other wives of their spouses' decoding ability.

For males the relationship between communication awareness and marital satisfaction was both weaker, and more complex. Moderate marital adjustment males were less aware than other males, while low marital adjustment males were less accurate than other males. High marital adjustment subjects, however, did show the highest level of awareness and were clearly the most accurate. It is possible that low marital adjustment husbands are more aware of their lack of communication skill than moderate marital adjustment husbands, even though they are lower on skills. Perhaps, as the relationship deteriorates, low marital adjustment husbands are forced to become more aware of their communication skill, or lack of it, for survival reasons. All the relationships studied were intact relationships, and this fact would lend support to such a possibility.

Message type effects

Differences related to message-type also showed a somewhat different pattern for males and females. Both males and females were better able to predict spouse responses for negative messages than for other types of message, but only for females was this related to a greater awareness of their own clarity at encoding negative messages. It seems that women, in particular, are fairly sensitive to the impact of their negative messages on their husbands. Noller (1980b) in a study of gaze behaviour in married couples to be described in detail in Chapter 10 found that unhappy wives monitored their husbands on negative messages, perhaps realizing the importance of being aware of the impact such messages were having.

In sharp contrast to the awareness of the wives of their clarity at sending negative messages, is the finding for the decoding of negative messages—that wives were less aware when they had misinterpreted a negative message. It could be that this finding is related to the finding of bias in decoding discussed in Chapter 5, with wives tending to make errors in decoding in a positive direction. Such a bias could be related to what Rosenthal and DePaulo (1979) refer to as "accommodation" in the females: "the well-documented result that females are interpersonally more polite and accommodating than men" (p. 69). On the other hand wives may defend against criticism from their husbands and assume that a message is not negative unless there is overwhelming evidence to the contrary.

Unlike the females, males were found to be more aware of their decoding for negative messages, although there was no relationship between this awareness of negative messages and marital satisfaction. Perhaps knowing when negative messages are wrongly interpreted (which means that they are interpreted more positively than intended) is not important to marital satisfaction. In fact, Gottman's (Gottman et al., 1976) "talk-table" study shows that it is discrepancies between intent and impact which are negative which are more likely to be related to marital adjustment.

So while the accuracy studies reported in Chapter 5 showed that it was the husband's skill at sending and receiving messages from the spouse that was important to marital satisfaction, the evidence from the present study is that for wives it is the awareness, particularly of her decoding accuracy and her ability to predict whether her spouse will understand her message that is important to marital adjustment.

References

DYMOND, R. (1954) Interpersonal perception and marital happiness. *Canadian Journal of Psychology*, **8**, 164–71.

GOTTMAN, J., NOTARIUS, C., MARKMAN, H., BANKS, S., YOPPI, B. & RUBIN, M. E. (1976) Behaviour exchange theory and marital decision making. *Journal of Personality and Social Psychology*, **34**, 14–23.

GOTTMAN, J. M. & PORTERFIELD, A. L. (1981) Communicative competence in the nonverbal behaviour of married couples. *Journal of Marriage and the Family*, **4**, 817–24.

KAHN, M. (1970) Nonverbal communication and marital satisfaction. *Family Process*, **9**, 449–56.

LOCKE, H. J., SABAGH, G. & THOMES, M. (1956) Correlates of primary communication and empathy. *Research Studies of the State College of Washington*, **24**, 118.

MACE, D. & MACE, V. (1974) *We Can Have Better Marriages if we Really Want Them*. London: Oliphants.

MILLER, S., NUNNALLY, E. W. & WACKMAN, D. B. (1975) *Alive and Aware*. Minnesota: Interpersonal Communications Program.

NOLLER, P. (1980a) Misunderstandings in marital communication: A study of couples' nonverbal communication. *Journal of Personality and Social Psychology*, **39**, 1135–48.

NOLLER, P. (1980b) Gaze in married couples. *Journal of Nonverbal Behavior*, **5**, 115–29.

NOLLER, P. (1981) Gender and marital adjustment level differences in decoding messages from spouses and strangers. *Journal of Personality and Social Psychology*, **41**, 272–8.

TIGGLE, R. B., PETERS, M. D., KELLEY, H. H. & VINCENT, J. (1982) Correlational and discrepancy indices of understanding and their relation to marital satisfaction. *Journal of Marriage and the Family*, **3**, 209–15.

ROSENTHAL, R. & DePAULO, B. (1979) Sex differences in accommodation. In ROSENTHAL, R. *Skill in Nonverbal Communication: Individual Differences*. Oelgeschlager, Gunn & Hain.

VENARDOS, C. (1982) Communication awareness in married couples. Unpublished Honours Thesis, University of Queensland.

WATZLAWICK, P., BEAVIN, J. H. & JACKSON, D. (1967) *Pragmatics of Human Communication*. New York: Norton.

8

The Use of the Different Channels in the Encoding and Decoding of Nonverbal Communication

Weakland (1976, p. 117) has claimed "that people are always sending and receiving a multiplicity of messages by both verbal and nonverbal channels, and these messages necessarily modify and qualify one another". The multiplicity of messages come from a number of sources: the visual channel, including information from the face, body, hands or feet, posture or gaze: the vocal channel which includes the various paralinguistic cues such as pitch, loudness and intensity; and the verbal channel which consists of the words spoken.

Two sets of questions are of particular interest with regard to channels:

1. How do encoders use the different channels? Do they rely more on one channel than another for sending particular types of messages? Do some encoders combine the verbal and nonverbal channels in particular ways, and is there any relationship between how encoders use the various channels, and marital adjustment? Do male and female encoders use the channels differently?

2. How do decoders use the different channels? Do they rely on one channel more than others, and does this reliance vary depending on the type of message, or on the sex of the encoder or decoder? Are there differences between the marital adjustment groups with regard to their reliance on the different channels?

Encoding

Studying the use of the different channels of communication in encoding is generally difficult. An important problem is the difficulty of getting data about encoding without using decoders. As we have seen in Chapter 5, encoders often do not succeed in sending the message they want to send or have been asked to send. For example, an encoder might consider both the visual and vocal channels as positive, while a decoder may detect some negativity in one of the channels and code it that way. If reliability between coders is checked and is high, then we can be fairly confident that the message has some negativity in it. But the problem is that this type of data does not strictly tell us how the encoder *uses* the channels, but rather how the encoding comes across to *decoders*.

The two most extensive studies of nonverbal communication in married couples, particularly with regard to the use of channels (Gottman *et al.*, 1977; Noller, 1982a) have both used trained coders to code the channels being studied separately, in order to determine the type of message present in the communication from that channel. The problem is that this coding may be affected by the decoding process, and we cannot be sure that there would be agreement between the encoder and the coder as to these ratings, nor can we be sure that the message would come across to the spouse in the same way as it comes across to the coder. Of course, if such discrepancies exist, they are of great interest to marital researchers.

In the study described in Chapter 5 (Noller, 1980) we found that encoding spouses frequently had difficulty getting across their messages to their spouses (the large number of encoding errors), but that there was a strong relationship between the perceptions of spouses and those of outsiders (the small number of decoding errors) since most messages seen as good communications by the judges were also correctly decoded by the spouse. In the studies to be described here, a distinction will be made between encoding and decoding, but it is important to keep in mind that the encoding is always judged by decoders.

As described in Chapter 3, Gottman and his co-workers (1977) carried out a study of the use of the channels by couples high and low in marital satisfaction. Couples were videotaped during discussion of an actual problem and then these videotapes were coded by trained coders using the Couples' Interaction Scoring System (C.I.S.S.). To recapitulate, the most important findings of their study for our purposes were:

1. That distressed and nondistressed couples could be better discriminated by their use of the nonverbal channels than the verbal channels.

2. That the use of negative affect discriminated between the distressed and nondistressed couples, while the use of positive affect did not.

Noller (1982) had couples interact with one another after filling in several questionnaires about their marriage, including the Short Marital Adjustment Test (Locke & Wallace, 1959) and the Areas of Change Questionnaire (Note 1). Couples were asked to discuss their reactions to filling in the questionnaires, telling each other as much or as little as they liked about their actual answers. Couples were generally keen to share their answers, to discuss their reactions, and in some cases, to work out solutions to problems that arose. These interactions were videotaped, the conversations were transcribed and divided into thought units, and four different codings were made:

TABLE 8.1. *Examples of Behaviours coded Positive, Neutral and Negative for each of the Channels*

Type of message	Channel		
	Verbal	Visual	Vocal
Positive	"I'm very happy with your appearance"	Smile, grin	Friendly tone, warm tone
	"I feel very happy with you at the moment"	Expression of surprise	Affectionate tone
Neutral	"Which friends would you like to see more?"	Absence of positive or negative characteristics	
	"I'm going to see your mother tomorrow"		
Negative	"There's not enough happiness in the marriage"	Frowns, scowls, etc.	Angry tone, shout
	"You never talk to me about anything interesting"		Tense voice etc.

1. *Verbal channel:* each thought unit was coded as positive, neutral or negative using only the words coded directly from the script. (Categories used by Raush and his colleagues (Raush *et al.*, 1974) for cognitive or neutral, affiliative or positive, and coercive or negative, were used in coding the verbal channel.)

2. *Visual channel:* each thought unit was coded as positive, neutral or negative using only the information available from the visual channel. To achieve this, a separate copy of the videotape was made, without the sound, and the unit numbers were added to the soundtrack. By using this procedure, it was possible to code the visual channel without reference to the script.

3. *Vocal channel:* each thought unit was coded as positive, neutral, or negative using only the vocal channel or sound track. This soundtrack included the verbal channel plus all paralinguistic information such as voice tone, pitch, loudness, speech rate etc. The affect codes from the Couples' Interaction Scoring System were used for coding both the nonverbal channels.

4. *Total channel:* each thought unit was coded as positive, neutral, or negative using the total information available from the videotape.

Examples of behaviours coded positive, neutral and negative for each of the channels are presented in Table 8.1. Subjects were given a set of 12 scores which were, for each of the channels, the percentage of thought units which were coded positive, neutral or negative. The scores were analysed using analysis of variance, and separately for each type of message, since the percentage of positives, neutrals and negatives in each channel summed to 100 per cent. Analysis of variance results are presented in Table 8.2. Results will be discussed for each message-type separately, with the focus being on the different ways the channels were used for the different types of messages.

TABLE 8.2. *Summary of Results for Analyses of Variance on Positive, Neutral and Negative Units*

Effect	Finding
Positive units	
Marital adjustment	Highs and moderates more positives than lows
Channel	Fewer in verbal channel than any other
Neutral units	
Marital adjustment	Fewer for lows
Sex	Males more than females
Channel	More in verbal channel than in any other
Marital adjustment × sex	Low marital adjustment males particularly used fewer neutral messages
Marital adjustment × channel	Lows fewer in total channel than other groups
Negative units	
Marital adjustment	Lows more than others
Sex	Females more than males
Channel	Fewer in verbal and visual than other channels
Marital adjustment × channel	Highs and moderates fewer negatives but lows fewer on visual channel than any other
Marital adjustment × sex	Low marital adjustment females particularly more than males

Positive messages

Positive messages were used more by subjects high or moderate in marital adjustment, and less by those low in marital adjustment (see Figure 8.1A). Interestingly, this finding is different from that of Gottman and his colleagues (1977) who found that distressed and nondistressed couples could be discriminated on their negative and neutral messages, but *not* on their positive messages. (See Table 3.6 for F-test results and means.) Birchler *et al.* (1975) found that subjects in distressed and nondistressed marriages could be discriminated on both negative and positive codes. These researchers used summary codes which took into account both verbal and nonverbal channels, while Gottman's analysis used nonverbal codings summed across content codes, and these differences may have been responsible for the results. Noller's (1982a) analysis included both the verbal and nonverbal categories, and resulted in an overall main effect for marital adjustment level. High and moderate marital adjustment subjects were different from other subjects on both verbal and nonverbal categories.

It is also possible that the way marital adjustment level was measured is relevant to the differing results, since Noller used the same method as that used by Birchler *et al.* (1975), while Gottman used a different measuring instrument. As well, in Gottman's study nondistressed couples self-selected on the basis that they felt their marriages were mutually satisfying, and results were based on data from only five couples in each group.

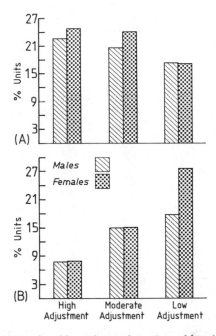

FIG 8.1. (A) Percentage of positive units sent by males and females at different levels of marital adjustment. (B) Percentage of negative units sent by males and females at different levels of marital adjustment. (Averaged across channels in each case.)

Gottman carried out another series of analyses where he used as the dependent variable the proportion of the eight content codes (using the C.I.S.S. codes as described in Chapter 3) for each of the three message-types (or affect codes). Multivariate analyses of variance were used to analyse separately for each type of message. There were no differences between husbands and wives for any of the message-types, but there were significant effects for the distress factor, for neutral and negative messages but again, not for positive messages.

A second finding of Noller's study was that there were fewer units coded positive in the verbal channel than in the other channels. This means that messages are frequently positive in the nonverbal channels, but are neutral in the verbal channels, relying on positive facial expressions or positive voice tone to make the message a positive one. As can be seen from Figure 8.2, the percentage of items coded positive in the total channel is considerably greater than the percentage of items coded positive in the verbal channel.

Such a finding implies that positive messages sent with neutral words tend to be successfully communicated at all levels of marital adjustment. However, if the findings of the earlier study using standard content messages (see Chapter 5) are taken into account, it becomes clear that positive messages

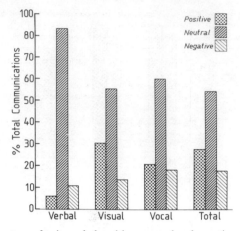

FIG 8.2. Percentage of units coded positive, neutral and negative over each of the communication channels (averaged across marital adjustment level).

with neutral words are not always clearly sent, and are encoded more accurately by females than by males, and by males high in marital adjustment more accurately than by those low in marital adjustment. Since the analysis of single channel scores indicates that these low marital adjustment husbands also send most of their positive messages with neutral words, one would expect that they may have problems getting these messages across to their wives. Preliminary analysis of a study examining the nonverbal behaviours of these couples showed that females tend to use more nonverbal behaviours than males, and that high marital adjustment husbands smile more on positive messages than other husbands (Gallois & Noller, Note 2).

Furnham, Trevethan and Gaskell (1981) carried out a study to see which channel of communication contributed most to the formation of impressions about the communicator in positive and negative messages. For positive messages, words were the least important, and tone of voice was the most important. Such a finding confirms that of Noller that positive messages particularly rely on the nonverbal channels.

Neutral messages

Perhaps the most interesting finding for neutral messages was that there were many more units coded neutral in the verbal channel than in any other. Figure 8.2 indicates that many messages were neutral in the verbal channel but were modified by either or both of the nonverbal channels to become other than a neutral message. This finding confirms the assumption of the standard content methodology, that couples do, in fact, communicate using neutral words and nonverbals that are other than neutral. Comments made by subjects during the experimental session seemed to indicate that couples thought that they generally used words to convey their messages more than they actually did in the interaction segment. In fact, the data show that the message was frequently carried by the nonverbal channels. The results also showed that low marital adjustment subjects used fewer neutral messages than other subjects, and that this difference particularly applied to the total channel: that is, low marital adjustment subjects had fewer of their messages coded neutral in the total channel. Thus while low marital adjustment subjects had about the same percentage of units as other subjects coded neutral on most channels, this was not true for the total channel—on this channel they had fewer units coded neutral than did other subjects. Since these low marital adjustment subjects had fewer positive messages over all channels than other subjects, it seems likely that they have fewer neutral messages because they have more negative messages.

A further result for neutral messages was that males sent significantly more neutral messages than females. Of course, the fact that males had a larger percentage of their units coded neutral than the females implies that the females had more of their units coded positive or negative. Females in the high and moderate marital adjustment groups had more of their units coded positive than did the males, while for the low marital adjustment group more units were coded negative for females than for males.

This finding of more neutral messages sent by the males would seem to be related to the general findings of lack of expressivity in males (Balswick & Avertt, 1977; Balswick & Peek, 1971). Notarius and Johnson (1982) also found that husbands were more neutral than wives (probabilities of observed neutral behaviours as coded using C.I.S.S. = .31 for wives and .50 for husbands). These researchers also found, however, that wives were more negative than husbands (probability = .34 for wives and .12 for husbands). This finding is quite different from that of Noller's (1982a) study, where it was only the wives in the low marital adjustment group who were more negative than their husbands. A comparison of the subjects in the two studies is presented in Table 8.3 and shows that the couples used by Notarius and Johnson (1982) are very similar in marital adjustment level to Noller's low marital adjustment group, and this could explain the similar results, with the wives having more negative units and fewer neutral units than their husbands. Notarius and Johnson's study is also based on data from a very small sample of couples.

As mentioned earlier, Noller (1982b) had the subjects in her study fill in the Areas of Change Questionnaire (Note 1) and these data were analysed using discriminant analysis to see whether there was a group of items which discriminated between the marital adjustment groups. The single most important item in discriminating between the couples was item 31, with wives in the low marital adjustment group wanting their husbands to express

TABLE 8.3. *Comparison of Samples for Noller (1982) and Notarius and Johnson (1982)*

	Study	
Sample details	Noller, 1982	Notarius & Johnson, 1982
N	15 couples in each group—high, moderate, low marital adjustment	6 couples
Locke-Wallace score	High marital adjustment group—both husband and wife above 120 (possible = 158)	106.3
Years married	Highs—$\overline{X}$ = 7.63 Lows—X = 12.44	$\overline{X}$ = 7.2
Age	Husbands $\overline{X}$ = 35 Wives X = 31	Husbands $\overline{X}$ = 34.3 Wives $\overline{X}$ = 31.7

their emotions clearly more often. It would seem from this finding that wives (or at least those in the low marital adjustment group) see the neutral communications of their husbands as not always desirable.

It would seem important for spouses of both sexes to be able to use all types of messages, including neutral ones when appropriate. While it seems that women are less likely to send neutral messages, we cannot be sure from the present data whether women have problems sending neutral messages, or see neutral messages as less often appropriate than do males. The results for the accuracy study (Chapter 5) showed that males and females were no different from one another in terms of the percentages of neutral "good communications" or on neutral encoding errors. In fact, females had a slightly smaller percentage of neutral encoding errors than did males. Hence females would seem to be as skilled as males at sending neutral messages, so the most likely explanation for the fewer neutral units in the interaction study is that females see neutral communications as less often appropriate, either because they feel neutral less often, or because they are more ready to express their positivity and negativity.

Negative messages

Again, as would be expected, low marital adjustment subjects had more of their units coded negative than did other subjects (see Figure 8.1B), and these subjects had proportionately fewer units coded negative in the visual channel than in other channels. This finding reflects a tendency for low marital adjustment subjects to send negative messages with smiles, a tendency which will be discussed in much greater detail in the next chapter on channel inconsistency (see Figure 8.3).

Other studies have also found that married couples high and low in marital adjustment can be discriminated on the proportion of their interaction which

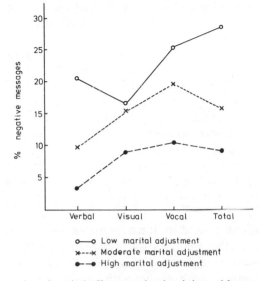

FIG 8.3. Interaction of marital adjustment level and channel for negative messages.
(Noller, 1982, p. 737)

is negative (Birchler *et al.*, 1975; Gottman *et al.*, 1977) but since the nonverbal channels were not analysed separately in either of these studies, we do not know whether results would have been similar for the visual channel. Gottman *et al.* (1977) summed positive, neutral and negative affect over all eight (C.I.S.S.) content codes and calculated the proportion of messages which fell into each category of affect. Birchler *et al.* (1975), on the other hand, combined verbal and nonverbal channels into a single rating of positive, neutral and negative.

A further interesting finding for negative messages was that over all levels of marital adjustment there were fewer negatives in the visual *and* verbal channels than in any other (see Figure 8.2). Thus the tendency for fewer negatives in the visual channel occurred over all marital adjustment levels, although it was stronger in the low marital adjustment group, particularly when related to the amount of negativity in the other channels. Again, this point will be taken up in the chapter on channel inconsistency.

The finding with regard to the verbal channel once again reflects the tendency to send messages which are neutral in the verbal channel and rely on the nonverbal channels to convey the full intention of the message. Sending negative messages in this way can allow the encoder to deny responsibility for the negative part of the message, particularly if the partner reacts very negatively. The encoder can then respond with "But all I said was. . . ." using neutral nonverbal, and thus deny the negative portion of the message.

The finding that there were fewer units coded negative in the visual and verbal channels than in other channels points to the vocal channel as being the key channel in negative messages, with the negativity being carried by the tone of voice, pitch, loudness etc. Furnham, Trevethan and Gaskell (1981), as mentioned earlier, carried out a study of the relative contribution of the communication channels to the impression conveyed by a communicator for both positive and negative messages. While their findings were the same as those of the present study for positive messages, they were quite different for negative messages, with the verbal channel contributing more to the overall impression than the nonverbal channels. There are at least two possible reasons why the results could be different:

1. Furnham *et al.* (1981) used only one encoder, and the result could be a function of his particular style of encoding.

2. The marital situation may be different from other situations.

We have already discussed the finding that spouses tended to rely on nonverbal channels rather than words to convey their positive and negative messages. As well, we have noted that negative messages tended to be accompanied by smiles. Both of these findings could be peculiar to the marital situation, and the sending of negative messages in the marital situation will be further discussed in Chapter 9.

Thus the overall finding for encoding is that positive and negative messages were frequently sent with neutral verbals, and relied on one or both of the nonverbal channels to convey the intention of the message. Such a finding confirms much of the earlier research on the importance of nonverbal behaviour to the communication process (Argyle *et al.*, 1970; 1972; Mehrabian, 1971; 1972). As well there were some findings with regard to marital adjustment level and sex.

Direct messages

Another type of message on which data were available, was the direct message—or the message on which all channels were coded the same, either positive or negative. An analysis was carried out comparing the percentage of direct negative messages, and the percentage of direct positive messages used by males and females at different levels of marital adjustment. Messages with all four channels coded neutral were not included in the analysis since the aim was to measure expressivity, which is more evident in the positive and negative messages. Mean scores for direct messages are presented in Table 8.4, and the results for the analysis of variance are presented in Table 8.5.

As can be seen from these tables, low marital adjustment subjects used more direct messages than high marital adjustment subjects (Newman Keuls, p < .01) and females used more direct messages than males. Follow-

TABLE 8.4. *Mean Percentages of Direct Messages sent by Males and Females of Different Levels of Marital Adjustment*

	Positive	Negative
High marital adjustment		
Males	1.5	0.0
Females	1.7	0.1
Moderate marital adjustment		
Males	1.2	1.3
Females	2.2	1.3
Low marital adjustment		
Males	0.9	1.2
Females	0.9	4.7

up tests were carried out, to explore the interaction of marital adjustment level and type of message, with each marital adjustment level being analysed separately. Results are summarized in Table 8.6. More direct positive messages than negative messages were sent by the high marital adjustment subjects, and more direct negative than positive messages were sent by the low marital adjustment subjects. Wives sent more direct messages than husbands, and wives in the low marital adjustment group particularly sent more direct negative messages than other subjects. Thus the results for direct messages followed a similar pattern to the results for the general use of the channels.

Messages with neutral verbal and nonneutral nonverbal channels

An analysis was carried out to compare messages with neutral words, and either positive or negative nonverbals for both males and females of

TABLE 8.5. *Summary of Significant Effects from Analysis of Variance on Direct Messages (with consistent channels), and Messages with Neutral Verbal and Consistent Non-neutral Nonverbal Channels*

Effect	Finding
Direct messages	
Main effect for marital adjustment level	More direct messages for lows than highs
Main effect for sex	More direct messages for females than males
Interaction of marital adjustment level and type of message	More direct positives for high marital adjustment group and more direct negatives for lows
Messages with neutral verbal and consistent non-neutral nonverbal channels	
Main effect for message type	Many more positives than negatives
Interaction of marital adjustment and type of message	From high to low positives decrease and negatives increase

TABLE 8.6. *Results of Follow-up Tests for each Marital Adjustment Level Separately on Direct Messages*

Marital adjustment level	Result
High	More direct positive messages than negative messages ($F(1,26) = 19.71, p < .001, d = 1.74$)
Moderate	No effect for type of message
Low	More direct negative messages than positive messages ($F(1,26) = 8.63, p < .01, d = 1.15$)

different levels of marital adjustment. Mean scores are presented in Table 8.7, while the results of the analysis of variance are included in Table 8.5. There were more messages with neutral verbal and positive nonverbal than there were messages with neutral verbal and negative nonverbal, implying that positive messages are more likely than negative messages to be sent in this indirect way. Such a finding confirms the earlier interpretation of the small percentage of units positive in the verbal channel. It is also important to be aware in this context of the problems which males, and particularly those low in marital adjustment had at communicating the positive versions of standard content messages. If these subjects are relying on neutral words accompanied by positive nonverbal for conveying positive messages, then they are likely to have problems getting such messages across to their spouse, and particularly is this true for husbands low in marital adjustment.

The interaction of marital adjustment level and message-type was investigated by analysing each message-type separately and each marital adjustment level. Results are presented in Tables 8.8 and 8.9. High marital adjustment subjects used more positives than low marital adjustment, and more positives than negatives. Moderate marital adjustment subjects also used more positives than negatives. Low marital adjustment subjects used more negatives than high marital adjustment subjects, but they used about the same number of positives as negatives.

Thus, while the low marital adjustment subjects used more direct negative messages than positive messages, for messages with neutral verbal there were no differences between the percentage of positive messages and the percentage of negative message used. In other respects, the results for these messages were similar to those for single channels, and for direct messages.

Decoding

With regard to decoding, the clearest data come from the accuracy study where spouses were asked to decode standard content messages from the video using only the vocal channel or only the visual channel. From this study, data can be obtained as to which channel leads to the most accuracy and which is most closely related to the coding using the total channel.

TABLE 8.7. *Mean Percentages of Messages with Neutral Verbal for Males and Females with Different Levels of Marital Adjustment*

	Positive	Negative
High marital adjustment		
Males	4.9	0.4
Females	7.5	0.4
Moderate marital adjustment		
Males	5.2	0.9
Females	5.1	2.1
Low marital adjustment		
Males	2.7	3.1
Females	3.1	2.9

TABLE 8.8. *Results of Follow-up Tests for Positive and Negative Messages with Neutral Verbal*

Message-type	Result
Positives	Highs use more than lows $F(2,78) = 6.44$, $p < .01$, $\eta = .38$, Newman Keuls $p < .01$
Negatives	Lows use more than highs $F(2,78) = 6.03$, $p < .01$, $\eta = .37$, Newman Keuls $p < .01$

TABLE 8.9. *Results of Follow-up Tests for Each Marital Adjustment Level on Messages with Neutral Verbal*

High marital adjustment	Use many more positives than negatives $F(1,26) = 40.37$, $p < .001$, $d = 2.49$
Moderate marital adjustment	Use more positives than negatives $F(1,26) = 11.18$, $p < .01$, $d = 1.31$
Low marital adjustment	Use a similar number of positives and negatives

Only a limited amount of data were available for these analyses, since each spouse decoded ten items from the partner using only the vocal channel, and ten using only the visual channel. Since the number of items was small, no attempt was made to analyse separately for message-type. Analysis of variance results can be seen in Chapter 5 and means can be found in Table 5.11 in that chapter. Results of the correlational analyses comparing scores on the single channel task with scores on the original decoding task for the same items are described in Chapter 5 and can be seen in Table 5.12.

Three kinds of data are important to the understanding of these results:

1. Relative accuracy in the total channel (original task) for the three marital adjustment groups.

2. Accuracy using the single channels for each group.

3. A measure of which channel is relied on most by the particular group (that is, which channel has the highest correlation with the total channel).

The findings for each set of messages (that is, husband to wife messages, and wife to husband messages) are presented separately.

Husband to wife messages

1. High marital adjustment subjects were more accurate than low marital adjustment subjects at decoding on the original task.

2. Accuracy was similar for each of the single channel tasks, whether the wives were using the visual channel or the vocal channel.

3. The visual channel was relied on most by wives in the high and moderate marital adjustment groups.

These findings suggest that relying on the visual channel, as the wives in the happier marriages do, leads to greater accuracy, even though, overall, accuracy on the single channel task was similar whichever channel was being decoded. A look at Table 5.11 shows a tendency for low marital adjustment wives to be less accurate on the visual channel than other wives. Rosenthal and DePaulo (1979) showed that females relied more on visual cues than did males, particularly when facial cues were available, and this was especially true for women who had good relationships with the opposite sex. Such findings seem particularly applicable to the data being presented in this section, since the wives high in marital adjustment were particularly likely to rely more on the information from the visual channel and to be more accurate at decoding. Hall (1979) found that females were particularly better than males at decoding visual cues. Hence these low marital adjustment wives seem to be particularly different from other wives (and women in general) in their decoding of the visual channel.

Wife to husband messages

1. No differences between the marital adjustment groups with regard to decoding on the original task.

2. Greater accuracy on the vocal channel than the visual channel.

3. Vocal channel relied on most by husbands in the high and moderate marital adjustment groups, while the visual channel was relied on most by those in the low marital adjustment group.

Such findings imply that relying on the vocal channel leads to greater accuracy for husbands decoding wives. This greater accuracy could be because husbands are better at decoding auditory than visual information, or because wives are more expressive in the vocal channel than in the visual channel. Buck et al. (1972; 1974) found that females were generally more facially expressive than males, and Hall (1979) also showed that females were more accurate senders of nonverbal cues, especially visual cues. These findings make it more likely that the males who rely on the vocal cues are more accurate decoders, because males are better at decoding vocal cues than they are at decoding visual cues, although there is no definitive data on this issue.

Summary

The results for the analyses of the use of the different communication channels indicate:

1. The tendency for people, at least in the marital situation to send many messages with neutral words, and to rely on the nonverbal channels to make the message positive or negative.

2. The greater likelihood of positive messages than negative messages being sent with neutral words.

3. The greater expressivity of females compared with males—as measured by their tendency to use positive or negative messages rather than neutral messages.

4. The greater positivity in the interactions of high marital adjustment subjects, and the greater negativity of low marital adjustment subjects—with direct negative messages particularly sent by low marital adjustment wives.

5. The tendency for low marital adjustment subjects to be different from other subjects when decoding, especially in their reliance on the least helpful channel.

Reference Notes

1. Weiss, R. L. & Perry, B. A. *Assessment and Treatment of Marital Dysfunction*, Oregon Marital Studies Program, University of Oregon, Eugene, Oregon.
2. Gallois, C. & Noller, P. (1983) A micro-analysis of nonverbal communication in married couples. University of Queensland, 1983.

References

ARGYLE, M., ALKEMA, F. & GILMOUR, R. (1972) The communication of friendly and hostile attitudes by verbal and nonverbal signals. *European Journal of Social Psychology*, 1, 385–402.

ARGYLE, M., SALTER, V., NICHOLSON, H., WILLIAMS, M. & BURGESS, P. (1970) The communication of inferior and superior attitudes by verbal and nonverbal signals. *British Journal of Social and Clinical Psychology*, 9, 222–32.

BALSWICK, J. & AVERTT, C. P. (1977) Differences in expressiveness: Gender, interpersonal orientation and perceived parental expressiveness as contributing factors. *Journal of Marriage and the Family*, 26, 1, 121–7.

BALSWICK, J. & PEEK, C. (1971) The inexpressive male: A tragedy of American society. *The Family Coordinator*, 20, 4, 363–8.

BIRCHLER, G. R., WEISS, R. L. & VINCENT, J. P. (1975) Multimethod analysis of social reinforcement exchange between maritally distressed and non-distressed spouse and stranger dyads. *Journal of Personality and Social Psychology*, 31, 349–62.

BUCK, R., MILLER, R. E. & CAUL, W. F. (1974) Sex, personality and physiological variables in the communication of affect via facial expression. *Journal of Personality and Social Psychology*, **30**, 587–9.

BUCK, R., SAVIN, J. V., MILLER, R. E. & CAUL, W. F. (1972) Communication of affect through facial expression in humans. *Journal of Personality and Social Psychology*, **23**, 362–71.

FURNHAM, A., TREVETHAN, R. & GASKELL, G. (1981) The relative contribution of verbal, vocal, and visual channels to person perception: Experiment and critique. *Semiotica*, 1/2, **37**, 39–57.

GOTTMAN, J., MARKMAN, H. & NOTARIUS, C. (1977) The topography of marital conflict: a sequential analysis of verbal and nonverbal behaviour. *Journal of Marriage and the Family*, **39**, 461–77.

HALL, J. (1979) Gender, gender roles and nonverbal communication skills. In ROSENTHAL, R., *Skill in Nonverbal Communication: Individual Differences*. Cambridge, Mass: Oelgeschloger, Gunn & Hain.

LOCKE, H. J. & WALLACE, K. M. (1959) Short marital adjustment and prediction tests: their reliability and validity. *Marriage and Family Living*, **21**, 251–5.

MEHRABIAN, A. (1971) *Silent Messages*. Belmont, California: Wadsworth Publishing Company.

MEHRABIAN, A. (1972) *Nonverbal Communication*, Aldine.

NOLLER, P. (1980) Misunderstandings in marital adjustment communication: A study of couples' nonverbal communication. *Journal of Personality and Social Psychology*, **39**, 1135–48.

NOLLER, P. (1981) Gender and marital adjustment level differences in decoding messages from spouses and strangers. *Journal of Personality and Social Psychology*, **41**, 272–8.

NOLLER, P. (1982a) Channel consistency and inconsistency in the communications of married couples. *Journal of Personality and Social Psychology*, **43**, 4, 732–41.

NOLLER, P. (1982b) Couple communication and marital satisfaction. *Australian Journal of Sex Marriage & Family*, **3:2**, 69–75.

NOTARIUS, C. I. & JOHNSON, J. S. (1982) Emotional expression in husbands and wives. *Journal of Marriage and the Family*, **44**, 483–9.

RAUSH, H. L., BARRY, W. A., HERTEL, R. K. & SWAIN, M. E. (1974) *Communication, Conflict and Marriage*. San Francisco: Jossey-Bass.

ROSENTHAL, R. & DEPAULO, B. (1979) Sex differences in eavesdropping on nonverbal cues. *Journal of Personality and Social Psychology*, **37**, 273–85.

WEAKLAND, J. (1976) Communication theory and clinical change. In GUERIN, P. J. (Ed.) *Family Therapy Theory and Practice*. New York: Gardner Press.

9

Channel Inconsistency in the Communications of Married Couples

Interest in discrepancies between communication channels—or channel inconsistency—has developed in recent years from three separate areas:

1. Clinical Psychology/Psychiatry with the work on the double-bind theory of schizophrenia (Bateson *et al.*, 1956). These researchers claimed that children who became schizophrenic were habitually faced with communication to which they were unable to respond, because at least two incompatible responses were being demanded at one time. They also maintained that a further problem for the child was that he/she did not feel free to comment on the impossibility of the situation. Messages with contradictory channels were seen as contributing to the confusion.

2. Counselling, with its emphasis on congruence in the counsellor (Rogers, 1957; Truax & Carkhuff, 1967), and confrontation of lack of congruence in the client (Alger & Hogan, 1967). Rogers has particularly emphasized the importance of the counsellor being genuine and open in his communication with the client, with consistency on all channels being seen as indicative of such genuineness. As well, incongruence or lack of consistency in client communications has been seen as indicating conflict and ambivalence on the client's part. "Good" counsellors are expected to help clients understand the reasons for such incongruence in their communications.

3. Social Psychology, with a large range of experiments where the messages sent by different communication channels have been manipulated to produce a certain effect—an example would be superiority being expressed in one channel, and inferiority being expressed in another channel (Argyle *et al.*, 1970). Studies in deception and leakage (DePaulo & Rosenthal, 1979; Mehrabian, 1971a) have involved subjects engaging in such activities as talking about someone they dislike as though they like them. As well, more naturalistic studies have compared the effects of messages with inconsistent channels, when the age and sex of encoder and decoder were varied (Bugental *et al.*, 1972). Bugental and her co-workers also compared the communications of families with disturbed children with those of normal

families, and found that mothers of disturbed children often made threatening or critical comments in a positive voice tone, or accompanied by a laugh (Bugental *et al.*, 1971). In another study (Bugental, 1972), parents of disturbed children were found to be extremely critical of their offspring, often with positive voice tone which didn't seem to detract from the disapproval. Bugental (1974) also found that fathers were much less expressive towards their children than were mothers, but were less likely to produce discrepant messages than were mothers.

Discrepant Communications in Married Couples

Noller (1982) carried out an analysis of the data obtained from the videotapes of couples interacting (see Chapter 8). Codings for each channel were compared in order to look for units where channel inconsistency occurred—that is, where one channel contradicted another, with one being positive and the other negative. Each subject was given a score representing the percentage of units where there was a discrepancy between the visual channel and the vocal channel, and between the visual channel and the verbal channel. A discrepancy was scored when one channel was coded positive and the other channel was coded negative. Scores were also calculated separately for each direction: for example, positive visual and negative verbal (+ −) was calculated separately from negative visual and positive verbal (− +).

Thus there were four types of discrepant communications used in the analyses:

    (a) positive visual, negative vocal

    (b) positive visual, negative verbal

    (c) negative visual, positive vocal

    (d) negative visual, positive verbal.

It is important to note that coding of the vocal channel was not totally separated from coding of the verbal channel since a filter was not used to minimize intelligibility. However by using an analysis which compares the verbal and vocal channels it is possible to see whether words alone, or words combined with tone of voice are more important in discrepant communications. Table 9.1 shows the mean percentages of different types of discrepant communications for each sex and marital adjustment level, with discrepancies being calculated as a percentage of the total number of communication units for each subject. Table 9.2 shows the results for the four-way analysis of variance (marital adjustment level × sex × type of discrepancy × direction). Low marital adjustment subjects sent more discrepant communications than other subjects, and females sent more discrepant communications than males. There were more communications with discrepancies between the visual and vocal channels than there were with discrepancies between the

TABLE 9.1. *Mean Percentages* of Different Types of Discrepant Communication for Each Sex and Marital Adjustment Level*

| | Channel | | | |
| | Visual/Vocal | | Visual/Verbal | |
Marital adjustment level	+ −	− +	+ −	− +
High				
Males	4.5	2.3	1.2	.19
Females	4.23	3.15	1.54	.7
Moderate				
Males	6.14	2.64	2.53	.0
Females	8.0	2.36	3.88	.49
Low				
Males	6.68	2.41	3.84	.31
Females	9.52	1.83	7.31	.00

Note + = positive message coding; − = negative message coding.
* As a percentage of the total number of communications (thought units).
(Noller, 1982, p. 738)

TABLE 9.2. *Results for Analysis of Variance on Discrepancies between the Visual and Verbal and Visual and Vocal Channels*

| | Results | | | |
Effect	df	F	$p <$	Magnitude of effect (d)
Marital adjustment	2,39	5.5	.009	.469*
Sex	1,39	6.8	.02	.833
Type of discrepancy	1,39	60.65	.001	2.49
Direction	1,39	56.9	.001	2.416
Marital adjustment × direction	2,39	7.3	.003	.522*
Sex × direction	1,39	4.6	.05	.687
Marital adjustment × sex × direction	2,39	3.13	.054	.372

* Effect magnitude given is η rather than d.
(Noller, 1982, p. 737)

visual and verbal channels, indicating that it was more often the tone of voice that was incongruent with the visual channel. The words, on the other hand, were likely to be neutral, given the evidence from the earlier studies. There were also more discrepancies with positive in the visual channel and negative in the verbal or vocal channels than there were discrepancies in the other direction. Hence discrepancies were most likely to involve positivity in the visual channel, and negativity in the tone of voice, or words plus tone of voice.

The interaction of marital adjustment level and direction indicated that

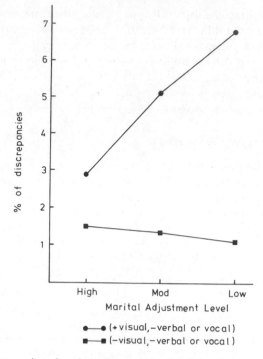

FIG 9.1. Interaction of marital adjustment level and direction of discrepancy
(+ = positive messages; − = negative messages). (Noller, 1982, p. 738)

the differences between the marital adjustment levels were greater for
discrepancies involving positivity in the visual channel, while there were no
differences between the groups for discrepancies involving negativity in the
visual channel, and this type of discrepancy also occurred relatively rarely.
Thus it would seem that the type of discrepancy which is of particular interest
to the marital researcher is the discrepancy which is positive in the visual
channel and negative in the verbal or vocal channels (see Figure 9.1).

The interaction of sex and direction indicated that differences between
males and females with regard to the percentage of discrepant communications among their utterances was also greater for discrepancies with positivity in the visual channel. As well, for both males and females, the percentage
of discrepant communications involving positivity in the visual channel
increased linearly from the high marital adjustment group to the low marital
adjustment group, with female scores generally being higher than male
scores. No such relationships existed for discrepancies with negativity in the
visual channel.

Thus the data indicate that discrepant communications, and particularly
those with positivity in the visual channel represented a larger percentage of

the communications of subjects low in marital adjustment, and particularly females. Hence it would seem likely that the use of such communications has a negative effect on marital adjustment. Such an interpretation seems particularly valid given the findings of Bugental and her colleagues (Bugental, 1972; Bugental *et al.*, 1971) that parents of disturbed children were also more likely to use discrepant communications than other parents. However, this issue will be discussed again in a later section.

Analyses to check for chance effects

Because of the possibility that these results related to discrepancies were affected by chance, Noller (1980; 1982) carried out several analyses to check for such effects—or whether the greater percentage of discrepant communications sent by the low marital adjustment females was due to the greater amount of negative interaction in that group, and the greater amount of smiling in the women generally.

For each subject the probability of making a negative statement was calculated, as also was the probability of using positive visual behaviour. These two probabilities were then multiplied together to give the probability of the co-occurrence of positive visual and negative verbal behaviour. Each subject was then given a score which was the ratio of the observed probability of the target behaviour (a negative statement accompanied by positive visual behaviour) to the expected probability of that behaviour. These scores were then transformed to logarithms and an analysis of variance was carried out using these log transformations as the dependent variable, and sex and marital adjustment level as the independent variables.

There was a main effect for marital adjustment level, $F(2, 78) = 3.9$, $p < .03$, $\eta = .3$, showing that when the amount of positive visual behaviour and negative verbal behaviour was controlled for, there was no sex difference—husbands were as likely as their wives to use a positive facial expression when making a negative statement. The marital adjustment effect, however, remained—even when amount of positive visual behaviour and negative verbal behaviour were controlled for, low marital adjustment subjects were still more likely than other subjects to use discrepant messages.

Comparisons of different types of negative messages

If we assume that there are basically three different ways that a negative message can be sent, then we can compare the frequency with which these different types of negative messages were used by males and females at the different levels of marital adjustment. The three different types of negative messages are:

1. A direct negative message—with verbal, visual and vocal channels all being negative.

TABLE 9.3. *Mean Percentages of Total Communications which were sent (a) as Direct Negative Messages, (b) with Neutral Verbal and Negative Nonverbals and (c) Discrepancies between the Visual Channel and the Verbal or Vocal Channels*

			Discrepancies	
Marital adjustment level	Direct negative	With neutral verbal	Visual/Vocal (+ −)	Visual/Verbal (+ −)
High				
Males	0.0	0.4	4.5	1.2
Females	0.1	0.4	4.23	1.54
Moderate				
Males	1.3	0.9	6.14	2.53
Females	1.3	2.1	8.0	3.88
Low				
Males	1.2	3.1	6.7	3.84
Females	4.7	2.9	9.5	7.31

2. With neutral verbal—both the visual and vocal channels are negative, but the words are neutral.

3. With positive visual, or smiles—the visual channel is positive, and the verbal, or verbal and vocal channels are negative.

Table 9.3 shows the comparison between these three types of message. As can be seen from the data, the preferred mode for sending negative messages (at least among the three modes discussed here) for both males and females at all levels of marital adjustment would seem to be with a smile, at least in the marital situation. Such a result would seem to support the findings by Mehrabian (1971b) that inconsistent messages are preferred more in informal than in formal situations, and that the verbal portion of the message tends to convey attitudes toward the actions of the person being spoken to, while the nonverbal portion of the message tends to convey attitudes toward the person him/herself. The discrepant communication is saying "I don't like your behaviour but I do like you".

If discrepant communications are the preferred way of sending negative messages even by highly satisfied couples, such a finding casts doubt on the notion that discrepant communications are bad for relationships. Gottman (1979) discusses research on channel inconsistency and concludes from the data presented that mothers of disturbed children were not more inconsistent, but more negative. A similar conclusion could be drawn about the data in Table 9.3, with low marital adjustment subjects sending more negative messages over all—and in all three modes. Another factor which needs to be kept in mind in considering these data is that there is evidence that a discrepant communication is not necessarily a negative one, and so the

TABLE 9.4. *Mean Positivity Ratings* for Utterances Accompanied by Positive, Neutral or Negative Facial Expression*

Type of Facial Expression	Positive	Neutral	Negative
Marital Adjustment Level			
High			
Males	2.1	2.0	1.9
Females	2.0	2.0	1.7
Low			
Males	1.9	1.8	1.8
Females	1.8	1.8	1.6

* Utterances were scored according to how positively they were rated in the verbal channel: 3 = positive; 2 = neutral; 3 = negative.

figures for discrepant messages in Table 9.3 will overestimate the percentage of discrepant negative messages since some of them would have been coded as positive in the total channel. This issue will also be taken up again in a later section.

Relationship of positivity of facial expression to words

An analysis was carried out to examine the relationship between positivity ratings of words and positivity ratings of facial expressions in order to see whether there were differences in the types of facial expressions accompanying different types of utterances, and whether such differences were related to sex and marital adjustment level. The analysis used was similar to that carried out by Bugental and her colleagues (Bugental, Love & Gianetto, 1971) when looking at the naturally-occurring utterances of mothers and fathers. For each subject in the high and low marital adjustment groups, mean positivity ratings were computed for each of the groups of utterances:

(a) Those accompanied by positive face.
(b) Those accompanied by neutral face.
(c) Those accompanied by negative face.

Positivity ratings were made on the basis of the coding of the verbal channel. Utterances coded as positive in the verbal channel received a rating of 3, those coded neutral in the verbal channel a rating of 2, and those negative in the verbal channel a rating of 1. Mean positivity ratings for each group of utterances are presented in Table 9.4 for males and females at each level of marital adjustment. An analysis of variance was carried out using these positivity ratings as the dependent variable and marital adjustment level (high or low), sex, and type of facial expression as the independent variables. Statements by subjects in the high marital adjustment group were rated significantly more positively than those by subjects in the low marital

TABLE 9.5. *Summary of Significant Effects from Analysis of Variance on How Items with Visual/Vocal Discrepancies were Coded in the Total Channel (Marital adjustment level × Sex × Direction × Type of Coding (+, 0, −))*

Effect	D.F.	F	P<	Finding
Main effect for type of coding	2,132	5.3	.001 $\eta = .27$	More coded positive
Interaction of type of coding and sex	2,132	3.7	.03 $\eta = .23$	More coded positive for males, not females
Interaction of direction and type of coding	2,132	10.8	.001 $\eta = .38$	+ visual − vocal coded negatively in the total channel while − visual + vocal coded positive in the total channel

adjustment group, suggesting a generally higher level of negativity in that low group over all message types and for both sexes, $F(1,25) = 14.17$, $p < .001$, $d = 1.04$. As well, utterances made with negative face were less positive than those made with positive or neutral face, $F(2,104) = 8.04$, $p < .001$, $\eta = .37$. Although females in the low marital adjustment group were no more positive when they were smiling than were males in the low marital adjustment group when they were frowning, the general indication from this analysis was for no sex differences in the positivity ratings of the channels, and no interactions with marital adjustment level. The main effect for marital adjustment level indicates that the main difference between the groups with regard to communications was related to the greater positivity in the high marital adjustment group, and the greater negativity in the low marital adjustment group.

How discrepant messages decoded

Since Bugental's work (Bugental, Kaswan & Love, 1970) had indicated that messages with positive in the visual channel and negative in other channels did not always come across as negative, a further analysis was carried out to see how units which involved discrepancies between the visual and vocal channels were decoded in the total channel. The dependent variable for this analysis was the percentage of thought units with discrepancies which were coded in each way in the total channel—that is, positive or negative. Results for the analysis are presented in Table 9.5, and indicate that messages with discrepancies between the visual channel and the vocal channel were more likely to be coded positive. Newman Keuls' tests showed that messages with discrepancies between the visual channel and the vocal channel were more often coded positive than neutral ($p < .05$), but the percentage coded negative was not significantly different from the percentage coded neutral.

Follow-up tests for each type of coding separately showed that for messages coded positive, there was a sex difference, with messages from males being more likely to be coded positive, $F(1,66) = 6.3$, $p < .02$, $d = .62$, but there were no effects related to sex for messages coded neutral or negative. So while messages from males were more likely to be coded positive than those from females, messages from males and females were equally likely to be coded neutral or negative.

There was a significant difference with regard to direction, with more messages with positive visual and negative vocal being coded negative than was true for messages with negative visual and positive vocal, $F(1,66) = 29.9$, $p < .001$, $d = 1.35$. For males, more messages with discrepancies between the visual and vocal channels were coded positive, $F(2,66) = 6.3$, $p < .005$, $\eta = .399$, while for females these discrepancies were equally likely to be coded positive as negative.

Thus Bugental's (1970) findings were confirmed and it became clear that communications which involved positivity in the visual channel and negativity in the vocal channel were not a single entity—and although such communications were more likely to be coded negative than positive, it could not be assumed that they were negative messages. Such communications from males were more likely to be coded positive, while those from females were equally likely to be coded negative as positive. For this reason it was decided to analyse negative messages separately, in order to better understand the relationship between discrepant communications and the expression of negativity in the marital relationship. This analysis will be reported in a later section. First, however, it is necessary to examine a section of the nonverbal literature which is particularly related to the decoding of discrepant communications.

The video primacy effect

Whenever the use of the various communication channels is discussed in the literature, the most frequently cited principle is the primacy of the visual channel—that is, that the visual channel has the largest effect on the way a message is coded overall. Osgood (1966) recognized that facial communication was unreliable, but saw the facial channel as relied on heavily by interactants. Bugental, Kaswan and Love (1970) found that the decoders of discrepant or conflicting messages relied heavily on facial information, with visual cues accounting for twice as much variance as either the words or the vocal cues, and other researchers have had similar results (DePaulo & Rosenthal, 1979; Mehrabian & Ferris, 1967).

DePaulo and Rosenthal (1979) claimed that the video primacy effect was moderated by four factors:

1. *The affect being decoded* (e.g. agreeableness, assertiveness, truthfulness, dominance)—visual cues have been found to be important in assessing dominance, agreeableness, and pleasantness, while vocal cues seem to be important in assessing assertiveness, truthfulness, and the intensity of the affect.

2. *The video channel conveying the affect* (body or face)—visual cues from the face tend to be more influential than those from the body.

3. *The sex of the decoder*—females rely more heavily on cues from the face, and are also better than males at decoding them.

4. *The degree of discrepancy between the channels*—as the degree of discrepancy between the visual cues and the audio cues increases, there is evidence that the visual cues become less influential. Degree of discrepancy for these researchers is defined as being discrepant on more than one dimension—that is, both positivity and dominance.

However, there are two other variables which would seem to be relevant to the issue of video primacy:

1. *The sex of the encoder*—males sending discrepant messages are more likely to be coded positive (perhaps seen as teasing) than females, who are as likely to be coded negative as positive.

2. *Whether the messages are being judged on the positivity dimension*—it seems that the channel conveying negative affect predominates, except when visual information is also available. When visual information is available, there is an interaction with sex of encoder, with the positive visual behaviour of males being seen as counteracting an otherwise negative message, while the positive visual behaviour of females is not necessarily seen as having this effect.

To summarize then, video primacy in the interpretation of discrepant communications seems to be moderated by the variables of sex of decoder, the video channel conveying the affect, the degree of discrepancy between the channels, and the affect being judged. When, however, the affect is being judged on the pleasantness or positivity dimension, there is an interaction between sex of encoder and positivity/negativity, with the positive visuals of males being more likely to counteract negativity in the verbal or vocal channels, while the positive visuals of females are much less likely to have this effect. When there is no visual information, negativity in either the verbal or vocal channels seems to override any positivity for either sex. This is, however, a complex issue.

Analysis of negative messages

As was mentioned earlier, because a full understanding of the relationship of discrepant communications to negative messages seemed important to a full understanding of the role of discrepant communications in the marital

TABLE 9.6. *Mean Percentages of* Negative Communications *which were sent as (a) Direct Negative Messages, (b) with Neutral Verbal and Negative Nonverbals, and (c) Accompanied by Smiles*

Marital adjustment level	Type of negative message		
	Direct negative	With neutral verbal	With smiles
High			
Males	1.43	4.52	29.15
Females	1.13	2.9	34.2
Low			
Males	3.01	11.7	22.69
Females	10.22	6.34	27.97

relationship, it was decided to examine the data for negative messages separately. Messages were classed as a negative message if they were coded as negative in the total channel. For these negative messages, three scores were calculated:

1. The percentage of negative messages which were direct—that is, negative in all channels.

2. The percentage of negative messages which had neutral words and negative nonverbal channels.

3. The percentage of negative messages which were positive in the visual channel—that is, accompanied by a smile.

An analysis of variance was carried out with these percentages as the dependent variable, and marital adjustment level (high or low), sex, and type of message (direct, with neutral verbal, and with a smile) as the independent variables. Table 9.6 presents mean percentages of each type of message for each group—as a percentage of their negative messages. It should be noted here that this typology clearly does not account for all the negative messages sent—many would seem to be sent with negativity in only one channel. An analysis of the use of the communication channels in negative messages will be discussed in a later section and will help to make the situation clearer.

Results showed no effects for marital adjustment level, and no effects for sex, indicating that for each of the groups a similar proportion of their negative messages were sent in each mode, irrespective of whether they were males or females in the high or low marital adjustment groups. There was, however, a main effect for type of negative message, $F(2, 104) = 40.67$, $p < .001$, with discrepancies being the preferred mode for sending negative messages for both sexes, irrespective of marital adjustment level.

Thus, when only negative messages are examined, it is clear that more negative messages are sent with smiles than in any other way. These results are quite different from the earlier results (Noller, 1982) which indicated

TABLE 9.7. *Number of Subjects using each of the Different Types of Negative Messages*

Marital adjustment level	Type of negative message		
	Direct negative	With neutral verbal	With smiles
High			
Males	1	4	10
Females	2	3	10
Low			
Males	5	10	12
Females	10	9	14

N = 14 for each group.

that low marital adjustment subjects, and particularly wives, had a greater proportion of their *total* messages discrepant. It would seem that the reason these subjects were more likely to send negative messages accompanied by smiles than other subjects was not because low marital adjustment subjects prefer this method of sending negative messages more than other subjects— but because they sent more negative messages. Table 9.7 presents the number of subjects who used each of the different types of messages (N = 14 for each group). As can be seen, most subjects sent negative messages accompanied by smiles, while few of the subjects high in marital adjustment sent direct negative messages, or negative messages with neutral verbal.

One of the problems with this study of married couples (Noller, 1982) is that some very important information is missing—how the discrepant communications were decoded by the spouses. Because this information is not available there are several questions with regard to discrepant communications which cannot be answered:

1. The first question unanswered from the present data concerns whether discrepant communications represent skilful communications or not. If spouses were intending to send a negative message when they smiled with negative in the other channels, then having it decoded as negative represents skill. On the other hand, if they were intending to tease and the message was coded as negative, then that represents lack of skill. Likewise, if they were intending to tease, and their messages with smiles were coded as positive, then that indicates skill. We know how the message came across to the coder, but we know neither the intention of the encoder, nor the way the message was decoded by the spouse.

2. The second question which is difficult to answer from the available data is whether sending negative messages with smiles makes it more likely that such complaints will be discounted or ignored, and thus the issues will not be resolved. The fact that the coders saw the overall effects of these messages as negative makes it likely that they will be recognized as negative even

though the smile may serve to make them more palatable. However, we cannot be sure that the spouse would decode the message in the same way as the coders.

3. The third question concerns whether spouses at different levels of marital adjustment interpret discrepant messages in the same way. It is possible that those who are happy and secure in their marriages are able to decode the negative comment and the positive expression about the relationship without any problems, while those low in marital adjustment, and less secure in their relationship would hear only the negative comment or be confused or angered by the ambiguity of the message.

Several findings discussed earlier are relevant to these questions:

(a) Gottman *et al.*'s (1976) finding that for unhappy spouses impact was often more negative than intent supports the contention that low marital adjustment spouses may decode such messages more negatively than other spouses.

(b) The findings of the bias analysis reported in Chapter 5 suggest that males would be likely to interpret such messages in a negative way, while females would be likely to interpret them in a more positive way, although it may be that the bias finding does not apply to discrepant messages.

(c) The findings from the study of communication awareness (Vernardos, 1982) which showed that wives were more confident of the decoding when they were wrong for incorrect negative messages than for incorrect positive or neutral messages. Since incorrect negative messages have to be decoded more positively, it seems likely that wives may miss hearing negative messages, and so fail to deal with the issues being raised by them. Since Venardos (1982) also found that it was particularly the wives in the low marital adjustment group who were confident when they were incorrect, they may be particularly likely to ignore negative communications.

The use of the communication channels in negative messages

A further analysis was carried out to examine the use of the different communication channels in negative messages. This analysis had three specific aims:

(a) To see which channel/s were most involved in negative messages between spouses.

(b) To gain some understanding of the large number of negative messages not accounted for by the typology presented earlier.

(c) To check for sex and marital adjustment level differences in the use of the communication channels in negative messages. For each subject, the percentage of negative messages which were coded negative in each of the channels (verbal, visual, and vocal) was calculated. Mean percentages for each group are presented in Table 9.8.

TABLE 9.8. *Mean Percentages of Negative Messages Coded Negative in each of the Channels of Communication*

Marital adjustment level	Communication channel		
	Verbal	Visual	Vocal
High			
Males	18.8	9.4	44.4
Females	14.6	14.0	38.3
Low			
Males	29.7	20.7	67.2
Females	43.5	23.8	68.8

An analysis of variance was carried out with these percentages as the dependent variable, and marital adjustment level, sex and channel as the independent variables. There were two significant main effects obtained in this analysis:

1. A main effect for marital adjustment level, $F(1,52) = 24.1$, $p < .001$, with low marital adjustment level subjects having a larger percentage of their messages coded negative on each of the channels.

2. A main effect for type of channel, $F(2,104) = 71.4$, $p < .001$ with negative messages being more likely to be negative in the vocal channel than any other.

The finding that low marital adjustment subjects had a larger percentage of their messages coded negative on each of the channels implies that negative messages sent by low marital adjustment subjects are more intense—that is, negative on more channels. Negative messages sent by high marital adjustment subjects, on the other hand, would seem to be less intense—and more often to be coded neutral, or even positive on some of the channels.

Such findings raise the question of whether the more intense negative messages are the more skilled messages. Since skill in communication involves getting the message across to the spouse, one could argue that direct or consistent communications should do this more efficiently. On the other hand, if the message is more negative than is needed to communicate the intention, is this skilful communication? Also, is it better for the relationship if the communication expresses some positivity to the spouse at the same time as the negativity?

Interestingly, although the wives in the low marital adjustment group had a significantly greater percentage of their communications rated as negative than did the husbands, and also sent more direct negative messages than their husbands, there was no sex difference in this present analysis. That is, when only the negative communications are taken into account (and there-

TABLE 9.9. *Mean Scores on Areas of Change Questionnaire
for Husbands and Wives of Different Levels of Marital
Adjustment*

	Sex	
Marital adjustment level	Males	Females
High	6.06	8.69
Moderate	15.75	13.69
Low	21.56	27.81

N = 16 for each group.

fore number of negative communications is controlled for), there is no sex difference with regard to the percentage of messages rated as negative on each channel—men's negative messages seem to be as intense as those of women, and presumably as expressive.

Several conclusions are possible as to why females send more negative messages than males, even though those from males are just as intense as those sent by females:

1. Females (at least those low in marital adjustment) are more prepared to communicate their dissatisfactions (hence they have more messages rated negative) than are males. However, when males (low in marital adjustment) do communicate their dissatisfactions, their messages are equally as intense or expressive as those of their wives. It should also be noted that the males were not more likely than the females to use negative words to express their negative feelings, although this possibility has been discussed by some writers.

2. Females low in marital adjustment are more unhappy than their spouses—or unhappy about more things, and this is the reason more of their communications are negative. Research has generally shown such a conclusion to be valid, and, for this sample, the results for the Areas of Change Questionnaire (Note 1) bear out such a conclusion (see Table 9.9). Scores on this instrument measure the amount of change a subject would like to see in their spouse's behaviour. Ratings are made separately for each item on a 7-point scale from +3 = I want my spouse to perform this behaviour much more, to −3 = I want my spouse to perform this behaviour much less, with 0 = no change required. Not only were wives' scores higher than those of the husbands for the low marital adjustment group, but wives scores discriminated significantly between the marital adjustment groups, $F(2,45) = 18.18$, $p < .01$, while those of the husbands did not. Hence we could conclude that husbands and wives low in marital adjustment differ with regard to how negative they feel about the relationship or how much change they want, but are equally clear about expressing the dissatisfactions they have.

3. A third possible conclusion is that the methodology employed could not identify subtle differences in intensity between husbands and wives. Certainly, using only a 3-point scale from positive to negative would be likely to mask any differences in extent of negativity within each channel. The fact that both males and females were coded as negative on a channel would not necessarily mean that they were equally negative. Using a scale with a greater range could lead to more accurate coding. However, it would seem important to keep in mind the data from the experimental study where spouses sent each other ambiguous messages. In that study males and females were equally accurate at sending negative messages. Of course, such data applies most directly to negative messages with neutral verbal, but skill at encoding these messages is likely to be highly correlated with general skill at sending negative messages.

The finding that negative messages were more likely to be coded negative in the vocal channel than the other channels seems to indicate that the vocal channel carries most of the negativity in communications between spouses, with the visual channel carrying least, for reasons we have already discussed in detail. The order of importance of the channels for negative messages in the marital situation is vocal, then verbal, then visual.

The fairly large discrepancy between the percentage coded negative in the vocal channel and that coded negative in other channels would seem to indicate that many of the messages not accounted for by the typology presented earlier are likely to be negative in the vocal channel only. Such a finding emphasizes the power of the tone of voice in messages between spouses. A negative message of this type could take a number of forms including:

(a) Asking a question e.g. Did you feed the cat? (with a negative tone of voice implying that the spouse has probably forgotten again).

(b) Giving information e.g. Yes I did. (with negative voice tone implying that the enquiring spouse never trusts the other one to do anything).

(c) Making a comment about the spouse to a third party e.g. She doesn't like the stereo playing loudly. (with negative voice tone implying that she's unreasonable in this respect).

In each of these commonplace situations the tone of voice (or vocal channel) could be expected to carry most of the negativity in the message.

The order of importance for the communication channels in negative messages is quite different from that found by Furnham and his colleagues (Furnham, Trevethan & Gaskell, 1981) in a study of the effects of communication channels on person perception. These researchers found verbal cues to contribute most to negative perceptions, then visual cues, and then vocal cues.

Several factors could account for the different results in the two studies:

1. It is possible that negative communications in the marital situation are different from those in other situations, particularly where long-term inti-

TABLE 9.10. *Comparison of Two Studies on Use of Channels*

	Furnham *et al*. study	Noller study
Type of stimulus	5 minute videotape of "Dr Brown"	10 minute videotape divided into "thought units" or turns
Type of rating	Semantic differential ratings of overall impression—28 scales	Unit by unit ratings by coder
Design	Totally between subjects Channel (Verbal, Visual, Vocal, Total) × Positivity (Positive or negative)	Within subject ratings of channels
	Tapes piloted so that each of the tapes judged to be equally negative on each of the nonverbal channels	Spontaneous interactions

mate relationships are not involved. Certainly, many of the results found for negative messages in this present series of studies are different from those found in studies using different populations. It is highly likely, given the results for discrepant messages discussed earlier, that the visual channel, in particular, is softening the message and preserving the relationship.

2. It is also possible that the different methodologies used in the two studies are related to the different results. Table 9.10 summarizes the relevant differences between the two studies. It could be that:

(a) Overall impression is judged differently from single communications.

(b) Spontaneous interactions are judged differently from videotapes, which have been carefully piloted so that the channels are equally negative.

What the data from the study of married couples suggests is that spontaneous negative messages are generally not equally negative in each channel, but some channels are more inclined to carry the negative message than others—particularly is this true for vocal channel. It is also important to note that this analysis really relates to what encoders do.

The Furnham *et al.* (1981) study, on the other hand, is about what decoders do and indicates that when the different channels are equally negative, the words will carry more weight than the face, and the face will carry more weight than the vocal channel—at least when the overall impression of a stranger is being gauged.

(c) The scales used by Furnham *et al.* (1981) for rating the videotape would not necessarily represent the dimensions on which spouse–spouse communications would be judged. Scales used for rating the tapes are presented in Table 9.11, together with an indication of those scales where the impression created by the single channel was different from the impression created by the total tape. As can be seen, differences between the vocal channel and the total channel occur on only six of the scales, and only on two scales do differences occur between the verbal channel and the total channel, and on five between the visual channel and the total channel. On the other hand, there are seventeen scales on which there are no differences

TABLE 9.11. *Scales used for Rating Tapes in Furnham* et al. *Study*

	Verbal	Vocal	Visual
Hostile			*
Unpleasant			
Relaxed			
Unemotional			
Sensitive			
Timid			
Naive			
Stimulating			
Submissive			
Confusing			*
Intelligent			
Untrustworthy		*	
Secure		*	
Civilized		*	
Insecure		*	
Complex			
Irrational		*	
Rigid			*
Serious			
Humble		*	*
Cold	*		
Tactless			
Introvert			
Unimaginative	*		*

at all between the impressions created by the channels and the total impression. In any case, for whatever reason, the present data indicate that for married couples the vocal channel seems most likely to be carrying the negativity in a negative message, while the visual channel is least likely to be negative.

There was, also, in this analysis of the use of the channels in negative messages, a significant interaction between marital adjustment level and type of channel, $F(2, 104) = 3.03$, $p < .05$. This result indicated that there was less difference between the groups on the visual channel than on the verbal or vocal channels. Thus happy and unhappy spouses would seem to differ most in the extent to which they use negative words and negative tone of voice in their negative messages.

Discussion

It seems then, that the interpretation made in the earlier work (Noller 1982) that discrepant communications would seem to occur more in unsatisfactory relationships needs to be qualified. While it is clearly true that subjects in the low marital adjustment group used more such messages, subsequent analyses indicate that these subjects send more discrepant communications basically because they send more negative messages.

The fact that the discrepant negative message was the most popular of the three modes of sending negative messages which were tested in this study—and the fact that these messages were the most popular for both sexes, and over all marital adjustment levels would seem to indicate that this type of message performs an important function in the marital relationship. The real difference between the marital adjustment levels was related to the intensity of the negativity often expressed by the low marital adjustment subjects. One is, in fact, tempted to conclude that the low marital adjustment subjects would have better relationships if they used more rather than fewer discrepant communications.

It would seem that the analysis to test for chance effects used by Noller (1982) was not totally suitable. Instead of asking about the probability of a smile with a negative message given the probability of positive visual behaviour and negative vocal behaviour, it may have been more appropriate to test for the probability of a smile with a negative message in that particular group. In the analyses that were carried out the expected probabilities for the high marital adjustment subjects were affected disproportionately by the high percentage of positive behaviour and the small percentage of negative behaviour, while the reverse occurred for low marital adjustment subjects.

The analysis which compared positivity ratings for words and facial expressions showed that, in general, the expected relationship between words and facial expressions occurs—that is, utterances made with negative face have more negative words than those made with neutral or positive face. However the low variability in the ratings of the words (see Table 9.4) with the total range being only from 1.6 (halfway between negative and neutral) to 2.1 (the midpoint of the neutral range) indicate the extent to which the words used by these married couples tended to be neutral.

Bugental's findings (Bugental, 1972; Bugental et al., 1971) with regard to discrepant communications seem mostly to be concerned with discrepancies with negative words and positive voice tone. As can be seen from Table 9.1, discrepancies between words and tone of voice are quite rare in the marital situation and although discrepancies with positive voice tone and negative words occur more often than negative voice tone and positive words (sarcasm) none of these discrepancies occur in more than 2 per cent of messages, even in the low marital adjustment group. Hence it would seem unlikely that the effects found by Bugental and her colleagues with regard to children in disturbed families and verbal/vocal discrepancies are relevant to the interaction between husbands and wives.

Bugental's (Bugental et al., 1970) finding of differences in the decoding of discrepant messages depending on sex of encoder were confirmed by the present study, at least for the coding of the total channel by the independent coder. We cannot be sure, however, that the spouses would necessarily decode the messages in exactly the same way. A study looking at family members' perceptions of communication is presently under way, and the data should help us to find out how spouses decode discrepant communications.

Summary

1. Discrepant messages (with positive in the visual channel, and negative words, or words plus tone of voice) occur more frequently in the communications of low marital adjustment subjects.

2. Discrepant communications seem to be the preferred mode for sending negative messages, by subjects of both sexes, whether high or low in marital adjustment. In fact, very few subjects in the high marital adjustment group send any other type of negative message.

3. Discrepant communications with positive in the visual channel and negative in the vocal channel are more likely to be coded as positive for males, but equally likely to be coded negative as positive for females.

4. Negative communications of unhappy couples are more direct or intense (negative on more channels) than those of happy couples—and it is possible that such messages are more intense than is needed to convey the desired message.

5. The vocal channel predominates in negative communications between spouses—negative messages are coded negative in the vocal channel much more frequently than in any of the other channels—and the visual channel is coded negative least of all.

Reference Note

1. Weiss, R. L. & Perry, B. A. *Assessment and Treatment of Marital Dysfunction*, Oregon Marital Studies Program, University of Oregon, Eugene, Oregon.

References

ALGER, I. & HOGAN, P. (1967) The use of videotape recordings in conjoint marital therapy. *American Journal of Psychiatry*, 123, 1425–30.

ARGYLE, M., SALTER, V., NICHOLSON, H., WILLIAMS, M. & BURGESS, P. (1970) The communication of inferior and superior attitudes by verbal and nonverbal signals. *British Journal of Social and Clinical Psychology*, 9, 222–31.

BATESON, G., JACKSON, D. D., HALEY, J. & WEAKLAND, J. (1956) Toward a theory of schizophrenia. *Behavioral Science*, 1, 251–64.

BUGENTAL, D. E. (1972) Inconsistency between verbal and nonverbal components in parental communication patterns: Its interpretation and effects. Cited in Bugental, D. E. Interpretations of naturally occurring discrepancies between words and intonation: modes of inconsistency resolution. *Journal of Personality and Social Psychology*, 30, 1, 125–33.

BUGENTAL, D. E. (1974) Interpretations of naturally occurring discrepancies between words and intonation: modes of inconsistency resolution. *Journal of Personality and Social Psychology*, **30**, 125–33.

BUGENTAL, D. E., KASWAN, J. W. & LOVE, L. R. (1970) Perception of contradictory meanings conveyed by verbal and nonverbal channels. *Journal of Personality and Social Psychology*, **16**, 647–55.

BUGENTAL, D. E., KASWAN, J. W., LOVE, L. R. & FOX, M. N. (1972) Child versus adult perception of evaluative messages in verbal, vocal and visual channels. *Developmental Psychology*, **2**, 367–75.

BUGENTAL, D. E., LOVE, L. R. & GIANETTO, R. M. (1971) Perfidious feminine faces. *Journal of Personality and Social Psychology*, **17**, 314–18.

BUGENTAL, D. E., LOVE, L. R., KASWAN, J. W. & APRIL, C. (1971) Verbal-nonverbal conflict in parental messages to normal and disturbed children. *Journal of Abnormal Psychology*, **77**, 6–10.

DEPAULO, B. M. & ROSENTHAL, R. (1979) Ambivalence, discrepancy and deception in nonverbal communication. In ROSENTHAL, R. *Skill in Nonverbal Communication: Individual Differences*. Oelgeschlager, Gunn & Hain.

FURNHAM, A., TREVETHAN, R. & GASKELL, G. (1981) The relative contribution of verbal, vocal, and visual channels to person perception: Experiment and critique. *Semiotica*, **1/2**, 37, 39–57.

GOTTMAN, J. M. (1979) *Marital Interaction: Experimental Investigations*. New York: Academic Press.

GOTTMAN, J., NOTARIUS, C., MARKMAN, H., BANKS, S., YOPPI, B. & RUBIN, M. E. (1976) Behaviour exchange theory and marital decision making. *Journal of Personality and Social Psychology*, **34**, 14–23.

MEHRABIAN, A. (1971a) Nonverbal betrayal of feeling. *Journal of Experimental Research in Personality*, **5**, 64–73.

MEHRABIAN, A. (1971b) *Silent Messages*. Belmont, California: Wadsworth Publishing Company.

MEHRABIAN, A. & FERRIS, S. R. (1967) Inference of attitudes from nonverbal communication in two channels. *Journal of Consulting Psychology*, **31**, 248–52.

NOLLER, P. (1980) *Marital Misunderstandings: A Study of Couples' Nonverbal Communication*. Unpublished Ph.D. Thesis. University of Queensland.

NOLLER, P. (1982) Channel consistency and inconsistency in the communications of married couples. *Journal of Personality and Social Psychology*, **43**, 4, 732–41.

OSGOOD, C. E. (1966) The dimensionality of the semantic space for communication via facial expression. *Scandinavian Journal of Psychology*, **7**, 1–30.

ROGERS, C. R. (1957) The necessary and sufficient conditions of therapeutic personality change. *Journal of Consulting Psychology*, **21**, 95–103.

TRAUX, C. B. & CARKHUFF, R. B. (1967) *Towards Effective Counseling and Psychotherapy: Training and Practice*. Chicago: Aldine.

VENARDOS, C. (1982) Communication awareness in married couples. Unpublished Honours Thesis, University of Queensland.

10

Gaze Behaviour in Married Couples

In the initial discussion of the scope of nonverbal communication in Chapter 1, gaze (or looking behaviour) was included among the nonverbal behaviours, and we now turn to a more comprehensive study of looking behaviour, particularly in the interactions of married couples.

Functions of Looking in Interaction

Looking behaviour performs several functions in interaction (Argyle *et al.*, 1973):

1. Sending information—we are all familiar with the fact that messages can be sent with a look—a warning look, a withering look, a loving look, a seductive look.

2. Collecting information—looking enables interactants to take in cues from facial expression, posture, spacing etc.; such information can perform two functions:

(a) help the interactant to understand the communications of the other interactant;

(b) give the interactant feedback on the other interactant's reactions to what he/she is saying—what we might call a monitoring function.

3. Synchronizing interaction—providing cues which enable smooth interaction with minimal interruptions.

An important issue in the literature has been whether looking is primarily affective (concerned with expressing feelings and attitudes), or primarily concerned with collecting information. Rutter and Stephenson (1979) argue that if looking were primarily affective friends should look at one another more than strangers, while if looking is primarily concerned with collecting information, then strangers should look more than friends. On four different measures:

(a) proportion of interaction time spent looking,

(b) eye-contact,

(c) length of looks,

(d) proportion of listening time spent looking,

these researchers found that strangers did look more than friends, supporting the hypothesis that looking mainly serves the function of collecting information.

Factors Affecting Looking Behaviour

There is also evidence that there are very large individual differences in the amount of looking people do in interactions (Argyle & Cook, 1976; Kendon, 1967) and that interactants are fairly stable in their looking behaviour, maintaining similar amounts of looking in different settings and over time (Argyle & Cook, 1976; Daniell & Lewis, 1972).

Looking behaviour has also been found to be related to a number of other factors apart from individual differences:
1. Sex.
2. Which role the subject is taking in the interaction at a particular point in time i.e. whether the subject is speaking or listening.
3. Personality differences.
4. Type of message or interaction.

The evidence related to each of these, and their possible relevance to the marital situation, will be examined in the following sections.

Sex, and whether the subject is speaking or listening

The evidence seems quite clear that women look more and are looked at more (Kendon, 1967). Some researchers claim that women particularly look more than men when listening (Exline & Winters, 1965) while other researchers have found more looking while speaking for women (Argyle & Dean, 1965; Exline, Gray & Schuette, 1965; Libby & Yaklevich, 1973). Libby and Yaklevich (1973) found that the main sex difference in their study was due to greater mutual gaze among pairs of female interactants. Argyle and Ingham (1972) found that mixed sex dyads showed less eye contact than pairs composed of either two males or two females.

Kleinke and his co-workers (Kleinke, Desautels & Knapp, 1976; Kleinke et al., 1973) found that amount of looking was evaluated differently by males and females, with females preferring an experimenter who looked at them a lot, while males preferred an experimenter who looked less. Exline (1972) showed that both sexes expressed a preference for about 50 per cent looking from those they interacted with, and felt that they would experience the most discomfort when they were speaking and their partner wasn't looking at them. Such a finding implies that looking while listening is more important to the interaction than looking while speaking, but other researchers have found that women like to see a person with whom they are interacting.

Personality

Various personality variables have been found to affect both amount of looking, and whether subjects look more when they are listening or when they are speaking. Table 10.1 summarizes the findings with regard to friendliness and sociability (Beekman, 1975), dependency (Exline, 1972; Exline & Messick, 1967; Nevill, 1974), dominance and desire to control (Ellyson, 1974) and need affiliation (Exline, 1963). These personality variables probably account, at least to some extent for the stability in looking behaviour (Argyle & Cook, 1976).

TABLE 10.1. *Personality Variables and Looking Behaviour*

Friendliness and sociability	More looking while listening for males but not females
High self control and low spontaneity	More looking while speaking for both sexes
Dependency	More looking at interaction partners
High dominance and desire to control others	Low visual dominance index—greater ratio of looking while speaking to looking while listening
High need affiliation (in cooperative situations)	Engaged in greatest amount of looking
Low need affiliation (in competitive situations)	Increased eye contact

Types of message or interaction

Type of message or interaction has been found to have an impact on the effect that looking behaviour has on interaction, the important dimensions being whether the material is positive or negative, and whether it is personal or impersonal. Ellsworth and Carlsmith (1968) found, for example, that interviewers who looked while making positive utterances were rated more favourably than those who did not, while those who looked while making negative utterances were rated more negatively than those who did not. Scherwitz and Helmreich (1973) found that when content was *impersonal* and *positive* high rates of looking produced liking, while when the content was *personal* and *positive* low rates of looking produced greater liking.

Other researchers have also examined the relationship between the looking behaviour of an interactant, and the reactions of others to him, and have generally concluded that looking can be used in different ways in interactions, and that the effect of the looking on others will depend on the context and the way the looking is being used. While there is clearly evidence for a looking–liking relationship of the type "the more you look at me (the more attention you give me) the more I will like you", there is also evidence for a relationship between looking behaviour and desire to dominate. Strongman and Champness (1968), for example, found that they were able to form a dominance hierarchy of a group using the maintenance of eye-contact as a measure of dominance.

Ellyson (1974) proposed a visual dominance index, which was the ratio of looking while listening to looking while speaking. That is:

$$\text{visual dominance index} = \frac{\text{looking while listening}}{\text{looking while speaking}}$$

Ellyson found that this ratio discriminated between subjects who were high and low in their desire to control others, as measured by the FIRO-B scale (Schutz, 1958). Ellyson (1974) noted that a lower ratio was related to high scores on dominance and competitiveness. Thus subjects who were strong in a desire to dominate looked more when they were speaking than when they were listening, independent of how much looking they actually did.

Looking Behaviour in the Interactions of Married Couples

Noller (1980) carried out a study of the looking behaviour of married couples using the videotaped interactions already discussed in Chapters 8 and 9. As in the earlier studies, the focus was on the relationship of looking behaviour to marital adjustment level, sex and type of message. The specific questions of interest included:

1. Do spouses, in interaction with one another, look more at each other when they are speaking or when they are listening, and is this relationship dependent on marital adjustment level, sex and type of message?

2. What is the relationship between marital adjustment level and sex and Ellyson's (1974) measure of dominance in interaction (the visual dominance index)?

3. For married couples, is there some relationship between the level of looking of one spouse and the level of looking of the other? Three particular questions were seen as important here:

(a) To what extent is the looking behaviour in a couple accounted for by individual differences?

(b) What is the relationship between one spouse's looking while speaking and the other spouse's looking while listening? To what extent do speaker and listener affect each other?

(c) What is the relationship between one spouse's looking while speaking and the other spouse's looking while speaking, and what is the relationship between one spouse's looking while listening and the other spouse's looking while listening? To what extent is there a characteristic pattern of looking for a couple?

(d) Do the relationships considered in the earlier questions vary depending on the marital adjustment level of the couple?

4. How do the findings with regard to looking behaviour relate to earlier findings on accuracy, use of the channels, and inconsistent messages?

Collecting the data on looking behaviour

Two trained coders worked through the videotapes of couples' interacting with one another—the same videotapes used in the earlier studies on the use of the communication channels, and on inconsistent messages. For each thought unit (or speaker turn) the coders recorded, for both the speaker and the listener, whether he/she looked at the spouse during that unit. Inter-rater and intra-rater agreement were calculated at 95 per cent and 92 per cent respectively. The criterion used was face-gaze (von Cranach, 1971) with looking behaviour being recorded only if the subject looked at the spouse's face during the unit.

For each subject, then, the percentage of units on which he/she looked at the spouse in different situations was calculated, for each type of message (positive, neutral or negative as judged by the rating of the total channel), and interaction role (whether the subject was speaking or listening). The following scores were obtained:

1. The percentage of units on which the husband was the speaker and he looked at his wife—calculated separately for positive, neutral and negative units.

2. The percentage of units on which the wife was the speaker and she looked at her husband—calculated separately for positive, neutral and negative units.

3. The percentage of units on which the husband was the listener and he looked at his wife—calculated separately for positive, neutral and negative units.

4. The percentage of units on which the wife was the listener and she looked at her husband—calculated separately for positive, neutral and negative units.

Variables affecting looking behaviour in couples

Marital adjustment effects. There was no main effect for marital adjustment level, but marital adjustment level interacted with type of message $F(4, 78) = 3.13$, $p < .02$, $\eta = .37$ (see Figure 10.1A and B). Analysis of simple main effects indicated that the important differences between the groups were related to negative messages, $F(2, 165) = 11.82$, $p < .001$, $\eta = .35$. High marital adjustment couples looked on a smaller percentage of negative messages than other couples (Newman-Keuls, $p < .05$) while both

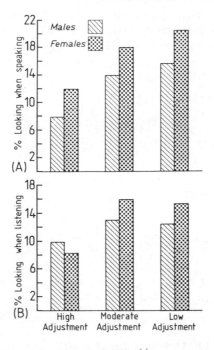

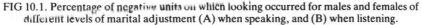

FIG 10.1. Percentage of negative units on which looking occurred for males and females of different levels of marital adjustment (A) when speaking, and (B) when listening.

lows and moderates looked more than the highs, and there were no significant differences between the lows and moderates with regard to their looking behaviour on negative messages. Such a finding fits with results related to the impact of looking on an interactant. The unhappy spouses seem to behave in similar ways to interviewers who were rated negatively— looking more on negative utterances with relatively small differences on negative messages related to whether they were speaking or listening (Ellsworth & Carlsmith, 1968). Looking on negative messages, particularly when speaking, could tend to be interpreted as attempts to dominate (Strongman & Champness, 1968), and as antagonistic or aggressive (Ellsworth, Carlsmith & Henson, 1972).

As well as being confrontational in itself, greater amounts of looking on negative messages for low marital adjustment couples could indicate a strong need to monitor the reactions of the partner when sending a negative message. Cook (1970) suggested that people in hostile relationships are the ones who need more visual information, since monitoring one another is very important to them, while Argyle and Cook (1976) contend that those in happy relationships may prefer closeness, and hence, less looking.

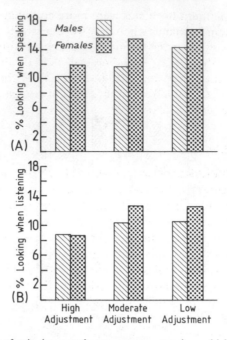

FIG 10.2. Percentage of units (averaged across message-type) on which looking occurred for males and females of different levels of marital adjustment (A) when speaking, and (B) when listening.

Sex effects. The analysis of the looking behaviour showed that females looked more than males over all groups and situations, $F(1,39) = 5.03$, $p < .03$, $d = .718$ since there were no interactions of sex with any other variable. Such a finding fits with other research which has generally shown women to look more than men in an interaction (Argyle & Dean, 1965; Exline, Gray & Schuette, 1965; Libby, 1970), although the sex difference has generally been related to interaction role (or whether the subject is speaking or listening). (See Figure 10.2 for percentages of looking by males and females at different levels of marital adjustment when (A) speaking, and (B) listening.)

Weitz (1976) showed some evidence for a "female monitoring mechanism" which she suggested could be a result of women generally having subordinate status to men. Similar findings with regard to monitoring and sensitivity in blacks in the United States (Gitter, Black & Mostofsky, 1972) give some validity to the explanation that the lower status person in the interaction is likely to monitor the interaction more.

Hall (1970) tested the "dealing-with-oppression" hypothesis as a possible explanation for women's superior ability at decoding nonverbal communication and found little support for such an explanation "since girls and women who described themselves as more equalitarian in their attitudes were better, not worse, decoders" (p. 57). There are, however, several problems with the data used to come to this conclusion since liberated or equalitarian women are also likely to be better educated and aware, and better decoders of nonverbal communication for this reason. Perhaps the relationship between decoding ability and female status is somewhat curvilinear, with the most oppressed and the most liberated being the better decoders. Hall herself (1979) suggests a further possible explanation related to sex of message-sender, since there is some very tentative evidence that ability to decode men may be related to status (negatively related, that is), while ability to decode women seems to be generally unrelated. However, since the data apply only to decoding a man's voice, the findings would not seem to be relevant to gaze behaviour. Some of these issues will be taken up again when sex differences are discussed in Chapter 11.

As mentioned earlier, Kleinke and his associates (Kleinke, Desautels & Knapp, 1976; Kleinke et al., 1973) found that females liked an experimenter who looked at them a lot, while males liked one who looked less. Such a result would suggest that in the marital situation males should look more and females look less (that is, if we assume they are seeking to please one another). Clearly this is not what happens at any level of marital adjustment.

If it is true that one of the functions of gaze is to communicate affect and attitudes and to send information, then it could be that the superior encoding of women described in Chapter 5 is related to their gaze behaviour. Perhaps some of the message, at least, is carried by the eyes and looking at the person enables that message to be conveyed more directly and clearly.

The finding reported in Chapter 5 and discussed again in Chapter 9 that the wives relied more on the visual channel than men when they were decoding would seem relevant to the sex differences in gaze behaviour. It seems that women are more aware of the information available from the visual channel and are more careful to make sure they get such information. The finding by earlier researchers that women prefer to see a person with whom they are interacting (Argyle, Lalljee & Cook, 1968; Ellsworth & Ludwig, 1972) further confirms the importance of the visual channel for women interactants.

Interaction role effects. In this study of married couples, more looking occurred when subjects were speaking than when they were listening, $F(1, 39) = 35.48$, $p < .01$, $\eta = 1.9$, but interaction role was also related to message-type, $F(2, 78) = 5.09$, $p < .01$, $\eta = .34$. Analysis of simple main effects showed that there was significantly more looking while speaking than while listening over all message-types, but the difference between the two measures was greater for positive messages and smaller for negative measures. Thus on positive messages speakers tended to look, while listeners tended not to look, probably reflecting a general embarrassment we have about receiving positive messages, or praise. The smaller difference between the amount of looking on negative messages for speakers and listeners would seem to imply that there is more likely to be eye-contact between the partners on a negative message than on other messages but that this is most likely to be a confrontational type of eye-contact.

The fact that more looking occurred when subjects were speaking than when they were listening implies that married couples use looking more for monitoring than for listening or gaining understanding, possibly monitoring the effects that their own messages seem to be having on the spouse so that he/she can tone down the message if that seems necessary. Perhaps this is how they decide whether a smile is needed (see Chapter 9). On the other hand, if subjects look less when they are listening, then many of these smiles may not be seen. It could be an interesting exercise to check whether smiling with negative messages occurs mainly when there is eye-contact established. As well, if subjects are aware that the smile may not be seen they may try to soften the message on the vocal channel as well and this could account for the fact that many of the negative messages, particularly from the high marital adjustment subjects were often negative on only one channel.

Message-type effects. Less looking occurred on neutral messages than on other messages, $F(2,78) = 32.97$, $p < .001$. This small amount of looking could have been related to the fact that couples were often consulting their questionnaires in order to compare answers. Such a situation would be similar to that used in Argyle and Graham's (1976) study where subjects used a map in planning a holiday. In fact, the amount of gaze found in the present study was higher than that found by Argyle and Graham (1976) but not nearly as high as the 50 per cent looking subjects tend to report that they prefer (Exline, 1972). However, when the presence of the questionnaires is taken into account, as well as the personal nature of much of the material discussed, the reasons become clearer.

Message-type also interacted with marital adjustment level, with looking on negative messages being more important in discriminating between the groups. As well, looking behaviour was related to interaction role, with the difference between speaker and listener being greater for positive messages. These effects have been discussed in the sections dealing with marital adjustment level effects and interaction role effects, respectively.

Visual dominance index. The visual dominance index suggested by Ellyson (1974) was also calculated for each subject. This index represents the ratio of looking while listening to looking while speaking. In the present analysis the index was the percentage of units on which the subject was the listener

TABLE 10.2. *Visual Dominance Index Scores*

Group	Males	Females
High marital adjustment	1.51	0.82
Moderate marital adjustment	0.91	1.03
Low marital adjustment	0.77	0.76

and looked at the spouse, divided by the percentage of units on which the subject was the speaker and looked at the spouse. Ellyson (1974), as discussed earlier, related low scores on the visual dominance index to high dominance, on the grounds that looking while speaking is more likely to involve a display of dominance or competitiveness than looking while listening, which is more likely to involve a desire to understand.

A two-way analysis of variance (marital adjustment level by sex) produced an interaction of marital adjustment level and sex, F(2,3) = 3.19, p < .05. The high marital adjustment husbands were the group with the highest visual dominance index (see Table 10.2) and hence the least display of competitiveness or dominance, while for both husbands and wives, the low marital adjustment subjects were the ones with the lowest visual dominance index. Given that Ellyson (1974) found that this index was able to discriminate between those who were high in their desire to control others, and those who were low, the findings in the present study would seem to indicate a high level of desire to control the partner in the low marital adjustment subjects, and a low level of desire to control the partner in the high marital adjustment husbands.

However, a warning needs to be sounded. Since speakers were highly likely to look on positive messages, it is clear that all looking while speaking is not confrontational. Nevertheless, since high marital adjustment wives sent the most positive messages and low marital adjustment subjects sent very few, the effect of looking on positive messages is likely to be higher on the high marital adjustment wives. Hence the mean visual dominance index for this group is likely to be unrealistically low, while those for other groups would be less likely to be distorted by the effect of positive messages.

Correlational analyses. Three sets of correlational analyses were carried out in order to examine the relationships between the looking behaviour of each subject in the different interaction roles and that of his/her spouse. The correlational analyses were designed to test three specific relationships:

1. The relationship between a subject's percentage of looking while speaking and the same subject's percentage of looking while listening—a measure of the importance of individual differences in looking behaviour.

TABLE 10.3. *Results of Correlational Analysis*

	Female speaking	Male listening	Female listening
Total group			
male speaking	.49†	.82†	.45†
female speaking		.54†	.83†
male listening			.61†
High marital adjustment			
male speaking	.49	.82†	.67†
female speaking		.57†	.89†
male listening			.67†
Moderate marital adjustment			
male speaking	.52	.89†	.54†
female speaking		.69†	.94†
			.68†
Low marital adjustment			
male speaking	.15	.77†	.28
female speaking		.19	.54*
male listening			.38

* p < .05.
† p < .01.

2. The relationship between a subject's percentage of looking while speaking, and the spouse's percentage of looking while listening—a measure of reciprocity, or the extent to which the speaker and listener affect each other with regard to patterns of looking.

3. The relationship between a subject's percentage of looking in a particular interaction role and the spouse's percentage of looking in that same interaction role—a measure of the extent to which the couple has a characteristic pattern of looking. These correlations and their results will be discussed in separate sections. The analyses were calculated for males and females over all marital adjustment levels and for each marital adjustment level separately.

Individual differences. As Table 10.3 indicates for both males and females the correlation between a subject's percentage of looking while speaking and the same subject's percentage of looking while listening was high and positive, and the correlations were significant for subjects at every level of marital satisfaction. The indication is that more than 60 per cent of the variance in looking behaviour is accounted for by individual differences, and that this is the greatest single effect on how much a person looks in an interaction. It would seem then that individual differences will be more important determinants of looking behaviour than situations or contexts. However, since all the data here is from the marital situation, the only conclusion that is justified is that in the marital situation individual differences are the most important determinant of looking behaviour, it is possible however, that some context and situations would have more powerful effects. However Argyle and Cook (1976) also found individual differences to account for a large amount of the variance in looking behaviour.

Reciprocity effects. The correlations were calculated between each subject's percentage of looking while speaking and the spouse's percentage of looking while listening. Again, as can be seen in Table 10.3 the correlations were both significant and positive, indicating that in a long-term relationship such as marriage the amount of looking one spouse does in a particular interaction role seems to affect the amount of looking the partner does in the reciprocal role. So, if the speaker is looking a lot, the listener is also likely to look a lot, while if the speaker looks only occasionally, the listener is likely to behave in a similar manner.

When the data were analysed separately for the three marital adjustment levels, it became clear that the strength of this reciprocity effect was different at different levels of marital adjustment. It was only for high and moderate marital adjustment couples that the correlations were high and positive. For the low marital adjustment subjects correlations were low, with little relationship between one spouse's looking while speaking and the partner's looking while listening. It would seem then that while couples in satisfactory marriages adjust their looking behaviour to that of the partner, those in unsatisfactory relationships do not.

Characteristic pattern for couples. The third set of correlations was related to the question of whether there is a relationship between one spouse's looking behaviour in a particular interaction role, and the partner's looking behaviour in that same role. Since the results for this set of analyses were more complex than those for other sets of analyses, with a different pattern of effects being found for speaking and listening, each role will be considered separately.

(a) *Speaking*. While the overall correlation for speaking was significant, with the correlation being positive, when the correlations were calculated separately for each marital adjustment level, there was no significant correlation at any level of marital adjustment between one spouse's looking while speaking and the other spouse's looking while speaking. Results are again presented in Table 10.3. However, the value of the correlation coefficient for the low marital adjustment subjects was much lower than for other subjects, indicating that the overall correlation was a function of a fairly weak relationship between the variables for those higher in marital adjustment. It would seem that, in general, the amount of looking a spouse does when he is speaking is more related to what he is saying than to any overall characteristic pattern for the couple.

(b) *Listening*. The results for looking while listening were again positive and significant, indicating that couples do tend to have a characteristic pattern with regard to amount of looking while listening. Also, when the different levels of marital adjustment were analysed separately a similar pattern emerged as for the reciprocity analyses—correlations were positive and significant for the high and moderate marital adjustment groups and low for the low marital adjustment couples. Thus those in happy marriages are more similar to each other with regard to looking while listening behaviour than are those in unhappy marriages.

Overall, the results for the correlational analysis would seem to indicate that low marital adjustment couples do not have the same tendencies to adjust to one another's pattern of looking as do other couples. Of course, the question arises as to whether the greater similarity found for happy couples is a result of the selection process or of an adjustment process. It could be that people feel more comfortable with those who have similar communication patterns to themselves and thus are more likely to form long-term relationships with such people. On the other hand it would seem equally plausible that couples adjust to one another's patterns over time. Such possibilities could only be explored by a longitudinal study which followed couples over time, or by a study which examined different couples who were at different stages of marriage. The adjustment hypothesis would seem to best explain the situation of the low marital adjustment subjects, since it is hard to come to terms with why these couples marry in the first place if one adopts the selection hypothesis.

Other writers have commented on the need for those in long-term relationships to adjust to each other's patterns of behaviour. Argyle and Williams (1969) found response matching over a wide range of nonverbal variables, and McBride (1975), in commenting on the special properties of relationships includes among these the tendency to adjust to one another's patterns of behaviour.

Summary

It seems, then, that looking behaviour does discriminate between couples at the different levels of marital adjustment. While the low marital adjustment group tended to look at their spouses more than other subjects, the pattern of looking also seemed to be different.

Low marital adjustment couples tended to look more when they were speaking and less when they were listening than other couples. High marital adjustment husbands were the only group who looked more when listening than when speaking—and thus, in Ellyson's (1974) terms showed less competitiveness and need to dominate.

Low marital adjustment subjects particularly looked more than other subjects on negative messages, suggesting a confrontation component to the looking—or a strong need to monitor the reactions of the spouse on negative messages. Low marital adjustment spouses were also less similar to one another in their patterns of looking than were other spouses, which could indicate a failure to adjust to one another in the same way as those in happier marriages.

Females looked more than males overall, especially when they were speaking, a possible indication of a female monitoring mechanism. While these results are useful in aiding understanding of the looking behaviour of married couples, care must be taken in generalizing these results to other situations.

References

ARGYLE, M. & COOK, M. (1976) *Gaze and Mutual Gaze*. Cambridge: Cambridge University Press.

ARGYLE, M. & DEAN, J. (1965) Eye-contact, distance and affiliation. *Sociometry*, **28**, 289–304.

ARGYLE, M. & GRAHAM, J. A. (1976) The Central Europe experiment: looking at persons and looking at objects. *Environmental Psychology and Nonverbal Behavior*, **1**, 6–16.

ARGYLE, M. & INGHAM, R. (1972) Gaze, mutual gaze and proximity. *Semiotica*, **6**, 32–49.

ARGYLE, M., INGHAM, R., ALKEMA, F. & McCALLIN, M. (1973) The different functions of gaze. *Semiotica*, **7**, 19–32.

ARGYLE, M., LALLJEE, M. & COOK, M. (1968) The effects of visibility on interaction in a dyad. *Human relations*, **21**, 3–18.

ARGYLE, M. & WILLIAMS, M. (1969) Observer or observed? A reversible perspective in person perception. *Sociometry*, **32**, 396–412.

BEEKMAN, S. (1978) Sex differences in non-verbal behavior. Paper presented at the meeting of the American Psychological Association, Chicago, 1975. Cited in Harper, R. G., Wiens, A. N. & Matarazzo, J. D. *Nonverbal Communication: The State of the Art*. New York: Wiley.

COOK, M. (1970) Experiments on orientation and proxemics. *Human Relations*, **23**, 61–76.

DANIELL, R. J. & LEWIS, P. (1972) Stability of eye contact and physical distance across a series of structured interviews. *Journal of Consulting and Clinical Psychology*, **39**, 172.

ELLSWORTH, P. C. & CARLSMITH, J. M. (1968) Effects of eye contact and verbal contact on affective response to a dyadic interaction. *Journal of Personality and Social Psychology*, **10**, 15–20.

ELLSWORTH, P. C., CARLSMITH, J. M. & HENSON, A. (1972) The state as a stimulus to flight in human subjects: a series of field experiments. *Journal of Personality and Social Psychology*, **21**, 302–11.

ELLSWORTH, P. C. & LUDWIG, L. M. (1972) Visual behaviour in social interaction. *Journal of Communication*, **22**, 375–403.

ELLYSON, S. L. (1978) Visual behaviour exhibited by males differing as to interpersonal control orientation in one- and two-way communication systems. Unpublished Masters Thesis, 1974. Cited in Harper, R. G., Wiens, A. N. & Matarazzo, J. D. *Nonverbal Communication: The State of the Art*. New York: Wiley.

EXLINE, R. V. (1963) Explorations in the process of person perception: visual interaction in relation to competition, sex and the need for affiliation. *Journal of Personality*, **31**, 1–20.

166 Nonverbal Communication and Marital Interaction

EXLINE, R. (1972) Visual interaction: the glances of power and preference. In COLE, J. K. (Ed.) *Nebraska Symposium on Motivation*, Vol. 19. Lincoln: University of Nebraska Press.

EXLINE, R. V., GRAY, D. & SCHUETTE, D. (1965) Visual behavior in a dyad as affected by interview content and sex of respondent. *Journal of Personality and Social Psychology*, 1, 201–9.

EXLINE, R. V. & MESSICK, D. (1967) The effects of dependency and social reinforcement upon visual behavior during an interview. *British Journal of Social & Clinical Psychology*, 6, 256–66.

EXLINE, R. V. & WINTERS, L. C. (1965) Affective relations and mutual glances in dyads. In TOMKINS, S. S. & IZARD, C. E. (Eds.) *Affect, Cognition and Personality*. New York: Springer, pp. 319–50.

GITTER, A. G., BLACK, H. & MOSTOFSKY, D. (1972) Race and sex in the communication of emotion. *Journal of Social Psychology*, 88, 273–6.

HALL, J. (1979) Gender, gender roles and nonverbal communication skills. In ROSENTHAL, R., *Skill in Nonverbal Communication: Individual Differences*. Cambridge, Mass: Oelgeschlager, Gunn & Hain.

KENDON, A. (1967) Some functions of gaze direction in social interaction. *Acta Psychologica*, 26, 22–63.

KLEINKE, C. L., BUSTOS, A. A., MEEKER, F. B. & STANESKI, R. A. (1973) Effects of self-attributed and other attributed gaze on interpersonal evaluations between males and females. *Journal of Experimental Social Psychology*, 9, 154–63.

KLEINKE, C. L., DESAUTELS, M. S. & KNAPP, B. E. (1978) Adult gaze and affective and visual responses of preschool children. Paper presented at the meeting of the Eastern Psychological Association, New York, 1976. Cited in Harper, R. G., Wiens, A. N. & Matarazzo, J. D. *Nonverbal Communication: The State of the Art*. New York: Wiley.

LIBBY, W. L. Jr. (1970) Eye contact and direction of looking as stable individual differences. *Journal of Experimental Research in Personality*, 4, 303–12.

LIBBY, W. L. Jr. & YAKLEVICH, D. (1973) Personality determinants of eye contact and direction of gaze aversion. *Journal of Personality and Social Psychology*, 27, 197–206.

MCBRIDE, G. (1975) Interactions and the control of behaviour. In WILLIAMS, T. R. (Ed.) *Socialization and Communication in Primary Groups*. The Hague: Mouton.

NEVILL, D. (1974) Experimental manipulation of dependency motivation and its effects on eye contact and measurements of field dependency. *Journal of Personality and Social Psychology*, 29, 72–79.

NOLLER, P. (1980) Gaze in married couples. *Journal of Nonverbal Behaviour*, 5, 115–29.

RUTTER, D. R. & STEPHENSON, G. M. (1979) The functions of looking: effects of friendships on gaze. *British Journal of Social and Clinical Psychology*, 18, 203–5.

SCHERWITZ, R. & HELMREICH, R. (1973) Interactive effects of eye contact and verbal content on interpersonal attraction in dyads. *Journal of Personality and Social Psychology*, 25, 6–14.

SCHUTZ, W. C. (1958) *Firo: A Three-dimensional Theory of Interpersonal Behavior*. New York: Holt, Rinehart & Winston.

STRONGMAN, K. T. & CHAMPNESS, B. G. (1968) Dominance hierarchies and conflict in eye contact. *Acta Psychologica*, 28, 376–86.

VON CRANACH, M. (1971) The role of orienting behavior in human interaction. In ESSER, A. H. (Ed.) *Behavior and Environment: The Use of Space by Animals and Men*. New York: Plenum Press, 217–37.

WEITZ, S. (1976) Sex differences in nonverbal communication. *Sex Roles*, 2, 175–84.

11

Sex Differences in Nonverbal Communication in the Marital Situation

Hall (1979) in a meta-analysis of more than 70 studies has shown that females are generally superior to males at both encoding and decoding nonverbal communication. This chapter aims to summarize the sex differences found in the series of studies which have formed the basis for this book. Four questions, in particular, related to sex and to the interaction of sex and marital adjustment, will be explored:

1. In what ways are males and females different from one another in their encoding and decoding of nonverbal communication in the marital situation?

2. In what ways are high marital adjustment husbands different from the low marital adjustment husbands?

3. In what ways are high marital adjustment wives different from low marital adjustment wives?

4. In what ways are the low marital adjustment husband and the low marital adjustment wife contributing to the communication problems in their relationship?

Sex Differences Related to Encoding

Accuracy

Although females were better encoders than males overall, the difference in skill at encoding between high and low marital adjustment subjects was greater for the males. High marital adjustment males were significantly better encoders of nonverbal communication than were low marital adjustment males. This finding will be discussed in a later section on differences related to both sex and marital adjustment.

Both males and females were better able to decode female strangers than male strangers, implying superior encoding by females. Females sent more good communications to the spouses, and had fewer encoding errors than did males, but this superiority was clearer on some types of message than others.

Positive messages. Female superiority at encoding positive messages was indicated by a number of findings:

1. Females sent more good communications than males, particularly positive ones.

2. Males made more encoding errors than females, particularly on positive messages.

3. Males made more encoding errors on positive messages than on other messages, while females made a similar number of errors on positive and negative messages.

4. Both males and females scored higher when decoding female strangers on positive messages, than they did when decoding male strangers.

Thus it would seem clear that females are better than males at encoding positive messages and would be better able to express affection and appreciation in the marital situation.

Neutral messages. There were no differences between males and females on either neutral good communications, or on encoding errors on neutral messages. There was also no clear evidence of superior encoding by either sex when the data on decoding strangers were examined.

Negative messages. Both males and females were better at decoding female than male strangers on negative messages, implying superior encoding by females. However, no differences were found when spouses were sending messages to one another. Both sexes were able to get their negative messages across to one another clearly.

Usage of different type of messages

Males and females were also different in their usage of the various types of messages. Females sent more direct messages than males—or messages that were coded positive in all channels or negative in all channels. Females also sent more positive and negative messages over all channels than did males, while males sent more neutral messages than did females. These findings could be related to expressivity since research has generally found that women are more expressive than men (Balswick & Peek, 1971). However, when just negative messages were analysed, there were no differences between males and females with regard to the intensity of their negative messages—or the percentage which were negative on each of the channels.

Messages with discrepancies between the visual channel and the vocal/verbal channels came across differently depending on whether they were encoded by males or females. These discrepant messages were more likely to be coded positive for males, but were equally likely to be coded negative as positive for females. Such a finding suggests that males and females are using these messages differently in their interactions. When negative messages were examined separately, there were no differences between males and females in the percentage of such messages which were accompanied by smiles. Males were as likely as females to send a negative message with a smile.

The finding of sex differences in encoding fits with results reported by Hall (1979), who was able to show on several different indices that studies of nonverbal encoding showed females to be more accurate encoders than males. In the present series of studies female superiority at encoding was supported both by the data from the accuracy study (Chapter 5) and that from the interaction study (Chapters 8, 9) with females being more accurate, and also sending more clear or direct messages than the males.

The fact that the wives were especially better at encoding positive messages in the accuracy study is particularly interesting, given the results in the interaction study with regard to the sending of positive messages. The data from that study showed that positive messages were highly likely to be sent with neutral or ambiguous verbal cues, and rely on the nonverbal channels to express the positivity. This finding implies that subjects would have the same problems in their general interaction as they had in the accuracy study—males would have real difficulty getting across their positive messages.

Male inexpressivity is particularly a problem of marriages but is almost certainly relevant to other aspects of the male sex role. Noller (1978) explored sex differences in parent–child interactions when parents were leaving their children at preschool. She found that fathers were less likely to express affection than were mothers, and the least affection was expressed between fathers and sons. Thus small boys both observe and experience that males are less expressive of affection than are females—they see their fathers express less affection than their mothers, and also experience less affection than their sisters. The socialization of male children could well account, at least in part, for the problems males have in sending positive messages.

These findings of sex differences on positive messages would also seem to fit with the idea that women are socialized to value close personal relationships and interpersonal skills such as empathy, nurturance, personal expression and interpersonal communication (Middlebrook, 1980; Stein and Bailey, 1973). Women could thus be expected to be more expressive of positive feelings of liking and affection while men, socialized to believe that the expression of such feelings is weak and feminine would be likely to have problems expressing them (Balswick & Peek, 1971). Komarovsky (1962) also claimed that male socialization inhibits expressivity by emphasizing reserve, and by identifying expressivity as feminine.

The finding that there were no differences between males and females with regard to the intensity of their negative messages argues against the conclusion that females are more expressive than males, at least when it comes to negative messages. Perhaps the greater percentage of negative messages sent by females is due not to their greater expressivity, but to their feeling more negative about the relationship, and being more prepared to say so. Lower scores for the females on the marital adjustment measure support such a contention.

It is interesting to note that in quite a different context Taylor and Epstein (1967) found that while males were typically more aggressive than females, when females saw themselves as being aggressed against they responded in kind.

Sex differences in the way messages with positive in the visual channel and negative in the vocal or verbal channel were coded, supports the conclusion that positivity in the visual channel may be discounted or ignored, especially when females are the message-senders. Bugental and her associates (Bugental, Kaswan & Love, 1970) also found that this type of message tended to be coded as positive for males and seen as a type of teasing, while being interpreted as negative for females. This encoder effect on the decoding of discrepant messages could mean that males actually engage in different behaviour when sending these messages, behaviour which countermands the negativity more effectively than the behaviour used by the females in the same situation. It is also possible, as Bugental *et al.* (1970) suggest, that women's smiles are responded to as friendly only when information from other channels is friendly as well.

Sex Differences Related to Decoding

There were generally few differences between males and females with regard to skill at decoding, at least when the spouses were decoding one another. While males and females made a similar number of errors in decoding each other's good communications, females tended to make errors in a positive direction (decode the message more positively than intended) while males tended to make errors in a negative direction (decode more negatively than intended). Wives also looked more at their spouses than husbands did, and tended to rely on the visual channels more when they were decoding.

As well, females had a larger percentage of their bad communications correctly decoded by the spouse. However, whether this result is related to the encoding of the wives or the decoding of the husbands is not clear.

Females were also better overall at decoding strangers than were males. Females scored higher than males when decoding positive messages. Also females scored higher than males when decoding the opposite sex on neutral messages and this result is most likely to be related to the superior decoding of females since there was no clear evidence that one sex was better than the other at encoding neutral messages.

When males and females were compared decoding the same subjects, again the females were better decoders than the males—particularly at decoding males, and the difference was clearer for negative messages.

The bias effect, with females tending to make errors in a positive direction could be related to Rosenthal and DePaulo's (1979) contention that females are more positive or accommodating in their decoding. It seems likely that the wives are assuming positivity when the evidence is quite minimal— perhaps any sign of positivity on the part of the males has a strong effect on the decoding wife. The finding of the heavy reliance by the wives on the visual channel would imply that where husbands showed that positivity in the facial expression, this was given a heavy weighting in the decoding.

The finding with regard to bad or idiosyncratic communications suggests that whatever private message system there is for these couples is particularly relevant when the wives are the message-senders and the husbands are the receivers. Since males are better decoders of people they know (Zuckerman *et al.*, 1975) it is possible that these males were particularly better at decoding their wives. On the other hand, females were generally better encoders than males, so it is possible that they were better at getting across these messages to their husbands.

The fact that there were no sex differences in accuracy when decoding spouses even though females were clearly superior when decoding strangers also relates to Zuckerman's (1975) finding with regard to acquaintanceship. When males are decoding someone they know, their decoding is as accurate as that of females.

Marital Adjustment Level Differences

Some marital adjustment level differences applied overall, while other differences applied to one sex but not the other. Overall differences were related to difference scores (or the relationship between ability to decode the spouse and ability to decode opposite-sex others), discrepant messages, gaze, and the use of positive and negative messages.

Difference scores

Low marital adjustment subjects obtained lower scores decoding their spouses than they obtained when decoding strangers and had a larger difference between these two scores than did other subjects. Such a finding implies that these subjects have more decoding skill than they are actually using with their spouses and that the decoding in the marital relationship is being affected by such factors as the history of that relationship, the way the spouses feel about each other, or the issue they are discussing.

These findings argue against the conclusion that nonverbal decoding skill (Friedman, 1979; Rosenthal, 1979) is a permanent or trait-type behaviour—rather, the implication is that accuracy in decoding depends on factors in the situation, at least to some extent. As well, it would seem that increasing nonverbal accuracy through skills training will not necessarily improve decoding in the marital relationship, unless the skills are taught in the context of that relationship. This issue will be taken up again in Chapter 12 when implications for counselling and therapy will be discussed.

Gaze

Low marital adjustment subjects looked at their spouses more than other subjects, particularly when they were speaking, and on negative messages more than other types of messages. It could be that these spouses feel a greater need to monitor the partner and to be aware of their reactions, because of the hostility in the relationship, or it could be that the gaze is used to add intensity, or confrontation to the negative messages. It is also possible that the looking serves both these functions at the same time.

High marital adjustment husbands were quite different from all other subjects in that they were more likely to look when listening than when speaking, suggesting a real desire to understand the spouse. It should be noted at this point that these husbands relied heavily on the audio channel—but since wives generally are facially expressive, extra information would certainly be gained from looking at the spouse. As well, these husbands seemed to be less involved than other spouses in confrontation or competitiveness.

High marital adjustment subjects were also more reciprocal in their pattern of looking—there was a positive relationship between how much one spouse looked in a particular interaction role and how much the other spouse looked in the reciprocal role. High marital adjustment spouses were also more similar to each other in their looking patterns, particularly for looking while listening. Such findings would seem to suggest a certain amount of adjustment in their looking patterns for the spouses in the happy marriages, which does not seem to have occurred for unhappy spouses.

Discrepant messages

Low marital adjustment subjects sent a larger percentage of discrepant messages (that is, messages with positive visual and negative verbal or vocal) than did other subjects, although this seemed to be related to the fact that they sent more negative messages than did other subjects. When amount of negativity was controlled for, there were no differences between the groups in the percentages of discrepant messages sent by each group of couples. Such a finding suggests that discrepant communications may perform a different function in the marital relationship than had been thought previously (Noller, 1982). It seems likely that the subjects smile in order to soften the impact of the negative message and to express positive feelings toward the spouse and thus maintain the relationship.

Negative messages

High and low marital adjustment subjects would also seem to be quite different in their use of negative messages. Low marital adjustment subjects sent more negative messages than other subjects and their effect occurred over all messages, and for the different types of negative messages such as direct negative messages, and messages with neutral verbal and negative in the nonverbal channels. There was also a different quality about the negative messages of low marital adjustment subjects. These messages seemed to be coded negative in more channels than were negative messages for other couples and generally seemed to be more intense. As well, these negative messages were more likely to be accompanied by a look. Such a picture fits with the complaints often made by unhappy spouses that their partners were hostile and coercive in their interactions with them, using criticism, insults, put-downs etc.

Gottman and his colleagues (1977; 1979) showed that low marital adjustment couples were also more likely to become involved in cycles of negativity, with one negative communication leading to another and another and another. These researchers also showed that low marital adjustment subjects were more likely to express agreement and engage in mindreading behaviours with negative nonverbal behaviour. Thus an important characteristic of the communications of low marital adjustment couples is the amount of negativity expressed.

Positive messages.

High marital adjustment subjects used more positive messages than low marital adjustment subjects, including more direct positive messages, and more messages with neutral verbal and positive nonverbals. Low marital adjustment wives complained that their husbands gave them too little attention and affection, and showed too little appreciation for them, probably reflecting this lack of positive communication. This issue will be discussed further in the next section.

Differences Related to Marital Adjustment Level and Sex

While low marital adjustment subjects were generally less accurate in communicating to one another, the differences between the groups were stronger for wife-to-husband communications than for husband-to-wife communications. Since high marital adjustment husbands were better at decoding their spouses than other husbands this result is likely to be related to this decoding difference. Such a finding also suggests that misunderstandings for unhappy couples are likely to occur when wives are the encoders and husbands the decoders.

Use of channels

The use of the different channels in decoding is complex, and seems to be related to both marital adjustment level and sex. For both wife-to-husband and husband-to-wife communications the low marital adjustment subjects relied on a different channel when decoding than did the other subjects. In the case of wife-to-husband communications the low marital adjustment subjects relied more on the visual channel, while subjects high and moderate in marital adjustment relied on the audio channel, the one which the accuracy data indicated would lead to fewer errors. It would seem that these husbands are relying on the least helpful channel, and could perhaps improve their decoding by becoming more sensitive to the audio channel.

For husband-to-wife communications on the other hand, the high and moderate marital adjustment wives relied on the visual channel when decoding, while for the low marital adjustment wives there was no significant relationship between the decoding of the separate channels and the decoding of the total channel. Such a finding suggests that when the low marital adjustment husbands are sending messages to their wives the channels may not be confirming one another—and the poorer encoding skill found for low marital adjustment husbands would support such an interpretation. Another possibility is that the wives lack any clear idea of which channel is most reliable and could best help them with their decoding. Perhaps these wives need to come to understand their spouses' visual cues better.

Awareness

High marital adjustment subjects of both sexes were better at predicting whether their spouses would accurately interpret their messages than were subjects in the other groups. Low marital adjustment wives were more confident of their decoding when they were incorrect than were other wives, suggesting that they were less aware than other wives of the possibility of making a decoding error.

High marital adjustment husbands were more confident than the moderate marital adjustment husbands when they were correctly interpreting their spouses' messages, implying that the moderate marital adjustment husbands were less confident about their decoding skill than other husbands. High marital adjustment husbands were also more aware of their encoding than other subjects and better able to discriminate between messages they sent clearly and messages not so clearly sent.

Encoding and decoding

There were no differences between high and low marital adjustment wives with regard to accuracy at encoding, but there were clear differences between the two groups of husbands. High marital adjustment husbands sent more good communications and made fewer encoding errors than low marital adjustment husbands, and the differences between the two groups were mainly related to the sending of positive messages.

High marital adjustment males were significantly better than low marital adjustment males at sending positive messages to their spouses. This finding also fits with that from the questionnaire data where an important variable discriminating low marital adjustment wives from high marital adjustment wives was that the low marital adjustment wives wanted their husbands to show them more appreciation and give them more attention. It would seem that these behaviours were not just perceived by these wives as lacking. We have empirical evidence that husbands had more difficulty than wives, and low marital adjustment husbands more difficulty than high marital adjustment husbands in sending positive messages, which were presumably what these wives were wanting. Snyder (1979) and Boyd and Roach (1977) also found that important variables relating to marital satisfaction are those involving the expression of appreciation and affection. What is underlined by the findings of the present series of studies is that even if the husbands try to send this kind of affectionate and appreciative message, they may not succeed—the message may come across more negatively than intended. Even the fact that the wives showed a bias to decode husbands positively did not seem to help in this situation.

High marital adjustment husbands were also better decoders of their wives' messages than were low marital adjustment husbands, and the husband's communication accuracy seemed to be a crucial factor in discriminating high and low marital adjustment couples.

Table 11.1 summarizes the main differences between high and low marital adjustment husbands for encoding, and aims to identify the important differences, not only with regard to accuracy but to other factors explored in this group of studies. The five main areas are accuracy, usage of different types of messages, awareness of communication, use of discrepancies, and

TABLE 11.1. *Differences between High and Low Marital Adjustment Husbands for Encoding*

Accuracy	Highs more good communications, and fewer encoding errors, particularly for positive messages
Usage of different types of messages	Lows more direct negative messages than highs and more intense negative messages; highs more positive messages
Awareness	Highs better able to predict whether spouse would decode message accurately and better able to discriminate own clearly sent and poorly sent messages
Discrepancies	Lows sent more discrepant messages, but no differences between the groups on percentage of negative messages which were discrepant
Gaze	Highs had lower visual dominance index—more likely to look when listening than when speaking; lows particularly likely to look more than highs on negative messages; more reciprocity of gaze for highs than lows

TABLE 11.2. *Differences between High and Low Marital Adjustment Husbands for Decoding*

Accuracy with spouse	Highs more accurate at decoding spouse than lows
Accuracy with strangers	Lows decoded spouse worse than strangers, while highs tended to decode the spouse better than they decoded strangers
Usage of channels	Lows tended to rely on visual channel while highs relied on audio channel (the one leading to greater accuracy for this context)
Awareness	Moderates were the less aware group with regard to decoding— not much difference between highs and lows
Gaze	Highs more likely to look when listening than lows; highs more similar to spouse in pattern of looking while listening for lows

TABLE 11.3. *Differences between High and Low Marital Adjustment Wives for Encoding*

Accuracy	No differences between highs and lows for good communications or encoding errors
Usage of different types of messages	Highs more direct positive messages and lows more direct negative messages; lows more negative messages overall, and negative messages more intense
Awareness	Lows less able than highs to predict whether spouse would decode message accurately
Discrepancies	Lows sent more discrepant messages but no differences between the groups on percentage of negative messages which were discrepant
Gaze	Lows more likely to look than highs, particularly on negative messages; highs more reciprocity of gaze than lows

TABLE 11.4. *Differences between High and Low Marital Adjustment Wives for Decoding*

Accuracy with spouse	No differences between highs and lows
Accuracy with strangers	Lows worse at decoding spouse than strangers while highs similar in each situation
Usage of channels	Highs tend to rely on visual channel while lows show little relationship between scores on single channel task and those for total channel
Awareness	Lows more confident when decoding incorrectly than highs
Gaze	Lows less likely to look while listening than highs; highs more similar to spouse in pattern of looking while listening

patterns of gaze. It is assumed that looking while speaking is related to encoding, although, as discussed earlier, it is also likely to be related to monitoring the reactions of the spouse.

Table 11.2 summarizes the main differences between high and low marital adjustment males for decoding. Again, the important differences are included for five areas: accuracy at decoding the spouse, accuracy at decoding strangers (particularly the relationship between these two accuracy scores), usage of the different channels in decoding, awareness of decoding, and patterns of gaze.

Tables 11.3 and 11.4 summarize the data for females in the same way, indicating where differences were found between those high and low in marital adjustment. In general, fewer differences were found for females than for males.

Contributions of males and females to communication problems

Using the data from the four tables one can also obtain a picture of the communication problems in the low satisfaction marriage—some of which come from both husband and wife, and some of which come from one or the other. Both husbands and wives:

1. Are generally more negative in their interactions, and they not only send more negative messages than other spouses, but their negative messages seem to be more intense.

2. Send fewer positive messages than other spouses.

3. Send more discrepant messages—but this finding seems to be related to the amount of negativity.

4. Are less able to predict whether the spouse will decode their messages accurately.

5. Are less likely to look at the spouse when they, themselves, are listening, and are more likely to look at the spouse when they, themselves, are speaking; they are also particularly likely to look at the spouse when they, themselves, are sending a negative message.

6. Show less reciprocity in their gaze patterns and are less similar to one another, particularly in their pattern of looking when they are listening.

7. Decode their spouses less accurately than they decode strangers.

Thus, over a wide range of communicative behaviours, both husbands and wives in the low marital adjustment group perform less well than other husbands and wives. These differences are not directly related to accuracy, but to the usage of different types of messages, the ability to predict the spouse's responses, gaze behaviour, and the relationship between skill at decoding the spouse and skill at decoding strangers.

Low marital adjustment husbands, but not wives, do have problems in both encoding and decoding as can be seen from the following summary. Low marital adjustment husbands are:

1. Poorer encoders, particularly on positive messages.

2. Poorer decoders of their wives' messages.

3. Seem to rely on the channel that gives least accuracy.

4. Are less aware of their own encoding and have difficulty telling a clear message from a not so clear one.

Low marital adjustment wives especially have problems with regard to decoding awareness—they are more confident than other wives when they are decoding incorrectly, and may be less likely to admit the possibility of misunderstandings occurring because of their decoding.

This series of studies, then, have indicated a number of ways in which husbands and wives in unsatisfactory marriages contribute to the communication problems in their relationship. In the next chapter we will discuss the implications of these findings for those engaged in marital or family therapy, marriage enrichment, or education for marriage.

References

BALSWICK, J. O. & PEEK, C. W. (1971) The inexpressive male: a tragedy of American Society. *Family Co-Ordinator*, **20**, 363–8.

BOYD, L. A. & ROACH, A. J. (1977) Interpersonal communication skills differentiating more satisfying and less satisfying marital relationships. *Journal of Counseling Psychology*, **24**, 540–2.

BUGENTAL, D. E., KASWAN, J. M. & LOVE, L. R. (1970) Perception of contradictory meaning conveyed by verbal and nonverbal channels. *Journal of Personality and Social Psychology*, **16**, 647–55.

FRIEDMAN, H. S. (1979) The concept of skill in nonverbal communication: Implications for understanding social interaction. In ROSENTHAL, R. (ED.) *Skill in Nonverbal Communication*. Cambridge, Mass: Oelgeschlager, Gunn & Hain.

GOTTMAN, J. M. (1979) *Marital Interaction: Experimental Investigations*. New York: Academic Press.

GOTTMAN, J., MARKMAN, H. & NOTARIUS, C. (1977) The topography of marital conflict: a sequential analysis of verbal and nonverbal behaviour. *Journal of Marriage and the Family*, **39**, 461–77.

HALL, J. (1979) Gender, gender roles and nonverbal communication skills. In ROSENTHAL, R., *Skill in Nonverbal Communication: Individual Differences*. Cambridge, Mass: Oelgeschlager, Gunn & Hain.
KOMAROVSKY, M. (1962) *Blue Collar Marriage*. New York: Random House.
MIDDLEBROOK, P. (1980) Social Psychology and Modern Life (2nd Ed.). New York: Alfred A. Knopf.
NOLLER, P. (1978) Sex differences in the socialization of affectionate expression. *Developmental Psychology*, **14**, 317–19.
NOLLER, P. (1982) Channel consistency and inconsistency in the communications of married couples. *Journal of Personality and Social Psychology*, **43**, 4, 732–41.
ROSENTHAL, R. (1979) *Skill in Nonverbal Communication: Individual Differences*. Cambridge, Massachusetts: Oelgeschlager, Gunn & Hain.
ROSENTHAL, R. & DEPAULO, B. (1979) Sex differences in accommodation. In ROSENTHAL, R., *Skill in Nonverbal Communication: Individual Differences*. Cambridge, Mass: Oelgeschlager, Gunn & Hain.
SNYDER, D. K. (1979) Multidimensional assessment of marital role satisfaction. *Journal of Marriage and the Family*, **41**, 813–23.
STEIN, A. H. & BAILEY, M. The socialization of achievement orientation in females. *Psychological Bulletin* (1973, 80), 345–366.
TAYLOR, S. & EPSTEIN, S. (1967) Aggression as a function of the interaction of the sex of the aggressor and the sex of the victim. *Journal of Personality*, **35**, 474–86.
ZUCKERMAN, M., LIPETS, M., KOIVUMAKI, J. & ROSENTHAL, R. (1975) Encoding and decoding nonverbal cues of emotion. *Journal of Personality and Social Psychology*, **32**, 1068–76.

12

Implications for Counselling and Therapy

Clearly, the research findings which have been presented throughout this book have implications for couples who are having problems with their communication, and those professionals who seek to help such couples find more constructive ways of relating to one another. The findings have implications at a general level, for decisions about the context in which couples may best be helped to communicate more effectively, and also at a more specific level, for decisions about the important aspects of communication, or communication skills that need to be included in such a programme.

General Implications

The fact that low marital adjustment subjects were able to decode strangers better than they were able to decode their spouses suggests that these subjects have more decoding skill than they are using in their marital interaction, and that problems in the relationship lead to some problems in the decoding. It would seem important then that a couple's communication problems be dealt with in the context of the marital relationship, not in the context of the individual and his/her individual skill. This is not to say that some benefit may not be obtained from individual communication skills training, but that the greatest benefit for the relationship will be obtained through training that takes place in the context of that relationship.

Satir (1976a) discussed this issue with regard to family therapy. She lists the advantages of dealing with communication problems in the context of family therapy as including the therapist being involved in examples of the family's interaction and thus being able to:

1. Observe the interaction.
2. Comment on the interaction.
3. Modify the interaction.

A professional who is clear about the behaviours which help and hinder effective marital communication can, through observing the couple in the therapy session and commenting on the interaction, help a couple to modify their communication patterns so that they communicate more helpfully and more effectively.

If communication problems of married couples are dealt with by counsellors in the context of the relationship, this also means that both members of the couple will need to be involved in the therapy. In Australian society, and no doubt in other similar societies as well, males have generally been unwilling to become involved in counselling situations for a number of reasons:

1. Men are more likely to be having their needs met in the marital situation than are wives.

2. Marriage tends to be less central to the lives of men than is true for women, particularly women who are totally involved in home-making.

3. Relationship issues, communication, emotions, tend to be seen as the proper interest of females, but not males.

4. Men are less likely than are women to admit that they need help.

5. Men tend to prefer a situation they feel they can handle, even if it has some undesirable qualities, and seem to fear that intervention might only lead to disruption.

However, since the data presented here have shown that it is the husband's skill at encoding and decoding nonverbal communication which is crucial to the marital relationship, it would seem not only highly desirable, but vitally important that males should be involved in any intervention, if that intervention process is to be maximally successful in helping the couple.

Thus the general implications from the research findings presented include the need for both members of the couple to be involved in any intervention process, and the need for communication skills to be "taught" in the context of the marital relationship.

Approaches to communication skills training

A number of writers have emphasized the need for marital therapists and counsellors to work at improving the communication skills of maritally distressed couples, including those theorists coming from a behavioural approach (Epstein & Williams, 1981; Jacobson, 1981; Liberman, Wheeler & Sanders, 1976; O'Leary & Turkewitz, 1978; Stuart, 1980; Thomas, 1977), those coming from a more systemic approach (Bodin, 1981; Satir, 1976a, b; Watzlawick, Beavin & Jackson, 1967) and those coming from a skills training (or preventative) approach (Garland, 1978; Guerney, 1977; L'Abate, 1981; Mace & Mace, 1974; Miller, Nunnally & Wackman, 1975). All of these approaches see improving the communication of the couple as essential to improving the relationship, and basically agree as to which communication behaviours help and hinder marital communication; the main differences between the approaches would be in the methods used to change the communication. Most of the approaches make some use of social learning principles although there are differences in the importance placed on the use of these principles. While Satir (1976b), for example, emphasizes that a family therapist should be both a "model of communication" (Bandura, 1977) and a "teacher of communication", communication skills would tend to be taught in the context of an ongoing therapeutic interaction with the therapist focusing on other issues, always modelling good communication and helping couples to come to an understanding of how they deal with problems and issues and the way this type of interaction is affected by the styles of communication which they use (compare example on p. 189).

Behavioural therapists, on the other hand, would concentrate on discrete observable behaviours (often communicative behaviours) which are desired by the partners. Spouses would be required to make lists of such behaviours, record the frequency of those behaviours and to work out exchanges or rewards contingent on those behaviours (Stuart, 1969). In the early days of Behavioural Marital Therapy spouses would exchange tokens but this is now less common (O'Leary & Turkewitz, 1978). (See O'Leary and Turkewitz (1978) for a discussion of problems related to the use of tokens.) Spouses are also encouraged to provide positive reinforcement for one another when desirable behaviours occur. O'Leary and Turkewitz (1978) for example, emphasize the skills of giving compliments, and acknowledging or reinforcing pleasing behaviours from the spouse.

Liberman, Wheeler and Sanders (1976) use therapist modelling, coaching, prompting, behaviour rehearsal, and feedback from therapists and group members. Thomas (1977) focuses on marital communication as operant behaviour controlled by its consequences, with each spouse affecting the other's communication by reinforcing (or failing to reinforce) and punishing certain behaviours. For example, paying a lot of attention to the spouse when he or she is being argumentative or aggressive, while ignoring or only minimally reinforcing compliments or affectionate behaviours will lead to the negative behaviour increasing and the positive behaviour decreasing.

He also emphasizes the way certain utterances of the spouse can become discriminative stimuli for the partner which indicate to him/her that certain behaviours are likely to be reinforced or punished. For example "I've had a lousy day" might signal "If you nag me now or pester me with questions I am likely to get angry", or "I feel like going to bed early" might signal "I'm really feeling romantic and would like to make love".

Thomas (1977) uses corrective feedback and instruction, including providing rules for interaction, stimulus control (where partners are taught how to stop or start certain behaviours on the part of the spouse by using certain responses), practice of skills in both role-playing and *in vivo* situations with feedback from the therapist, setting up operant response contingencies to modify each other's behaviours, and setting up contracts.

A further technique which can be useful in teaching communication skills in a therapy content is the use of videotape playback (Berger, 1978) where couples are exposed to a videotaped segment of their interaction. Nadelson (1978) discusses the use of videotape feedback from a psychoanalytical perspective and sees the technique as useful in dealing with communication issues, as well as transference and countertransference. She maintains that when seeing him/herself on videotape has a strong positive or negative impact on the client, the result is greater involvement in the therapy and more rapid change. Epstein and Williams (1981) discuss videotape playback from a behavioural perspective and see it as having "considerable therapeutic utility" and as being "a valuable aid in communication work" (p. 264). Sager (1981) summarizes the value of this technique when he says:

> "videotaping and audiotaping of sessions is an excellent way to observe the interactional patterns at work. Instant playback confronts the couple directly with how they deal with each other. With these techniques we can often help patients turn more quickly to less injurious transactions" (p. 177).

Preparing for training in communication skills

Before specific communication skills can be taught, however, couples may need help in two other very important areas:

1. Understanding the importance of communicating so that they can express their needs to one another, make mutually satisfying decisions, establish and work towards joint goals, and solve problems effectively.

2. Dealing with their fear of communicating, particularly of revealing their true feelings or attitudes.

Understanding the importance of communication

Couples are often aware of the importance of communication and of the problems that lack of communication is causing them, but in a very vague and general way. Counsellors can help client couples to be aware, in a more specific way, of the problems that arise because of lack of communication. Such problems could include:

1. Feelings and attitudes that have not been expressed cannot be taken into account in decision-making.

2. Behaviours that irritate the partner cannot be changed unless they are identified.

3. Negativity which is not expressed frequently leads to resentment which continues to affect the relationship and is often "leaked" at inappropriate times.

4. When putting a decision into effect requires the cooperation of the spouse, that cooperation is more likely to be forthcoming when that spouse knows that his/her own point of view has been taken into account in the making of that decision. This latter situation underlines the importance of the partners' being prepared to listen to one another and to understand one another's position on an issue.

Reasons couples may stop communicating

Many couples have retreated into "noncommunication" because attempts at communication have so often led to unsatisfactory outcomes. Outcomes which are likely to be particularly negative for the one who attempts to communicate are:

1. Lack of listening on the part of the spouse.
2. The spouse becoming defensive and attacking back—or the couple generally becoming involved in a cycle of negativity.
3. Rejection from the spouse.
4. Flight on the part of the spouse—or refusal to communicate further on the issue.

Satir (1976b) comments on the catastrophic fears that clients frequently have about the effects of communication, and gives examples of how she would burlesque such fears through statements such as:

"Mother and Dad won't drop dead if you simply comment on what you see and hear",

"You seem to act, Mary, as if Joe will fall apart if you simply report on what you have observed" (p. 210).

The fact remains, however, that if couples have generally found attempts at communication unrewarding or distressing, they may need a lot of help from the therapist before they are ready to make significant attempts at communicating to one another again. Satir (1976a) points out that therapists can help their clients by being prepared to reveal themselves, and their feelings and attitudes, with clarity and without fear, and showing that such communication can be useful and does not lead to catastrophic outcomes.

Understanding the communication process

As well as being convinced of the importance of communication, and being helped to deal with their fear of communicating, couples may also need help in understanding the communication process itself, particularly the fact that message sent does not always equal message received, and that misunderstandings can occur as a result of either the encoding process, the decoding process, or both. Couples also need to be aware that misunderstandings can occur for many reasons related to the verbal channel, the nonverbal channel or a combination of the two.

Problems related to the verbal channel are likely to occur because:
(a) The words are ambiguous.
(b) Words have different connotations for the interactants.
(c) Pronouns are used without clear referents.
(d) Complex sentence structure makes the message confusing.

Problems related to the nonverbal channel are likely to occur because nonverbal communication is "a noisy and unreliable system", as Osgood (1966) noted with regard to facial expression. This ambiguity and unreliability mean that spouses need to learn to check out the meaning of their communications and ensure that the spouse has received the message they actually sent.

Unfortunately, those working in the area of nonverbal communication who talk and write as though there were a dictionary of nonverbal behaviour, and every gesture, posture, or facial expression had its own unique and unambiguous meaning, only confuse the situation. Communication is not that simple. It is important for people to be aware of the messages they may be sending with their bodies, faces and paralinguistics, and to be aware of the possible interpretations of such behaviours. However, it is equally important that those making such interpretations learn to check with the "message-sender" to ensure that they are interpreting him/her correctly. Nonverbal cues can help us make guesses or form hypotheses about what is happening in a situation, but these hypotheses still need to be tested.

As well, an interaction is a reciprocal situation which is a series of communications and responses, each of which has some effect on the other. A misunderstanding may cause a spouse to respond negatively, but unless the other partner realizes that the negative response is based on a misunderstanding, the members of the couple are likely to become involved in a cycle of negativity or what Gottman (1979) called negative affect reciprocity. Perhaps unhappy couples are more likely to become involved in these cycles of negativity because they are:
(a) More likely to misunderstand one another.
(b) Less likely to check out each other's meanings.

It is important then, that spouses are helped to appreciate the importance of communication, and of seeking to understand the partner's point of view. They also need help to overcome their fears of communication, and to respond to the complex nature of the communication process. The important question then becomes, what are the specific communication skills which can be taught in the context of the husband–wife relationship, and which are likely to help the couple to be more effective in their communication?

Communication Skills and the Marital Relationship

In this section, the various skills that have been shown to be important in marital communication will be discussed under six different headings:

1. Sending clear messages.
2. Sending messages from one's own point of view.
3. Listening.
4. Responding in a way that shows you've heard.
5. Metacommunication.
6. Negotiation.

Tables 12.1 and 12.2 summarize the methods a therapist might use in teaching each of these skills, both through modelling, and through more direct teaching.

Sending clear messages

Messages can be unclear for a number of different reasons, including the following:

(a) The person is not being expressive enough.
(b) The person is "leaking" some underlying feeling or attitude.
(c) The message is not consistent on all channels.
(d) The message may be inappropriately strong or intense.

Positive messages seem to cause the most problems with regard to expressivity, particularly for husbands, and it would seem to be particularly interesting that husbands not only sent fewer positive messages in the interaction segment, but had problems sending such messages, even when they were given permission by the experimenter to encode them. In fact, the demand characteristics of the experimental situation were particularly high, and yet these husbands still had difficulty getting across their positive messages. Clients could be helped to make their messages more positive by either being positive on more channels (e.g. tone of voice as well as face), or being more explicitly positive on the verbal channel. However, given the finding that positive verbals were used relatively infrequently by all groups, it may be difficult to get clients to make this change. The therapist may use the technique of giving the spouses specific tasks in this area such as thinking of something they like about the partner and communicating it (Stuart, 1980). If the spouse is able to receive such a message, and reinforce the partner for sending it, then progress may be made toward increasing skills in this area (O'Leary & Turkewitz, 1978). As well, the therapist may comment on the degree of positivity, or expressiveness, or have the spouse comment on how positively the message came across to him/her.

Messages can also be affected by underlying feelings which "leak" through the message, making it less clear. Such feelings could include resentment towards the spouse because of some earlier incident, or they may not be related to the spouse at all. It is possible for a husband, for example, to be angry about something at work, annoyed with a child, worried about his chances of promotion, concerned about a difficult decision he has to make,

TABLE 12.1. *The Therapist as a Model of Communication*

Skill	Method	Example
Sending clear messages	Taking care to express own feelings and attitudes clearly; Being appropriately expressive; Using words where possible	I feel disappointed when you agree to do some work between sessions and then you forget about it
Sending messages from own point of view	Being careful to send messages to the client from own point of view	I feel confused. *not* You're confusing me
Listening	Commenting on nonverbal aspects of the message; Being clear about the data being used in making an interpretation	When you say "yes" in that tentative way, I get the impression you still have some reservations. Is that right?
Responding	Using paraphrasing, summarizing, reflection of feeling, "active listening" etc.	It's disappointing for you when you put in so much effort and A.... doesn't seem to notice
Metacommunication	Commenting on the process of interaction whenever that seems appropriate or necessary; Particularly commenting when the message seems incongruent or discrepant	J...., the last three times A.... has tried to tell me how he/she feels about this issue, you have interrupted him/her. I find it difficult to understand what's been happening when everyone talks at once. When you say you are glad to see me with a frown on your face, I feel confused
Negotiation	Through negotiating a contract for the therapy; Through presenting alternatives, negotiating homework etc.	Could we talk about what you might do to work on this problem between now and the next time I see you?

TABLE 12.2. *The Therapist as a Teacher of Communication*

Skill	Method	Example
Sending clear messages	Giving feedback when message seems unclear to the therapist;	I'm not clear what you meant by that statement.
	Asking spouse to indicate what message was received and compare with what was intended;	A . . . what did you think J . . . means by that statement?
	Giving clues as to how a message might have been made more clear	If you had said that more softly it might have been clearer what you meant
Sending messages from own point of view	Insisting that clients speak for themselves;	I'd like to hear what J . . . thinks about this matter.
	Not allowing any member of the family to speak for another or to mindread other members	Let's ask J . . . to tell us what he/she thinks
Listening	Encourage clients to be aware of, and to indicate, data on which interpretations are based;	What did J . . . do which led you to think he/she was annoyed about that?
	Helping clients to take account of the nonverbal aspects of the message	What did you think that wink of J . . . 's meant?
Responding	Encouraging clients to use paraphrasing, reflection of feeling etc.	J . . . can you tell A . . . what you thought was meant? . . . what he/she seemed to be feeling?
		Is that right J . . . ?
Metacommunication	Encouraging clients to comment on the process of interaction;	Would you like to tell J . . . how you react when you are interrupted so often?
	Encouraging spouses to explore their confusion with one another particularly discussing aspects of the message which seemed to contribute	Would you like to tell A . . . what it was about the message that confused you?
Negotiation	Encouraging couples to express needs, consider alternatives, decide between alternatives etc.	What alternatives do you see as possible in this situation? Could we explore the advantages and disadvantages of each?

or just plain tired—any or all of these feelings could lead to a message he was trying to send to his wife coming across more negatively than he intended. Such situations can be improved by couples being made aware of the possibility of leakage, and being encouraged, where possible, to declare negative feelings so that the partner has some idea of what the problems are and can both adjust his/her behaviour to suit such a mode, and make allowances for the bad feelings when decoding messages. Declaring such feelings also precludes the possibility that the spouse will think that he/she is somehow to blame for the negative mood.

Stuart (1980) maintains that "as a general rule, couples should be taught to use both verbal and nonverbal channels whenever they wish to express positive feelings but to rely heavily on words when they wish to communicate negative feelings" (p. 213). Applying such a rule could also help those unhappy spouses who were sending negative messages on all channels at once.

Gurman (1978) accuses behavioural therapists of denigrating the expression of feelings and trying to eliminate such behaviours as criticism, fighting and complaining from the interactions of married couples. He accuses such therapists of having too narrow a focus on the behaviour itself rather than on the broader implications for the relationship. What looks like "disrespect" at a content level may communicate great "respect" at the meta-level. Wife says to husband "when it comes to politics, your head is really up your you-know what". Behaviour therapists call this a "D" (very destructive). However, the relationship message may be something like, "I have enough confidence in our relationship and enough respect for your strength that I can let go, lose my temper, and bounce a few insults off you—I know you aren't fundamentally wounded by this" (Gurman, 1978, p. 496).

However, couples who are like those described by Gurman in this passage may not need marital therapy, and those who do are unlikely to have such positive feelings about insults or such feelings of security about their relationship.

Another reason that messages may be unclear is because of inconsistency in the channels—particularly if one channel is negative and the other is positive. Satir (1976a) gives as one of the important rules for teaching communication, "The therapist will help the patient be aware of messages that are incongruent, confused or covert" (p. 196). In the same chapter she illustrates how she would do this by the following transcript from a therapy session,

"Th: (to husband) I notice your brow is wrinkled, Ralph. Does that
      mean you are angry at this moment?
H: I did not know that my brow was wrinkled.

Th: Sometimes a person looks or sounds in a way of which he is not aware. As far as you can tell, what were you thinking and feeling just now?

H: I was thinking over what she (his wife) said.

Th: What thing that she said were you thinking about?

H: When she said that when she was talking so loud, she wished I would tell her.

Th: What were you thinking about that?

H: I never thought about telling her. I thought she would get mad.

Th: Ah, then maybe that wrinkle meant that you were puzzled because your wife was hoping you would do something and you did not know that she had this hope. Do you suppose that by your wrinkled brow you were signalling that you were puzzled?

H: Yeh, I guess so.

Th: As far as you know, have you ever been in the same spot before, that is, where you were puzzled by something Alice said or did?

H: Hell, yes, lots of times.

Th: Have you ever told Alice you were puzzled when you were?

W: He never says anything.
       (a therapist comment omitted here)

H: I think she knows." (Satir, 1976a, p. 192).

Later in the transcript it became clear that Alice has tended to interpret these puzzled looks as meaning:

"He don't want to be here. He don't care. He never talks. Just looks at television or he isn't home". (p. 194). This segment of interaction actually illustrates a number of points:

1. The ambiguity of nonverbal signals (in this case, a wrinkled brow accompanying a message).

2. How easily such a signal can give a completely wrong message.

3. How unaware a person can be of the nonverbal messages he/she is sending.

4. How easily a message can be affected by underlying feelings or thoughts (in this case, the feeling of puzzlement about an earlier comment).

5. How useful it can be for therapists or counsellors to help couples clarify the meaning of such messages, both as a way of helping them understand the complexity of the communication process, and as a method of teaching them to clarify messages.

One of the problems about inconsistent communications, as we illustrated in Chapter 1, is that the messages may be inconsistent for a number of reasons. Such reasons would include:

(a) Having strong feelings on an issue (not necessarily related to the topic under discussion) and not realising that those feelings are being revealed through the nonverbal channels.

(b) A lack of social skill leading to lack of ability to communicate clearly and consistently on all channels—or to communicate what is intended.

(c) Ambivalence about an issue, with the verbal channel perhaps expressing one attitude, while the nonverbal channels express a contrary attitude.

(d) Deception, or pretending—with the words expressing a socially desirable position, while the nonverbal channels "leak" the real attitude.

(e) Using one channel to express an opinion, and the other channel to express one's feelings toward a person—as when one wants to criticize a person's behaviour, but at the same time let the person know that you care about them.

Each of these situations can be dealt with, at least to some extent, by the therapist or the spouse letting the person know about the inconsistency (if it is causing confusion) so that he/she can clarify the message intended. The therapist can also help the clients to be aware of how frequently this kind of communication situation arises for them in their everyday interaction, just as Satir did in the transcript presented earlier. Such a procedure aids generalization of skills, learned in the therapy session, to the "real world" situation.

A further problem concerned with message-sending is the need to ensure that the intensity of the message is appropriate to the situation, and that the message is presented in such a way that the spouse has a chance of dealing with it. It certainly seemed that the couples in the unhappy marriages sent very negative messages, and it would seem likely that better communication would occur if they could learn to "tone down" such negative messages. O'Leary and Turkewitz (1978) note that it is also important for couples not to express negative feelings about something the spouse cannot change.

Miller, Nunnally and Wackman (1975) discuss the frequent use in interpersonal relationships of what they call "Style II" behaviours—including blaming, directing, defending, speaking for the other, closed questions, and frequent use of "you", "always", "never", "should", "ought" (e.g. you never consider me, you always do as you please, you should consider your wife more etc.). Along with other writers in the interpersonal communication area, Miller and his colleagues note the importance of people learning to express their feelings and attitudes from their own point of view, in a nondefensive and nonblaming manner. The way such a goal can be achieved will be discussed in the next section.

Sending messages from one point of view

Many of the programmes available these days for assisting people in their interpersonal relationships teach first person skills (Dick, 1983), or the

I-message (Dinkmeyer & McKay, 1976; Gordon, 1970; Miller, Nunnally & Wackman, 1975). Dick (1983) describes the skill as being able "to convey information to another without threat" (p. 82). The I-message doesn't blame or attack or defend but states "This is my point of view, how I react, feel etc. in this situation, and I'd like you to be aware of that and take my view into account". Dick suggests that such a message is most informative if it gives information about:

> "the specific behaviour of the other person;
> the material consequences for the speaker;
> if relevant, the assumptions the speaker forms, particularly about the other's motives;
> if relevant, the way the speaker feels;
> if relevant, the way the speaker intended or intends to react".

Miller and his colleagues (1975) comment on the way that such self-disclosure skills, when used appropriately, lead easily into a problem-solving phase, whereas the use of "Style II" messages leads only to self-defence or counter-attack and the oft-mentioned cycle of negativity. Once the cycle of negativity has begun, there is little possibility of problem-solving unless there is a cooling-off period, and a new start to the communication process. It may be important for therapists to teach clients not only the self-disclosure skills, but also how to stop the cycle of negativity and call a halt to the communication. At this point it is important for couples to set a time to communicate on the issue after they have had time to calm down, and to think about the problem. Setting the appointment ensures that the matter is discussed again, and not avoided.

However, while the sending of messages is clearly important, another aspect of the communication process, which is just as important for married couples, is listening. In the next section the many facets of the listening process will be discussed.

Listening

A major contention of low marital adjustment couples is that their complaints and criticisms are not listened to by their spouses. In the series of studies described in this book, there were many indications of problems in listening. Low marital adjustment subjects, for example, were more likely to look at the spouse when they were speaking than when they were listening. However, looking while listening would seem to be important in aiding understanding of the spouse, and in ensuring that the nonverbal behaviour available on the visual channel can be taken into account. Spouses could be helped to use looking patterns more related to seeking understanding. The therapist could increase awareness of the visual channel by commenting on information which he/she obtains from the visual channel, just as was done by Satir (1976a) in the interaction reported earlier in this chapter. It may also be important for spouses to gain understanding of the way each uses the different communication channels when encoding, and the therapist, teaching communication in the context of the relationship would be able to help here, by making the spouses aware of each other's communication, as he/she comments on the process.

Miller and his colleagues (1975) also emphasize the need for couples to be aware of their own process of interpretation. Since the low marital adjustment husbands were poor decoders, and since the low marital adjustment wives were particularly unaware of their own decoding, it would seem important for both these groups to be made more aware of the decoding process. Of great importance for those in close relationships is the need to be aware of the data on which they are basing their interpretation of the message from the partner. The data of prime importance is the behaviour occurring in the present situation—the frown, the wrinkled brow, the smile, the laugh, the tear, the turned up nose or the downcast look. The problem is that interpretations are often made so quickly that the data is lost, in favour of the interpretation, and the interpretation is treated as though it were fact. However, because nonverbal behaviour is generally ambiguous, such interpretations can be wrong, but they will still tend to be dealt with as though they were facts. Helping subjects to be more aware of the data on which they make interpretations can be very important. For example in the segment from Satir (1976a) the wife was made aware that the wrinkled brow which she interpreted as rejection, was actually expressing confusion and puzzlement.

A further problem is that interpretations are frequently not based on the data available in the present situation, but on expectations which come from past experience (Raush et al., 1974). Recall the wife who felt that her husband didn't like spending money on holidays and who interpreted all three of his messages (positive, neutral and negative) as indicating that he didn't want to go on the trip. When interpretations are based on expectations, however, it is very difficult for relationships to change. Even when a spouse tries to say something different, it is likely to be interpreted according to the old norms, unless he/she is very direct and explicit, particularly on the verbal channel.

While listening to the message itself is clearly very important to marital interaction, the way that couples respond to each other's communications is also important. Couples need to respond to one another in such a way that the spouse knows that he/she has been heard and understood. In the next section, various responses used by couples will be discussed.

Responses which show the spouse he/she has been heard

Gottman and his colleagues in a handbook for couples (1976) describe two behaviours common in low marital adjustment couples—summarizing self and cross-complaining, each of which has been discussed in Chapter 2. Each of these behaviours indicates that the spouse has not really heard the partner's point of view, and certainly is not taking that point of view into account.

Again, the various programmes designed to help parents in their communication with their children provide a technique for helping couples respond to one another in such a way that each knows their point of view has been heard by the other. The skill of active listening (Dinkmeyer & McKay, 1976; Gordon, 1970) involves paraphrasing the communications of the spouse and reflecting the feeling contained in the message so that the person knows the extent to which his communication has been understood. Such a process allows the spouse to demonstrate his/her understanding, and also increases the likelihood that any misunderstandings will be revealed and clarified.

Since these skills of paraphrasing and reflecting feeling are part of the general repertoire of the counsellor, they would be modelled frequently in the therapy situation. However, it may also be important for such skills to be taught more directly. A therapist could encourage a client to tell his/her spouse what was heard so that meaning sent and meaning received could be checked out. A therapist may also encourage clients to be more aware of their own feelings, and also of the feelings being conveyed by the spouse, so that they would be more able to label feelings and communicate to the spouse that their feelings have been recognized and understood.

As a warning, O'Leary and Turkewitz (1978) provide a rather humorous example of the inappropriate use of empathic listening. In this example the husband communicated clearly and the wife responded reflectively, but she used this technique to avoid dealing with the issue.

He: You said you'd call the insurance agent today.
She: You really think it's important that I call.
He: Yeh, what happened? How come you didn't?
She: You're starting to get angry thinking about how I didn't call.
He: Well, did you not want to call or did you forget?
She: You're not sure what happened.
He: That's right, damn it; why don't you answer me?
She: Now you're really angry.

Metacommunication

Another important skill which couples need to learn if they are to communicate with one another effectively, is metacommunication—or commenting on the communication process. Such a skill is particularly important when subjects are confronted with discrepant or incongruent communications. As Bandler and his colleagues (1976) comment,

"When the messages which the receiver accepts are congruent, he has no difficulty in understanding the meaning of what the communicator intends. When the communicator presents incongruent messages, whether or not the receiver has organized the conflicting messages so that he is aware that they do not fit, he will reach a conclusion that something about the communication didn't work for him. This will either occur in the receiver's awareness, and then he will have the freedom to gracefully present the dissenting conclusions he has reached from the dissenting messages and, possibly, even give the communicator specific feedback. . . . If the receiver has not been aware of the particular conflicting messages . . . he will, typically, reach the conclusion that he is confused. When the receiver is sensitive to his own experience and recognizes his confusion, he is free to comment on it and has the choice of requesting the assistance of the communicator in resolving it. What is really important here is that the receiver and the communicator both have the choice of exploring their communication without their self-esteem being threatened . . . (p. 114)."

It would seem, then, that there are a number of important issues involved in successful metacommunication:

1. The receiver needs to be aware of some confusion created for him by the message sent.

2. The situation may be more easily resolved if the receiver is aware of the parts of the message which are contributing to his confusion (for example, the words expressing pleasure at seeing the receiver, while the nonverbal channels seem to indicate displeasure—flat voice, frown etc.).

3. The receiver needs to feel that it's alright for him/her to communicate this confusion to the sender without being afraid of being attacked, put-down etc.

4. The sender needs to be able to accept the comments of the receiver without feeling that his/her self-esteem is under attack.

5. The sender needs to feel free to make a further attempt to communicate the message, and to discuss his/her ambivalence, or physical discomfort, or lack of skill, or whatever is causing the message to create confusion for the receiver.

6. The receiver, on the other hand, has to feel free to explore the possibility that his/her own expectations, or mood might be contributing to the confusion.

The therapist can help a couple to deal with each of these issues—to become more aware of what they experience in the communication context, to feel free to comment when they are confused, to accept comments from the partner when the partner is confused, and to explore the meaning and process of their interactions. The therapist can help the couple achieve these skills both through modelling metacommunication him/herself, and commenting on the process of interaction when that seems appropriate or necessary, and by more direct interventions aimed at encouraging the spouses to comment for themselves.

However, metacommunication is not only about confusion. Spouses may communicate about many other aspects of the communication process, such as their reactions to silence, or interruptions, their reactions to the volume of the partner's speech, to the use of posture or spacing or gaze, or to any other part of the communication process which is causing problems. However, it should always be kept in mind that in situations where there is a great deal of control of one partner by the other, metacommunication is much more difficult (Bateson *et al.*, 1956). In this situation the therapist may need to deal with the power issues before emphasizing metacommunication.

Negotiation

There would seem to be no doubt that one of the reasons that couples low in marital adjustment have problems in negotiation and decision-making is that they are generally poor communicators, having problems in many of the areas discussed both in this chapter and throughout this book. Thus the communication process tends to break down before such couples reach the negotiation phase because they become involved in the cycles of negativity described earlier. For this reason, some writers in the area (e.g. Bach & Wyden, 1969; Dayringer, 1976) have emphasized the need to teach couples to "fight", or to negotiate fairly. Dayringer (1976) describes a process in which the therapist acts very much like a referee in a boxing match.

Members of the couple are put into separate "corners" and the therapist works with them one at a time, helping them to work out what to say to the spouse at that point in the process. Such skills as clearly stating a complaint from one's own point of view, responding to that complaint without attacking the spouse etc. are taught in this way. The "beef" or complaint to be dealt with is selected by both the therapist and the couple, with just one "beef" being worked on in any one hour session. Clients are also encouraged to thank the spouse for listening, so that listening and appropriate responding are reinforced.

Other writers also emphasize the use of negotiation, but do not teach it in such a dramatic way. Miller and his colleagues (1975) teach what they call Style IV skills—such as self-disclosure skills, awareness of others skills, discussing issues in the present, and focusing on the self, and stating feelings and attitudes from one's own point of view. Many of these skills are similar to the ones discussed earlier in this chapter, and serve to air feelings and formulate the issue. For the actual problem-solving or negotiation phase, these writers teach Style III skills which include the use of open questions, of making suggestions in exploratory and tentative ways, of looking at alternatives, and of considering possible outcomes.

Another important factor in learning to negotiate is to learn different styles of conflict resolution, and the issues for which each of them is appropriate. Many couples, unfortunately, tend to use only one style, and then find problems insoluble when they don't fit that style. Mace and Mace (1977) describe three ways of dealing with issues in order to resolve the conflict:

1. *Capitulation* which they define as "a loving fight" and not "anything resembling a humiliating process" (p. 120).

2. *Compromise* which involves concession by both parties, so that the final solution meets both sets of needs as far as possible.

3. *Coexistence* which involves "an agreement to accept the current difference, because at the present time it seems impossible for either to give ground to the other".

Behavioural therapists, in particular, have tended to use contingency contracting (Jacobson, 1981) which is based on the principle of reciprocity in social exchange. Epstein and Williams (1981) discuss the various types of contracts which have been used. Those involving coercive demands and including punishment; those which are *quid pro quo* (that is, if you do A, I'll do B) but which are positive and use rewards for compliance rather than punishment for non-compliance, and good faith contracts where I agree to do A regardless of your behaviour, and you agree to do B regardless of my behaviour. Liberman, Wheeler and Sanders (1976) have called contingency contracting "a temporary aid in structuring positive exchange and fairness as well as an opportunity to practice communication and problem-solving skills".

Some research has been carried out on the value of contingency contracting in marital therapy. Knox (1973) concluded that behaviour contracts are helpful for some couples and while they are useful during the counselling phase the practice does not necessarily have to be continued to maintain happiness. There has also been some work carried out in comparing the effects of different types of contracts as well as in trying to separate the effects of contracts from the effects of communication skill. Jacobson (1978b) carried out a study of mildly to moderately distressed couples and concluded that *quid pro quo* and good faith contracts were interchangeable. Ewart (1978, Note 1) also compared these two types of contracts in severely distressed couples and found that the two were equivalent, but that contracting as a procedure was no more effective than noncontingent goal setting.

Liberman and his colleagues (1976) addressed the question of whether training in communication skills or formal contracting was most important in dealing with marital distress and concluded that "contingency contracting is worth just about the paper it's printed on without the family members having adequate communication skills" (p. 32). Jacobson (1978b) also questioned whether the reason that *quid pro quo* and good faith contracts were equivalent was that communication and problem-solving training were the main causes of improvement in any case. Ewart (1978, Note 1) carried out an experiment where he was able to separate the effects of communication and problem solving training from those of contracting and concluded that contracting had an important effect "over and above improvements due to the communication and problem-solving training" (Epstein & Williams, 1981).

Thus it would seem that *both* communication skills and a separate emphasis on skills of negotiation such as generating alternative solutions, resolving conflicts and making contracts are important. Teaching skills of this kind to the couple can be an important adjunct to teaching the communication skills discussed throughout this book. As with the other skills, clients can be helped to resolve issues using these methods during the actual therapy session.

A model for teaching communication in a therapy context

Figure 12.1 presents a model for teaching communication skills in a therapy context, beginning with the therapist's use of metacommunication in the therapy session so that couples become more aware of their unhelpful or destructive uses of communication. This metacommunication needs to be based on a thorough knowledge of empirical findings with regard to marital communication, and the types of communication which cause problems. As the metacommunications of the therapist lead to greater awareness on the part of the clients, it is also important for the therapist to encourage them to use metacommunicative statements themselves. Couples who are able to comment on the communication process are more likely to be able to express their confusion, seek clarification and deal with such difficult situations as double-binds. A couple's awareness of the communication process and ability to comment on the process may be increased by the use of videotape feedback of their interaction (Berger, 1978). The use of this technique could make them more aware of the actual interaction process and of the specific behaviours they engage in, and the effects these have on the partner. As well, they may be able to see their own interaction with some degree of distance, and therefore objectivity (Nadelson, 1978).

From the point of view of behavioural therapists it would be important to build into the model some reinforcement for each other for appropriate behaviours such as clear expression of feelings, metacommunication,

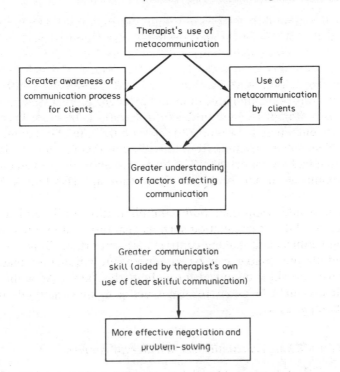

FIG 12.1. Model for improving communication skills in therapy context

empathic responses etc. As well couples must learn to guard against punishing the partner for performing behaviours that they want to see increased by, for example, reacting negatively to metacommunications.

Crucial to the whole process, however, is the therapist's ability to communicate in clear and effective ways and to help couples to do the same. The therapist also may need to give reinforcement to couples for improvements in communication effectiveness.

Finally, skills of negotiation and problem-solving need to be taught so that the use of appropriate communication skills can lead to problems actually being resolved—a very reinforcing event, in itself. As well, these skills need to be modelled and taught in such a way that solutions can be found to present problems and the skills can also be applied to other situations as they arise in the future.

Contexts other than therapy

The teaching of the communication skills discussed here can also be carried out in other contexts apart from the therapy setting. Marriage enrichment, particularly models which involve both members of the couple in a small group situation (Mace & Mace, 1974) can also be useful for teaching these skills, particularly where the relationship of the couple is basically sound. Most couples seem to find that they benefit from input about communication skills, since these are rarely part of education programmes and many feel the need to relate more effectively to those with whom they are in regular contact. As well, the most frequently taught skill—assertiveness—is frequently taught in a way that encourages people to consider their own needs above those of others. In the marital context it is necessary for people to learn to resolve issues in ways that best meet both sets of needs, and to be prepared to subsume individual needs to the needs of the relationship when that seems important—and this is true for both males and females (Scanzoni, 1981).

In conclusion

Finally it needs to be recognized that in this volume we have focused on one important facet of the marital relationship—communication. While all would agree that communication is vital to the marital relationship, there are other aspects of the relationship that are important, as well. Two other factors which need to be mentioned here are commitment and cooperation (or willingness to give and take). Learning to express one's true feelings and attitudes, clearly, and from one's own point of view may not help too much if the partner has no commitment to the relationship, or believes that things should always be done his/her way. However, learning to communicate effectively may help couples talk about such issues as levels of commitment to the relationship, who should make what decisions, and how mutually satisfying solutions to problems can be found. Effective communication can also help to provide an atmosphere in which both cooperation and commitment can grow.

Reference Notes

1. Ewart, C. K. Behavior contracts in couple therapy: An experimental evaluation of *quid pro quo* and good faith models. Paper presented at the American Psychological Association, Toronto, 1978 (cited by Epstein and Williams (1981)).
2. Ewart, C. K. Behavioral marriage therapy with older couples: Effects of training measured by the Marital Adjustment Scale. Paper presented at the Association for Advancement of Behavior Therapy, Chicago, 1978 (cited by Epstein and Williams (1981)).

References

BACH, G. R. & WYDEN, P. (1969) Marital fighting: A guide to love. In ARD, B. N. & ARD, C. C. (Eds.) *Handbook of Marriage Counseling*. Palo Alto: Science and Behavior Books, pp. 313–21.

BANDLER, R., GRINDLER, J. & SATIR, V. (1976) *Changing with Families*. Palo Alto, California: Science and Behavior Books.
BANDURA, A. (1977) *Social Learning Theory*. Englewood Cliffs, N.J.: Prentice-Hall.
BATESON, G., JACKSON, D. D., HALEY, J. & WEAKLAND, J. (1956) Toward a theory of schizophrenia. *Behavioral Science*, 1, 251–64.
BERGER, M. (1978) *Videotape Techniques in Psychiatric Training and Treatment*. New York: Brunner/Mazel.
BODIN, A. (1981) The interactional view: Family therapy approaches of the Mental Research Institute. In GURMAN, A. S. & KNISKERN, D. P. *Handbook of Family Therapy*. New York: Brunner/Mazel.
DAYRINGER, R. (1976) Fair fight for change: a therapeutic use of aggressiveness in couple counseling. *Journal of Marriage and Family Counselling*, 2, 2, 115–30.
DICK, R. (1983) *Communication Skills Workbook*, University of Queensland.
DINKMEYER, D. & McKAY, G. (1976) *Systematic Training for Effective Parenting:* Parent's Handbook. Circle Pines, Minn: American Guidance Service, Inc.
EPSTEIN, N. & WILLIAMS, A. M. (1981) Behavioural approaches to the treatment of marital discord. In SHOLEVAR, G. P. *The Handbook of Marriage and Marital Therapy*. New York: Spectrum Publications.
GARLAND, D. R. (1978) *Couples Communication and Negotiation Skills*. New York: Family Service Association of America.
GORDON, T. (1970) *Parent Effectiveness Training*. New York: Peter H. Wyden.
GOTTMAN, J. M. (1979) *Marital Interaction: Experimental Investigations*. New York: Academic Press.
GOTTMAN, J., NOTARIUS, C., GONSO, J. & MARKMAN, H. (1976) *A Couple's Guide to Communication*. Champaign, Illinois: Research Press.
GUERNEY, B. G. JR. (1977) *Relationship Enhancement*. San Francisco: Jossey Bass.
GURMAN, A. S. (1978) Contemporary marital therapies: a critique and comparative analysis of psychoanalytical, behavioral and systems theory approaches. In PAOLINO, T. J. & McCRADY, B. S. *Marriage and Marital Therapy*. New York: Brunner/Mazel.
JACOBSON, N. S. (1978) Specific and nonspecific factors in the effectiveness of a behavioral approach to the treatment of marital discord. *Journal of Consulting and Clinical Psychology*, 46, 442–52.
JACOBSON, N. S. (1981) Behavioral marital therapy. In GURMAN, A. S. & KNISKERN, D. P. *Handbook of Family Therapy*. New York: Brunner/Mazel.
KNOX, D. (1973) Behavior contracts in marriage counseling. *Journal of Family Counseling*, 1, 22–8.
L'ABATE, L. (1981) Skill training programs for couples and families. In GURMAN, A. S. & KNISKERN, D. P. *Handbook of Family Therapy*. New York: Brunner/Mazel.
LIBERMAN, R. P., WHEELER, E. & SANDERS, N. (1976) Behavioral therapy for marital disharmony: an educational approach. *Journal of Marriage and Family Counselling*, 2, 383–95.
MACE, D. & MACE, V. (1974) *We Can Have Better Marriages if we Really Want Them*. London: Oliphants.
MACE, D. & MACE, V. (1977) *How to Have a Happy Marriage*. Nashville: Abingdon.
MILLER, S., NUNNALLY, E. W. & WACKMAN, D. B. (1975) *Alive and Aware*. Minnesota: Interpersonal Communications Program.
NADELSON, C. C. (1978) Marital therapy from a psychoanalytic perspective. In PAOLINO, T. J. & McCRADY, B. S. *Marriage and Marital Therapy*. New York: Brunner/Mazel.
O'LEARY, K. D. & TURKEWITZ, H. (1978) Marital therapy from a behavioral perspective. In PAOLINO, T. J. & McCRADY, B. S. *Marriage and Marital Therapy*. New York: Brunner/Mazel.
RAUSH, H. L., BARRY, W. A., HERTEL, R. K. & SWAIN, M. E. (1974) *Communication, Conflict and Marriage*. San Francisco: Jossey-Bass.
SAGER, C. J. (1981) Couples therapy and marriage contracts. In GURMAN, A. S. & KRISKERN, D. P. *Handbook of Family Therapy*. New York: Brunner/Mazel.
SATIR, V. (1976a) Family communication and conjoint family therapy. In ARD, B. N. & ARD, C. C. *Handbook of Marriage Counseling*, 2nd Ed. Palo Alto, California: Science & Behavior Books, pp. 175–85.

SCANZONI, J. & FOX, G. L. (1980) Sex roles, family and society: the seventies and beyond. *Journal of Marriage and the Family*, 42, **4**, 743–56.
STUART, R. B. (1969) Operant-interpersonal treatment for marital discord. *Journal of Consulting and Clinical Psychology*, **33**, 675–82.
STUART, R. B. (1980) *Helping Couples Change: A Social Learning Approach to Marital Therapy*. New York: The Guildford Press.
THOMAS, E. J. (1977) *Marital Communication and Decision Making*. New York: Free Press.
WATZLAWICK, P., BEAVIN, J. H. & JACKSON, D. D. (1967) *Pragmatics of Human Communication*. New York: W. W. Norton.

Author Index

Subject Index